D1487056

VIKINGS

VIKINGS

RAIDERS, TRADERS AND MASTERS OF THE SEA

RODNEY CASTLEDEN

CHARTWELL BOOKS

CONTENTS

PART 1.
The Viking Age

PART 2.
Viking Violence

PART 3.
Viking Myths, Religion & Beliefs

PART 4.
Viking Social Network

PART 4. (CONTINUED)

PART 5.

Celebrity Vikings: Kings & Bards

PART 6.

The Lasting Legacy

INTRODUCTION

It began in about AD 790 with an outburst of raiding by sea and lasted for 300 years – it was called The Viking Age.

The early Vikings were pagan and the monasteries of Christian communities were targets for attack and plunder. It was not that the Vikings were anti-Christian, just that they saw monasteries and churches as wonderfully undefended stores of treasure. Those raids continued on a large scale through the ninth and tenth centuries and became the Vikings' trademark.

By the time of the Norman Conquest of England, the raiding was dying down, though in Ireland it went on longer. Magnus Bare-Legs, who was born in 1073 and became king of Norway in 1095, died while raiding in Ulster in 1103. Viking raids on Wales continued after that, into the twelfth century.

The Hebrides were still under Norwegian rule until 1266, Orkney until 1468, Shetland until 1469. So the Viking Age did not have a sharply defined end. At the same time, after the Norman Conquest of England, the 'Vikingness' of the Scandinavian presence softened. It was at this time that the Vikings were converted to Christianity, and that changed the nature of Viking culture.

By 1100, what we think of as the Viking Age was over. It was a distinctive phase of European history with far-reaching effects – not least because the Vikings' geographical reach was so extensive.

WHO WERE THE VIKINGS?

The name Viking has an uncertain origin. It may come from a place-name in the south of Norway, the Oslo Fjord, which is also known as *Viken* (The Bay). More likely, it comes from the Old Norse word *vik*, meaning 'bay'. As seamen, the Vikings valued bays as harbours, refuges, bases for ship repair, potential trading posts and places to settle.

Another possibility is that the word may be a borrowing from the Latin word *vicus*, meaning 'trading post', or its Anglo-Saxon form *wic*, which was found in the Anglo-Saxon name for London, Lundenwic. Behind the Viking image is a quieter Viking nature, the trader, and trading was just as important an activity as pillage and plunder.

RAIDING AND TRADING

Whatever the original meaning of the word, after the Viking Age two Old Norse words existed side by side. A *víkingr* was someone who was away from home with a group on a military expedition. A *víking* (only one letter different) was a group activity away from home, usually raiding, but sometimes trading.

It looks as if it was this second word that was picked up by the English, who rendered it *wicing*, and used it to mean 'pirate', and usually 'pirate from Scandinavia' at that. The difference between the two Old Norse words is rather like the difference in meaning between 'adventurer' and 'venture'.

These words were apparently not in widespread use in the Viking Age. In the contemporary Latin texts several other words were used instead – *Nordmanni*, *Dani*, *piratae* and *pagani*, meaning 'Northmen', 'Danes', 'pirates' and 'heathen'. English texts refer to 'Northmen' and 'Danes'. Germans called them *Ascomanni*, 'the Ash-men'.

Gaels called them *Lochlanach*, 'Norsemen'. Welsh and Irish texts refer to 'foreigners', distinguishing between 'white' and 'black' groups, which implies that the Welsh and Irish could differentiate between two kinds of Vikings, though no-one knows now what that distinction was.

'Viking' has become a name we cannot do without. No other word really covers the broad population of Scandinavia in the eighth to eleventh centuries and the many groups of descendant colonies scattered across Europe and beyond. 'Scandinavian' scarcely has the same flavour or overtones. But it is as well to remember that few of the people we call Vikings would have called themselves that.

THE UNALTERABLE PAST

We still have a surprisingly vivid memory of the Viking Age, even though it ended 900 years ago, but how well do we really know the Vikings? Our image of them has shifted with time and continues to shift.

Logically, the past ought to be unalterable; it has happened and should lie beyond the possibility of change, yet it does change, just as a landscape changes as we pass through it on a train. Our place in time is relative, and the place of the past in relation to us is also relative. Our values and preoccupations alter through time, so we notice different aspects of the past and evaluate them differently.

For us, today, the name Viking has a very particular meaning, a meaning with an alarming sharpness of focus. A Viking is a terrifying warrior hell-bent on rape and pillage, and we usually think of him (never her) wielding an axe and charging ashore from a newly-beached longship, heading towards the nearest monastery. But how close is this image to the historical reality? And how close is it to the way the Vikings saw themselves?

Dawn raiders.

PART 1.

THE VIKING AGE

CHAPTER 1.

THE VIKING HEARTLAND

The homelands of the Vikings lay in Scandinavia – Norway, Denmark and southern Sweden. Today, Denmark consists of the peninsula of Jutland, two large islands, Fyn and Sjaelland (Zealand), and a scattering of smaller islands. The drowned glacial landscape is distinctively low-lying and flat – a tame terrain for a once-wild people.

THE DANEVIRKE

In the Viking Age, Denmark was larger, encompassing a large area of southern Sweden, the provinces of Skåne (Scania), Blekinge and Halland. In Jutland, the border with what is now Germany lay further to the south and, as the one short land border, it was marked by a series of defensive earthworks, called the Danevirke, which had a single gap for the Haervej, the Army Road. This was the main land communication with routes traversing the Northern European Plain; south of the Danevirke lay the lands of the Saxons, Frisians and Wends. Denmark was really two lands: the west, a desolate sandy heath and the east, a fertile till plain.

Eleventh century commentator, Adam of Bremen, described the large eastern island of Sjaelland as 'famous for the valour of its people and for the richness of its produce'. It was on this fertile island, at Roskilde, that the Viking monarch of Adam's day, King Sveinn Estridsson, had his royal seat. Denmark, with its islands and winding inlets, has a very long coastline. A Danish Viking was never more than 35 miles from the sea. It is not surprising that the Vikings should have become a great seafaring people.

VIKING SWEDEN

Modern Sweden is huge and physically diverse. In the Viking Age it was only the southernmost quarter that was significantly inhabited, though even that contained several different landscapes. Skåne, in the deep south, was a fertile lowland like the Danish islands, but north of that was the infertile low plateau of Småland. North of that were two fertile regions, the Svear and the Götar. The Svear was the dominant region, where the royal seat at Old Uppsala was located. To the north lay Norrland, a huge expanse of largely empty forest.

THE NORTH WAY

Norway was, and still is, different again: a huge chain of high, snow-capped mountains with an astonishing fjord coastline 12,500 miles long. Again the coastline draws attention to the sea. It can be a rough, inhospitable coastline, but the scatter of hundreds of small islands in front of it creates a sheltered sea-route, the 'North Way', that gave its name to the country.

There are sheltered patches of farmland at the heads of the Norwegian fjords, but the most significant lowland region lies at the head of the Oslo Fjord, which became a great route centre.

In the far north there was a region the Vikings called Halogaland, which perhaps means Land of the Northern Lights. In about 880 a trader from Halogaland found his way to the English court of King Alfred, and the king was interested in having his account of Norway recorded.

The trader, called Ohthere, described for Alfred his own expedition to the far north, to find out how much further Norway stretched. After six days the land curved eastwards, which means Ohthere reached North Cape.

From there he went eastwards and then southwards for another nine days and reached 'a river' and a settlement; this might have been Arkhangel. It seems from this episode that even modest traders like Ohthere were

startlingly adventurous and inquisitive travellers.

The account was evidently censored for politically sensitive material. King Alfred must have pressed for information about the political situation in Scandinavia, yet there is no mention of it in the surviving version of Ohthere's account.

These, then, were the Vikings' homelands from which they set off on adventures, the familial heartlands to which they returned from their raids with all their plunder and treasure.

THE VIKINGS' NEIGHBOURS

Immediately to the south of Denmark lay the kingdom of the Franks. Originally these were several separate Germanic tribes, but they gradually joined together to form a single kingdom, and this expanded to its greatest extent in the reign of Charlemagne, who was king of the Franks from 768 to 814. In 800, Charlemagne took the title emperor – he was crowned 'Carolus Augustus' – and his Carolingian empire was the greatest European power of the time. In contrast to his Viking neighbours to the north, Charlemagne was a Christian.

In a belt across the northern fringe of Charlemagne's empire was a zone of Anglo-Saxon colonization, of which England, Wales and Lowland Scotland were part. In the sixth century, the western half of Britain had managed to retain its separate 'British' cultural identity, but by the eighth century Anglo-Saxon influence was felt, even in the west. Only Ireland and the Scottish Highlands and Islands remained culturally and politically distinct.

To the east of Charlemagne's empire lay the lands of the non-Christian Slavs, consisting of several tribes. The Slavs had their own traditions of dress and ornament and their own brands of jewellery, which were different from the Carolingian and the Viking. They nevertheless had regular and frequent trading contacts with Scandinavia.

The southern Baltic coastline was a good location for trading stations that could act as go-betweens for the Vikings and Slavs. There were several great rivers in eastern Europe that were brought into play as trade routes. In the tidal flow of trade, Baltic amber found its way south-eastwards, and Islamic coins found their way to the Baltic.

There were also several tribes described as Balts, living in what is now Latvia, Lithuania and north-west Russia; they were culturally similar to the Slavs.

The Danevirke fortification.

CHAPTER 2.

VIKING EXPANSION

As the Vikings spread out from their homelands, raiding, pillaging, sometimes settling, they had an impact on other communities, far and wide. They were at best interlopers, at worst thieves, vandals, bandits and murderers.

The arrival of the Vikings outside Scandinavia was understandably always felt as a negative experience, and that in turn affected the way events were reported. The Christians living in western Europe in particular gave them a bad press. The English had nothing good to say about them in the Anglo-Saxon Chronicle.

What was it that fed this expansion, this explosive onslaught of raiding? It is easier to say what did not cause it. It was not the Vikings' undoubted technical skill in shipbuilding; the ships provided the means, not the motive.

It was not a pagan reaction to over-zealous Christian missionaries. Nor was it a simple response to over-population in Scandinavia. Most of the early raids were hit-and-run, without any intention of settlement. It was difficult to make a living in Norway, though certainly not in flat and fertile Denmark.

Viking warriors and explorers coming ashore.

THE OPPRESSION OF KINGS

One driver was the high value placed on military prowess; fighting well and fearlessly was a route to increased status. It may be that young men were driven by the need to raise the 'bride price' so that they could marry.

The medieval sagas say it was the oppression of kings that drove men from their homes. This could well have been part of the story. Royal dynasties were growing stronger and there was increasing centralization of power, which probably led to conflict. Unsuccessful and marginalized contenders may have decided to try their luck elsewhere.

There were individual reasons too. Erik the Red was exiled from both Norway and Iceland for violent crimes, forcing him to sail the oceans.

YOU NEED FRIENDS

Fighting was necessary to defend the property rights of the family and fulfil social obligations. A very high value was put on friendship.

I was young once. I walked alone.
Soon I went off my path.
I felt rich when I found a friend.
Man is man's delight ...

Don't think about giving lavish gifts.
Respect can be cheaply bought.
With half a loaf and a near-empty bottle
I have gained a real friend.

Friendship went far beyond sentimental ties, mutual entertaining and gift-giving; it became a contractual obligation that necessitated acts of support. This could entail fighting someone else's battle.

But the main thrust behind the Viking adventures was greed: the desire to acquire wealth that would maintain and enhance the raiders' status back in the homelands.

In Scandinavia it was the custom for inherited wealth to be divided among several relatives, and this tended to disperse and reduce wealth. This was probably a major underlying factor in driving raiding expeditions.

LIGHTNING STRIKES

In the late Viking Age there were full-scale organized invasions of England, and these were part of the Danish kings' program of imperialist expansion.

We tend to think of Vikings as criminal raiders and their victims as peaceful, passive and virtuous. But the Vikings were by no means alone in Europe in behaving as they did. Many of the peoples they came in contact with were similarly dominated by aggressive military elites with similar values to the Vikings.

The most distinctive feature of the Viking raids was their swiftness, the lightning strikes from the sea, which were so effective in catching people unawares, and leaving before any effective opposition could be mustered.

The ninth century was a period of growing trading opportunities, of commercial expansion. New trade routes were opened up and networks of coastal and riverside trading centres were being established. Wealth was being created.

The escalation in the number of raids at this time was at least partly linked to the growing scale of the rewards. If more wealth was being created, there was more wealth to steal. The scale of the new wealth can be seen in the astonishing scale of the buy-offs.

The Vikings were able to demand 10,000 lbs (4,500 kg) of silver in return for 'protecting' (i.e. not destroying) a region or a city in the ninth century. By the twelfth century that figure had increased almost five times over, and some rulers were, somehow, able to pay ransoms of this size over and over again.

PAYING FOR PROTECTION

On a small scale, archaeology can reveal some of the Vikings' plunder. Irish and Anglo-Saxon decorative metalwork has a distinctive design, and pieces of it are regularly found in Viking graves in Scandinavia and even in Britain and Ireland. Often the bullion value of these pieces is low, which may explain how they survived intact; some pieces have been adapted to make brooches.

One piece of plunder was a highly decorated triangle of gilt-copper, which was originally made to decorate the corner of a chest, reliquary, shrine or book. It is easy to imagine this being seized from an Irish monastery during a Viking raid; it was found among the grave-goods of a Viking woman in Dublin.

Sometimes the monks were so desperate to keep their most hallowed treasures that they were ready to pay the raiders to be allowed to keep them. Some treasures were in effect ransomed. A richly decorated gospel book called the *Codex Aureus*, the Golden Book, contains a marginal note telling us that it was ransomed 'from the heathen army with pure gold' and that this gold was provided by a pious Anglo-Saxon couple.

Western Settlement
GREENLAND
ICELAND
Norwegian Sea
Skraelingar
Middle Settlement
Faeroes
Shetland
Orkneys
Eastern Settlement
Hebrides
SCOTLAND
North Sea
VINLAND
(NORTH AMERICA)
IRELAND
ENGLAND
WALES
Normandy
ATLANTIC OCEAN
FRANCI
SCANDINAVIAN SETTLEMENT
Eighth Century
Ninth Century
Tenth Century
Eleventh Century
Denotes areas subjected to frequent Viking raids but with little or no Scandinavian Settlement
IBERIAN KINGDOMS
al Andalus

Saami (Lapps)
PERMIA (Bjarmland)
NORWAY
Finns
SWEDEN
VOLGA
BULGARS
Chuds
RUS
STATES
SKANE
Letts
DENMARK
Lithuanians
Wends
Prus
West Slavs
East Slavs
KHAZAR
KHAGANATE
South Slavs
Bulgars
Black Sea
ITALY
BYZANTINE EMPIRE
Caspian
Sea
Sicily
Shirvia
Daylam
Mediterranean Sea
ABBASID
CALIPHATE

CHAPTER 3.

MOVING OUTWARDS

THE NORTHERN ISLES

A short voyage across the North Sea brought the Vikings to landfall in Shetland, Orkney or the mainland of Scotland. It would not be surprising if the early phase of expansion brought many raids in these areas.

The truth is that so far there is little archaeological evidence to show how early the Vikings settled Shetland or Orkney. The graves that have been excavated show that the Vikings were settled in the Northern Isles in the eighth century.

Nor is it clear what means the Vikings used to colonize the Northern Isles and the Scottish mainland. Was it by conquest or by peaceful negotiation or by friendly assimilation?

DNA EVIDENCE

Some historians point to the replacement of all the earlier place-names in the Northern Isles by Norse names as evidence of a take-over by force, evidence of ethnic cleansing, but it may not be so. For a long time it was assumed that the swamping of Kent and Sussex by Anglo-Saxon place-names meant that the earlier, native British, population was massacred. DNA studies now suggest that a large proportion of the British population was left alone.

The aristocratic landowners might have been driven out or murdered but the bulk of the work-force, the serf class, was left alone. So we should not read too much into the prevalence of Norse place-names in the Northern Isles. Large-scale exterminations are unlikely.

THORFINN THE MIGHTY

Excavation has shown that productive native Pictish farms were taken over by the Vikings. Jarlshof in Shetland and Buckquoy in Orkney are examples of such farms. Buckquoy looked across a tidal inlet to an island, the Brough of Birsay, where there was a major Pictish village; metal-working went on there, including the manufacture of jewellery.

This village of oval or figure-of-eight stone-walled houses was taken over by the Vikings and replaced by a village of rectangular houses; the artifacts show that the way of life did not change much, so it looks, at least to the archaeologist Anna Ritchie, like a story of continuity.

A Pictish stone on Birsay showing three warriors in long gowns and carrying shields suggests that it was high-status Pictish site. Then it became the power base of the greatest Viking earl of Orkney, Thorfinn the Mighty, which again could be interpreted as a sign of smooth continuity.

Pictish brooches of the type made at Birsay were found, hidden in a hoard of silver treasure at St Ninian's Isle on the southern tip of Shetland. This native Pictish treasure was buried in a wooden box under the floor of a chapel in about 800, almost certainly to stop it from falling into the hands of Viking raiders, who targeted churches and monasteries in particular.

At Buckquoy, the ninth and tenth century houses contained pottery and other objects made in the Pictish style, and this is strong evidence for assimilation; the Picts went on making the same kinds of objects as before, but for their Viking masters.

VIKING CEMETERY

We know the Vikings settled in Orkney. There is a small Viking cemetery at Westness on the island of Rousay; the grave-goods buried there with dead Viking settlers give an idea of their lifestyle.

The men still saw themselves as warriors, as their weapons were buried with them, but

they were also farmers and fishermen. They had their boats buried with them too, showing they had not given up the sea, and depended on it; maybe it also showed that the afterlife would be spent voyaging on to new places.

LIVING IN COMFORT

A Viking farmstead has been excavated at Jarlshof on the southern tip of Shetland, a site that had been occupied before the Vikings arrived; in fact it had been occupied since the bronze age. The first Viking dwelling there was a bow-sided house 75 feet (23 meters) long, built of drystone and turf. Inside were two rooms, a living room and a kitchen.

The living room or hall had a long central hearth, with platforms on each side for sitting and sleeping. The outbuildings included a byre to house livestock in winter, a barn for fodder, stables, a forge and another small building, close to the house, that may have been a sauna.

The settlers who lived here in reasonable comfort were mainly farmers, but fishing became more important, possibly prompted by population growth.

REACHING THE HEBRIDES

These early footholds to the west of the North Sea were used as stepping stones to other places in the same archipelago. After Shetland and Orkney, the Hebrides, the Isle of Man, north-west England and Ireland.

Many Viking burials in the Hebrides are known, but few settlements have been excavated. One, the Udal, on the sandy coast of North Uist, was a farmstead very similar in layout to Jarlshof and, again as at Jarlshof, a pre-existing settlement site was taken over in the ninth century. The characteristic bow-sided drystone houses with long central hearths were built among the ruins of pre-Norse buildings.

Native houses were destroyed and replaced by Viking houses. Here the archaeologist Ian Crawford saw the changeover as violent; the native population was expelled, killed or suppressed. Rather similar evidence has been interpreted quite differently.

The pattern of Viking settlement in the Hebrides is not fully understood, but it was uneven: denser in some areas than others. This is reflected in the distribution of place-names. In Skye, only the northern half of the island has a significant number of Viking place-names.

King Orry's Grave, Laxey, Isle of Man.

SEIZING THE ISLE OF MAN

The scatter of Viking colonies through the Hebrides led south towards the Irish Sea. The Viking graves on the Isle of Man, such as the warrior buried in his boat in the Christian graveyard at Balladoole, suggest that the earliest settlements were being established at the end of the ninth century, the same time that they were being set up in north-west England.

It is likely that the Isle of Man was seized and occupied by Viking warriors, who then married local Manx women. Viking settlements on Man include defended homesteads. A familiar sight now is the massive bow-sided hall at the Braid, which replaced the round houses that were there before.

The Viking heritage of the Isle of Man lives on in its status independent of the UK, under the British Crown but with its own parliament, the Tynwald. This assembly still meets annually in the open air. Man remained a Scandinavian possession until 1266; then its king accepted the overlordship of the Scottish King, Alexander III.

MOVING ON TO IRELAND

A small Viking cemetery on Rathlin Island off the north-east coast of Ireland implies a Viking settlement there too. The main concentration of Scandinavian settlements was round new Viking towns – Dublin especially, which was first set up as winter-base in 841. In 902, the Irish succeeded in expelling the Vikings from Dublin, and the refugees set up a colony in north Wales. They were pressed to move on, into England.

NORTH-WEST ENGLAND

Vikings settled in north-west England (Cumbria and Lancashire) in the early tenth century. We know this from burials, and also from a hoard, the Cuerdale hoard, which was buried in about 905 beside the River Ribble. This consisted of over 90 lb (40 kg) of silver: more than 7,000 coins, ingots and ornaments, mostly cut into pieces. This is the biggest Viking treasure ever found in the West.

It is likely that a great many farms set up in north-west England during the Scandinavian colonization lie hidden under their modern successors, but there are some that were set up on marginal land and were subsequently deserted.

OCCUPYING YORK

One such is Ribblehead in West Yorkshire. It consisted of a bow-sided stone-built hall with outbuildings, including a detached kitchen and a workshop, arranged round a yard; drystone walls radiated from it across the high limestone moor.

Three coins struck in York show that it was occupied towards the end of the ninth century. The archaeologists found no Scandinavian artifacts, so it is possible that this farmstead was occupied by either Anglo-Saxons or Vikings; it is the date that suggests a Viking initiative.

THE ISLANDS OF SHEEP

After Cumbria, Man and Ireland, the Vikings sailed further afield, moving on to the Faeroes, halfway between Shetland and Iceland, then Iceland itself.

The Vikings were not the first to settle the Faeroes. Irish hermits were there before them. In 825, the Irish monk Dicuil described the islands as being settled 'for roughly a hundred years. Now, because of Norse pirates, they are empty of anchorites, but full of innumerable sheep and many kinds of sea-fowl.'

It was the Vikings who called them the Faeroes, or Sheep Islands. At the modern settlement of Kvívík, a Viking farmstead has been excavated. It consisted of a bow-sided stone hall with a long central hearth and, right next to it, a second similar structure divided into stalls as a cattle byre.

CHAPTER 4.

FURTHER AFIELD – ICELAND AND GREENLAND

COLONIZING ICELAND

The Irish monk, Dicuil, knew about the existence of Iceland too. It seems there were already Irish hermits there too when the Viking settlers arrived, though 'they went away because they were not prepared to live here in company with heathen men.' Iceland was given its name by a Viking called Floki, on account of the first harsh winter he spent there in about 860.

THE FIRST VIKING SETTLERS

The main phase of colonization and land claim was from 870 to 930. Icelandic sources record the names of the men who are considered to have been the first 400 settlers. Of those, at least one-seventh came from Britain and Ireland. DNA studies also show that the modern 'Scandinavian' population of Iceland has a very strong component of ancient British ('Celtic') stock.

This in turn suggests that the Vikings who settled in the Highlands and Islands of Scotland, Ireland, Man and north-west England acquired British and Irish wives – and probably British and Irish slaves – before the move on to Iceland.

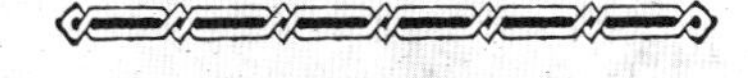

ICELANDIC FOUNDATION

Icelandic historians in the middle ages believed that the Vikings sailed to Iceland to settle in order to escape the tyranny of King Harald Fair-Hair. This was, as genetic studies show, almost certainly not the only reason, and perhaps not a reason at all, but the idea of the Vikings setting up an independent republic in the face of tyranny was attractive. History is often bent in this way to create a palatable foundation myth.

DECLARING CHRISTIANITY

Iceland has the oldest (though revived) national assembly in Europe. It is known as the Althing and it met in the open air each summer at Thingvellir, a plain flanked by lava cliffs. It is said that the first meeting of the Althing was in 930. At the 999 or 1000 meeting, Iceland was declared to be a Christian country; everyone was to be baptized, though pagans were allowed to follow their religion in private.

THE CHIEFTAIN'S HALL

The first Viking settlers in Iceland built farmsteads very similar to those seen at Jarlshof and Kvívík, with farmhouses that were long narrow halls. One, at Hofstadir in north Iceland, was unusually long, 130 feet (40 meters) long, and probably belonged to a chieftain. The large hall was to entertain a band of people and accommodate feasting on pagan festivals.

House design was developed in Iceland, dividing up the building to create a series of specialized rooms, much like a modern house, in fact. The houses were also made more compact, probably in response to the more severe weather conditions.

A NEW LAND TO THE WEST

A sequence of chance events led to the Viking colonization of Greenland and the Viking discovery of North America. The principal player was Erik the Red. It was violence – 'some killings' – that drove him and his father into exile from Norway in around 980.

But young Erik was no more peaceable than his father, and some more killings in Iceland led to Erik's second banishment. A

land to the west had been discovered about sixty years earlier by Gunnbjorn Ulfsson, who had been blown off-course while sailing from Norway to Iceland. In 978, Snaebjorn Galti also sighted its barren glaciated east coast.

DESTINED FOR GREENLAND

This nameless land to the west of Iceland is where Erik headed. He rounded Cape Farewell and found the ice-free south-west coast, with sheltered fjords and patches of pasture. He set up two settlements and stayed there for three years before going back to Iceland with encouraging stories about the land he cunningly called 'Greenland'.

Twenty-five ship loads of Icelanders set off for Greenland in 985, though only fourteen ships arrived. The most favourable areas for settlement were the Eastern and Western Settlements which were unfortunately 300 miles apart.

THE LAND OF THE INNUIT

It was a difficult land to live in because there were no trees, but there was plentiful driftwood, which must have suggested to Erik and the other settlers that a substantial forested land lay not far distant; this would turn out to be Labrador.

The most valuable exports came from the north: polar bear furs and walrus ivory, which took the Vikings further and further north to trade with the Innuit. They were lured into exploring the entire west coast; iron longship rivets have been found on the coast of Ellesmere Island.

They made a living of sorts, and the Greenland settlements flourished in the mild climate of the late tenth to twelfth centuries. After that the colonies went into decline and Greenland became once more a land of the Innuit, the people the Viking Greenlanders referred to contemptuously as *skraelingar*, 'feeble stunted people'.

Brattahlid, the eastern Greenland settlement, founded by Erik the Red.

CHAPTER 5.

VINLAND AND THE NEW WORLD

From the springboard of the Greenland settlements, the Viking adventurers were able to make one more significant voyage to the west – the one that brought them to the New World. It was Bjarni Herjólfsson who discovered Vinland by chance in 986.

ADAM'S VINLAND

All kinds of stories revolved round the mysterious Vinland in the middle ages, but there is one early account which can claim to be a historical record. This is the account by Adam of Bremen, who was writing his Gesta in the eleventh century.

In his account he mentions a 'he'; this is the king of Denmark, Sveinn Estridsson, who died in 1074 and was known to Adam personally. This is what Adam wrote;

He related an account of one of the many islands discovered in that ocean. It is called Vinland, because vines spring up wild there bearing excellent grapes. That crops abound there unsown we have learned not from fable and fancy but from a factual report given by the Danes. Beyond that island, he said, there is no habitable land to be found in the ocean; everything beyond it is full of impenetrable ice and utter darkness.

FOR THE SAKE OF THE STORY

There are lots of problems with this passage. If Vinland is an island, is it Newfoundland? If so, it could scarcely have supported vines. Nor was it isolated; the mainland of Canada lies not very far away across the Cabot Strait in the south-west and Belle Isle Strait in the north.

There was land to the west of Newfoundland, and it was habitable. The grapes and the crops that need no tending sound like a piece of story-telling rather than a geographical description.

MEADOW LAND

It may be that the name Vinland has been misunderstood, both in recent times and back in the eleventh century too. Vin is a common place-name element on Norwegian farms of Norse age, and today the word means 'pasture'.

A related name existed in Old English in the name of the village of Woolland in Dorset. In the Domesday Book this was written *Winlaude* and interpreted to mean 'meadow land' or 'pasture land'. So it is possible that the Viking discovery of Vinland in North America had less to do with vines, more to do with meadows for grazing.

L'ANSE AUX MEADOWS

So, were the voyage to Vinland and the Viking discovery of North America pure fantasy?

In 1960, the Norwegian explorer Helge Ingstad visited the coast of northern Newfoundland. At a place called L'Anse aux Meadows, he was shown some ruins of what appeared to be turf houses. His wife Anne Ingstad was an archaeologist and she subsequently excavated the site.

What has emerged is a Viking Age settlement, with buildings of the type seen in Greenland and Iceland. There were further excavations in the 1970s undertaken by Birgit Wallace. The main buildings were in three groups lined up on a north-facing terrace, each group with its own house. This could have provided accommodation for up to 90 people.

L'Anse aux Meadows, World Heritage Site, Newfoundland, Canada.

NOT MUCH TO GO ON

There was a fourth building complex, next to a freshwater stream, which was industrial. It included a charcoal kiln and a smelter for smelting bog-iron. The site has been radiocarbon dated to the early eleventh century, so the Viking incomers introduced the iron age to North America.

There were tantalizingly few personal possessions to link the site with the Vikings, but there was a distinctive bronze pin, which was recognizable as a type found in Viking settlements in Britain, Ireland, the Faeroes and Iceland. Not much, but just enough evidence to prove that the Vikings landed on North American soil and set up a settlement there.

WINTER REFUGE

L'Anse aux Meadows was a substantial building complex, but what was it? It was evidently more than temporary accommodation of the sort Leif Eriksson would have needed on his expedition, yet it did not look as if it was equipped for permanent settlement.

Apart from anything else, there was no evidence of any agriculture there. Probably the complex was used as an overwintering refuge, dependent on food supplies gathered elsewhere. Walnut timber and butternut squash seem to show that the Vikings who used this site voyaged at least another 600 miles further south, as far as eastern New Brunswick; significantly, this is a place where grapes grow wild.

This all seems to point to Newfoundland not being Vinland, but the gateway to Vinland, which was further to the south and encompassed the shores of the Gulf of St Lawrence and land to the south. L'Anse aux Meadows was a staging-post for Viking settlements which have yet to be discovered.

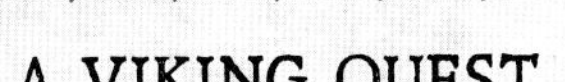

A VIKING QUEST

Both Canadians and Americans have understandably been keen to find more evidence of early colonization of North America. There has been a steady stream of claims for 'Viking' sites to show that Vikings penetrated further and established more and longer-lasting settlements.

At Terrebonne and Laval on the St Lawrence near Quebec people have claimed to find the ruins of Viking fortresses and burial mounds and even a Viking mooring stone. It became virtually a quest for a lost civilization.

NORDIC IMMIGRANTS

But the various stone structures and burial mounds that have so far been claimed as Viking have turned out to be palaeo-Indian or Innuit in origin. Some finds of apparently Scandinavian origin were discovered further south along North America's eastern seaboard. But they are in areas where large numbers of nineteenth century immigrants lived, so the sites were 'contaminated' by later Scandinavian settlement.

It is possible that Vikings travelled as far south as Godard Point in Maine, where an eleventh century Norwegian coin has been found. So far there is only one well attested Viking site in the New World, and that is L'Anse aux Meadows, in Canada.

HISTORIC VOYAGE

There is an element of irony in the decision by the Smithsonian Institution in Washington to stage a major exhibition in 2000 about the Vikings to celebrate the millennium of Leif Eriksson's historic voyage. As far as the documentary and archaeological records are concerned, Canada was visited and settled, though as far as we can tell not (quite) the USA.

The editors of the book accompanying the exhibition showed good judgement in acknowledging that there is no evidence for long-term settlement by Vikings in the United States. But the search will surely continue, and it may be that more Viking settlements will one day be found.

THE VINLAND MAP

The Vinland Map may have been forged in order to bolster the fragile evidence for the Vikings' visits to the New World. It first appeared in 1957, bound into a book with a short medieval text called *Hystoria Tartaorum*. In that year it was offered to the British Museum by a London book dealer, Irving Davis, on behalf of a Spanish-Italian dealer, Enzo Ferrajoli de Ry.

The British Museum declined to buy it and Ferrajoli sold it instead to an American dealer, who offered it to Yale University. There were suspicions about the authenticity of the map from the start, because the wormholes in it did not match the wormholes in the text.

But then Irving Davis produced another book, *Speculum Historiale*, and it was found that the wormholes could be made to match if the Vinland map had been originally bound into the front of the *Speculum* and the *Hystoria* into the back.

PLASTIC THREAD

But there were other worries. The rebinding of the *Speculum* without the map or the *Hystoria* had been bound with plastic thread, which meant that it had been done after 1950. All traces of former ownership of the *Speculum* had been removed, so neither the map nor the texts had any provenance.

Vinland is shown in the extreme top left hand corner of the Vinland map as an island larger than Greenland. In its east coast it has a river, which might be Churchill River in Labrador, and a large inlet which might be the Gulf of St Lawrence. The island itself is helpfully labelled *Vinlanda Insula*, Vinland Island.

MODERN FORGERY

On the face of it, it is a fifteenth century map, drawn about fifty years before the landmark Columbus voyage of 1492. There are several reasons why academics have rejected it as a fake.

One is that the coastline of the east side of the Atlantic Ocean has evidently been modelled on Portuguese maps drawn in the sixteenth century: in other words it shows greater geographical knowledge of that coastline than would have been available in the fifteenth century.

A second reason is that Greenland is shown as the island that we now know it to be, but this was *not* known in the fifteenth century; in fact it was not discovered until 1902. It is also odd that Greenland is drawn with far greater accuracy than Norway, when it should be the other way round.

A third reason, the decisive one, is that ink used in drawing the map contains a titanium dioxide pigment that was not used until the 1920s. This forensic evidence emerged in 1972, and in 1974 the conclusion was reached, probably correctly, that the Vinland map was a twentieth century forgery.

STOLEN BOOKS

The *Hystoria* and the *Speculum* were displayed at an 1892 event in Madrid to celebrate Columbus, but there is no record of a map being displayed with them. The two texts were examined again in 1926 by a Spanish scholar, but again no map was mentioned.

Many books were stolen from the Zaragoza Cathedral Library in the 1950s, which is when the two (unprovenanced) texts were probably stolen, and the map was probably drawn and added then, just before its appearance in 1957. Ferrajoli was eventually convicted in connection with the thefts.

Intriguing though the Vinland map is, it must remain under strong suspicion. Yale's position is to regard the map as 'an extremely interesting and controversial document ... We watch the scholarly work on it with great interest.'

REMOTE OUTPOSTS

The Vikings apparently visited Newfoundland and Vinland a number of times, but ultimately these far western outposts – and that went for Greenland too – were too remote, even for the Vikings.

No regular chain of communication existed between the North American colonies and the rest of the Viking world. We are very lucky to have the surviving archaeological evidence of L'Anse aux Meadows, as there cannot have been many Viking settlements or camps in North America: nor can they have been substantial or long lasting.

On the other hand the existence of one genuine Viking settlement means we can suppose that at least a few more must once have existed and will eventually come to light. It seems reasonable to hope so.

(*Right*) Viking bronze spear with a decorated silver shaft.

CHAPTER 6.

CONTACT WITH THE EAST

VIKINGS IN UKRAINE

In the tenth century, Vikings of Swedish origin, and known as the Rhos, controlled a region of Ukraine. Whether they still thought of themselves as Scandinavian is not known, but they were still speaking a Scandinavian language. On the other hand their personal names were becoming more and more Slavonic through time.

This Viking presence persisted, and still persists; though in the mid-twentieth century it was scarcely possible to mention that part of Ukraine had been thoroughly infiltrated, and long ago, by Vikings.

IN CONSTANTINOPLE

The Vikings penetrated eastern Europe by using the river systems – and of course their ships. The authorities in Constantinople were understandably nervous when the ships appeared, as the intention was not always clear.

The first mention of these eastern adventurers was in the *Annals of St Bertin*, written by Bishop Prudentius of Troyes. For the year 839, he describes envoys sent by the Byzantine Emperor Theophilus to the Holy Roman Emperor Louis the Pious, who was then at Ingelheim.

[Theophilus] sent with them certain men who said that they – their race, that is – were called Rhos. Their king had directed them to him [Theophilus] in friendship, they claimed. In his letter, Theophilus requested that by favour of the [Holy Roman] emperor they might have help and opportunity to return home through his territories since the roads they had taken to get to Constantinople led through cruel and barbarous tribes of extreme savagery. He did not want them to return that way, fearing they might encounter danger. After carefully investigating the reason for their coming, the [Holy Roman] emperor found them to be a race of Swedes.

PENETRATING EAST

This account shows that the Vikings had penetrated right across eastern Europe and reached Constantinople. But it is also interesting in showing that they were not always confident that they could look after themselves – a side we do not often see.

The way the Rhos travelled about in eastern Europe, crossing Ukraine by river, was written about a hundred years later by Constantine Porphyrogenitos;

Wooden boats come down to Constantinople from outer Russia; some come from Novgorod, some from the walled town of Smolensk and from Lyubech and Chernigov and from Vyshgorod. All these come along the River Dnieper and converge on the fortress of Kiev.

The Slavs who are bound to pay the Rhos tribute hew the hulls in their wooded hills during the winter, and when they have them ready, at the seasons when the frosts dissolve, they bring them to the lakes nearby. Since these discharge into the River Dnieper, these people come to the Dnieper, make their way to Kiev, drag their ships along for fitting out and sell them to the Rhos.

The Rhos buy the plain hulls, and from their old ships, which they break up, they supply oars, rowlocks and whatever else is needed. So they

fit them out. Moving off down the Dnieper in June they come to Vitichev and gather there for two or three days. When all the ships are assembled they set off and make their way down the Dnieper ... [negotiating the nine notorious rapids on the Dnieper by using poles or hoisting the boats up onto the shoulders of slaves].

On the island of St Gregorios they conduct sacrifices because of the huge oak that stands there. They sacrifice live birds ... They come out to the River Dniester. When they come to the River Aspros they have a rest and come to the Selinas, a branch of the River Danube [on the Danube delta].

VIKING MEMORIAL

If this sounds too fantastic to be true, a typically Viking memorial was found along the route. At the mouth of the Dnieper is a standing stone with the inscription, 'Brand made this grave for his partner [business partner] Karl.' This was not a gesture of sentiment; Brand needed the world to know that the business (and the profits) were now solely his, and no longer shared by Karl.

REALMS OF ISLAM

The Rhos, or Rus as they were sometimes known, were active in parts of Russia, Ukraine and Byelorussia, mainly using the Dnieper, the Volga and the Don to take their vessels to the Black Sea, to reach the realms of Byzantium and Islam.

Their main base was in Kiev, and from there they made a number of expeditions to Constantinople. They were merchants and their envoys negotiated treaties to make commerce easier.

TRADING NOT RAIDING

These eastern Vikings were mainly traders, not raiders, but it is revealing that the terms of the trade treaties attempted to exclude misbehaviour. The Byzantine authorities stipulated that 'Your [Rus] prince shall personally order any of the Rus who come here [to Constantinople] not to commit acts of violence in our town and our territories.'

They were required to enter the city by one particular gate, unarmed, and reside in a particular quarter. They were to be kept under tight control. Suspicions about the Rus were fully justified; they attacked Constantinople in 860, 907, 941 and 1043.

PROTECTED INTERESTS

A treaty of 912 protected the interests of those Rus who were serving in the Byzantine emperor's army; this was something that Harald Hardrada, later to become king of Norway, would do a century later.

Another treaty dating from 945 dealt with documentation; the grand prince of the Rus decreed that appropriate documents should be sent straight to the Byzantine authorities, detailing how many ships were being despatched; this was to reassure the Byzantine emperor that the Rus came in peace, which was certainly not always the case. Failure to produce documents would result in arrest.

ISLAMIC CALIPHATE

The one remaining empire the Vikings had dealings with – a huge and powerful empire – was the Islamic Caliphate. This huge empire centred on the Middle East, and sprawled eastwards into central Asia and westwards along the north coast of Africa to Morocco and Spain.

The Caliphate had a sophisticated money-based economy that was built on access to large resources of gold and silver. It commanded large fleets of commercial ships, ports for trading and extensive networks of land routes too; situated at the western end of the Silk Road, it was in a position to control markets in oriental spices, silk and exotic luxury goods.

CITY OF BAGHDAD

The Vikings wanted to deal with the Caliphate because it offered possibilities

Byzantine and Islamic coins from the eleventh century.

of trade with even more distant trading partners, like India. The experience must, even so, have been a bewildering one.

Nothing in Scandinavia, indeed nothing in northern Europe, could compare in size or magnificence with the glittering capital of the Caliphate, Baghdad, a city that was then known as Madínat-al-Salām.

This astonishing city was the seat of the ruler, the caliph. When the Rus came in contact with Baghdad in the 800s, the caliphate was at its peak and already beginning to show signs of fragmenting. It was ethnically diverse, and there were squabbles between rival dynasties.

INCREDIBLE OUTREACH

The reach of the Vikings was by any standards astonishing. They travelled east to Kiev and south-east to Constantinople and Baghdad. They sailed west to Britain and Ireland. They roved north-west to Iceland, Greenland, Labrador, Newfoundland and the Gulf of St Lawrence.

They sprang from a relatively small and, it has to be said, unpromising heartland, the homelands of southern Scandinavia. Their reaching out to both east and west was incredible.

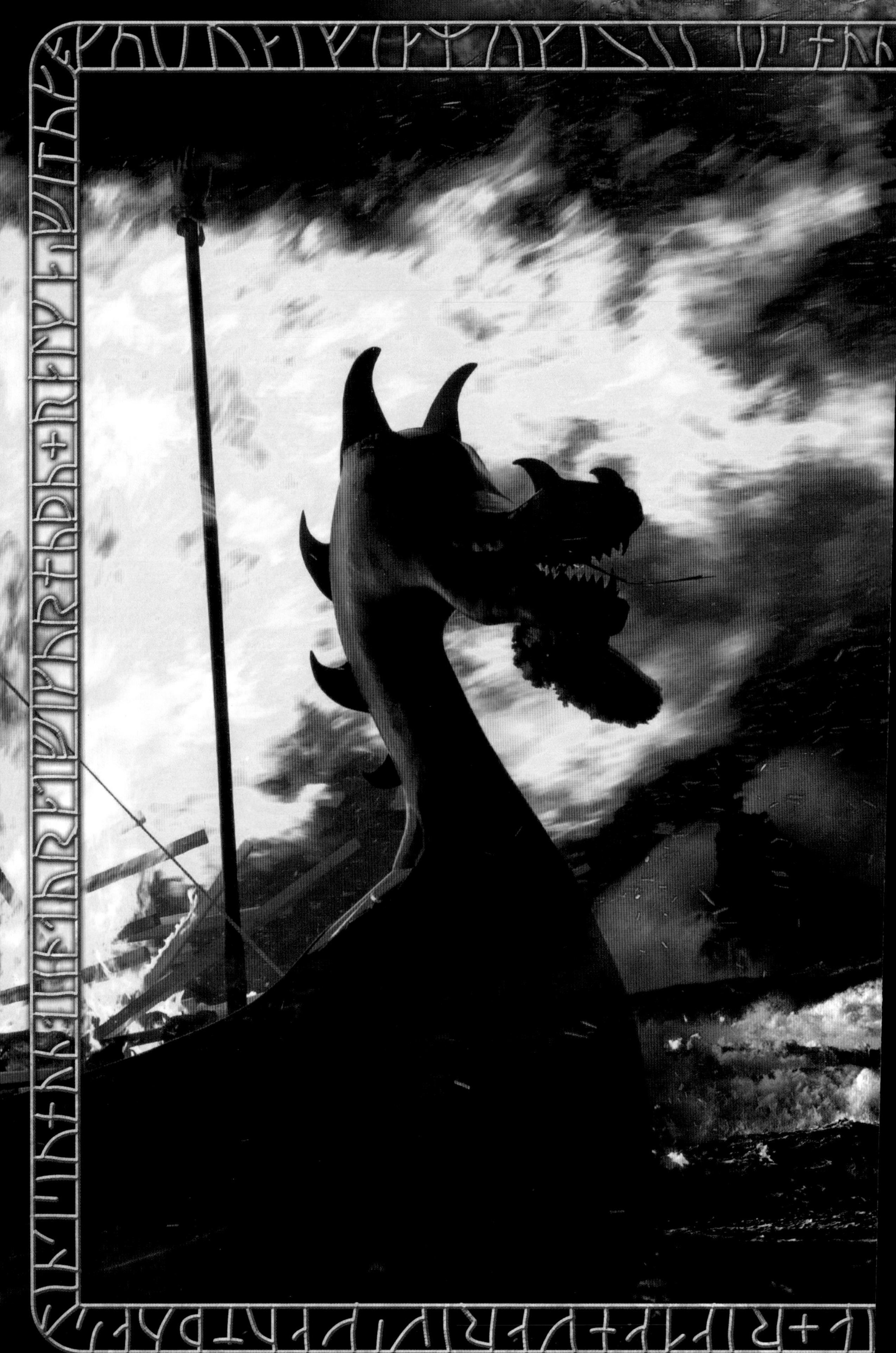

PART 2.

VIKING VIOLENCE

CHAPTER 7.

WEAPONS & WARFARE

GOING BERSERK

The berserker (an Old Norse word) was the epitome of the Viking warrior, though not all Viking warriors were berserkers. They were a special caste of warriors. According to the saga tradition, which was based in historical fact, the berserker fought naked or at any rate scantily clad. He fought in a deliberately induced battle frenzy, which transformed him into a super-warrior, gave him superhuman strength, and allowed him to be wounded without feeling pain. He appeared to be in a delirium. Some of the Lewis chessmen are shown chewing their shields to indicate that they are berserkers.

SHAPE-SHIFTERS

Another aspect to the transforming powers of the berserker was his ability to shape-change into a wolf or a bear. Among the Vikings and in other ancient societies as well, beliefs in shape-shifting were widespread. Under certain circumstances, it was believed, people could change into animals, and animals could change into people. Vestiges of these beliefs have survived in fairy tales like *The Frog Prince*.

If such transformations were possible, and it seems people believed that they really were possible, it would be useful for a human warrior to change into a wolf or a bear, in order to acquire the strength of a wild beast. A matrix for making a metal helmet panel from Sweden shows the actual moment of shape-shifting. On the left is a fully human warrior, in the midst of performing a ritual dance with two spears. To the right, immediately beside him, is the wolf-man into which he is about to be transformed.

Norse chessmen, Isle of Lewis, Scotland. The one biting his shield is a berserker.

FULL-BODY TATTOOS

Warriors did whatever they could to make themselves look extraordinary. Viking warrior graves from many locations show that warriors routinely filed their teeth, adding a distinctive horizontal groove halfway up. They wore eye make-up and tattoos. An Arab observer described Rus warriors on the Volga; 'From the tips of his toes to his neck, each man is tattooed dark green with designs.' Another Arab commentator noted that both men and women in Hedeby in Denmark wore eye make-up. Anything that made warriors more exotic, disconcerting or alarming gave them an extra advantage in battle. This is reminiscent of the practice among Celtic warriors, and no doubt many other warriors of the ancient world, of contorting their faces into grotesque and frightening masks. Maori warriors still do it.

UNRIVALLED MOBILITY

The Viking raiders defeated their enemies by a variety of means. Extreme violence and savagery on the battlefield was one. What is known today as empathy deficit was another – they often displayed greater skill and cunning than their enemies. They also had very well-made weapons and armour and the unrivalled mobility of their longships. These vessels were deployed in relatively small numbers at first, with raiding squadrons of three to five ships. But by halfway through the ninth century the Norse fleets comprised thirty or more vessels, and by 875 the invaders arrived with hundreds of ships.

A remarkable feature of Viking warfare was the ability to sustain warriors in the field, far away from home, for years at a time. Their longships enabled them to carry substantial volumes of supplies, and these were replenished from the plundered proceeds of their raids.

CONQUEST & SLAVERY

The motive for raiding was variable. Sometimes a raid was no more than a hit-and-run attack, for the sake of the food, livestock or loot that might be stolen. Sometimes the raid was a more systematic expedition, for example, trawling for slaves who might be lucratively sold on. Sometimes the intention was to find a plot of land to settle, while other raids focussed on conquest, ownership and political dominion.

The chronicle accounts make it clear that many of the raids involved as few as three ships and a correspondingly small number of men. But there were also major expeditions like The Great Army, as the Anglo-Saxons called it, which seems to have been a federation of many small bands.

The Great Army was a very effective force, which in the 860s and 870s succeeded in conquering the armies of the Anglo-Saxon kingdoms of Northumbria, East Anglia and Mercia – and came very close to conquering Wessex too. In 1016, a Viking army was able to conquer the whole of England.

The Vikings were very active in Ireland, but less successful in establishing large territories there. They succeeded in setting up coastal colonies (towns) with adjacent hinterlands, and the native Irish chieftains were unable to dislodge them.

The record in Scotland is much less complete, but the sagas suggest that Viking rulers in the end not only controlled large areas of western and northern Scotland, but also the Northern and Western Isles.

THE STEEL OF ISLAM

Viking weaponry was advanced. Basic spears, axes, bows and arrows were cheap as they used relatively little iron; it was also the case that spears, bows and arrows had a second, non-military use; they could be used for hunting as well, while axes could double as domestic tools. Shields too were fairly inexpensive as the iron boss could be re-used and the rest of the shield could be remade as necessary.

On the other hand there was no such thing as a cheap sword. Even a basic design took a lot of iron or steel and a great deal of technical skill to forge it. Analysis of swords

shows that the Vikings were using crucible steel made in the Islamic world and imported from there. Rus warriors used swords made of steel produced in central Asia. Armour too was expensive. The manufacture of both helmets and mail shirts took a lot of iron or steel, as well as intensive labour.

Written accounts and contemporary illustrations show that warriors almost always had helmets and mail shirts, and it does indeed seem likely. It was certainly true among the Anglo-Saxons. Aethelred II ordered that every man in the kingdom should have a mail shirt and a helmet; judging

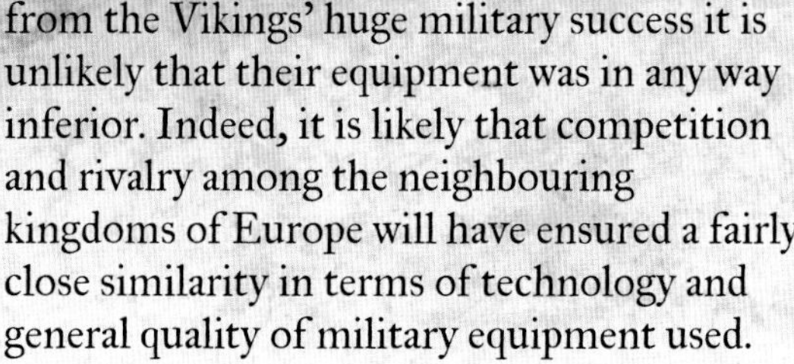

from the Vikings' huge military success it is unlikely that their equipment was in any way inferior. Indeed, it is likely that competition and rivalry among the neighbouring kingdoms of Europe will have ensured a fairly close similarity in terms of technology and general quality of military equipment used.

LETHAL WEAPONS

In the last few decades, views of Anglo-Saxon and Frankish military organization at the start of the Viking Age have moved away from the old idea of Germanic communities of free men sharing a duty and a right to bear arms as the basis of warfare, towards an idea of warfare as a more elite activity, with a focus on aristocrats, their households and followers, and a motivation driven more by personal gain. This is much closer to the Viking approach. Maybe we should not only review our image of Vikings, but start seeing the Anglo-Saxons differently too.

The Vikings had good weapons, but they did not necessarily make them themselves. In fact, many of their best weapons were imported. Frankish laws of the early ninth century actually forbid the provision of horses or weapons to the Vikings, which tells us that it must have been going on. This is confirmed by the occasional Viking poem that refers to Viking use of 'Western spears and Frankish swords'.

The sword hilts are often distinctively shaped and highly decorated, so these are not anonymous objects by any means. Carolingian hilts (sword hilts made in the Frankish empire) are found right across the Viking world, from Ireland to Ukraine. In addition to the importation of Frankish swords (whole swords with hilts), there was also a flourishing trade in sword blades, and the Vikings imported many of these, fitting them with Scandinavian hilts. Either way, it was only the rich who could afford swords.

Iron Viking swords with decorated hilts.

SPECTACLE FACEGUARD

We might expect to find that the Vikings made their own trademark winged or horned helmets, but there is no evidence that these ever existed. Helmets from the era just before the Viking Age, pre-Viking helmets, were very distinctive, borrowing a number of features from late Roman cavalry helmets, incorporating nasals and cheek-pieces to protect the face and neck. These features continue into the ninth and tenth centuries.

A tenth century helmet found in Norway has a 'spectacle' faceguard and a mail aventail or neck-guard. The spectacle face protector was also part of the eighth century Viking helmet. A truly wonderful survival from this time is the Vendel helmet, found in Grave 1 at the Vendel Cemetery at Uppland in Sweden. This has a basic hemispherical form, but with the addition of a nasal, spectacle faceguard and a crest.

But images from the Viking Age show a roughly bullet-shaped helmet with a nasal or nose-guard, so we must assume this was the commonest form of helmet. The basic forms were shared with the Anglo-Saxons, Slavs and Franks, so the Vikings would not have looked markedly different.

SWORD CHAPES

Another piece of armour that has survived archaeologically is the sword chape. This is a decorative openwork metal fitting to protect the lower end of a sword scabbard. Although it may seem like an unimportant detail, the chape was always on display, unlike the sword blade itself, which most of the time would have been hidden inside the scabbard. The decoration on the chape therefore sent an important signal of identity.

PLAYING MIND GAMES

Just as the weapons were part of a shared heritage and a shared technology, many elements in the style of warfare were shared. The Old English poem *The Battle of Maldon* describes a real battle in 991 between an English army commanded by Byrhtnoth, ealdorman of Essex, and a mixed band of Vikings led by Olaf Tryggvason.

The Vikings characteristically try to blackmail the English into giving them money to go away. This parleying episode is presented as a *flyting* match; the same sort of thing is described in Norse sagas. It represents a real feature of Viking warfare.

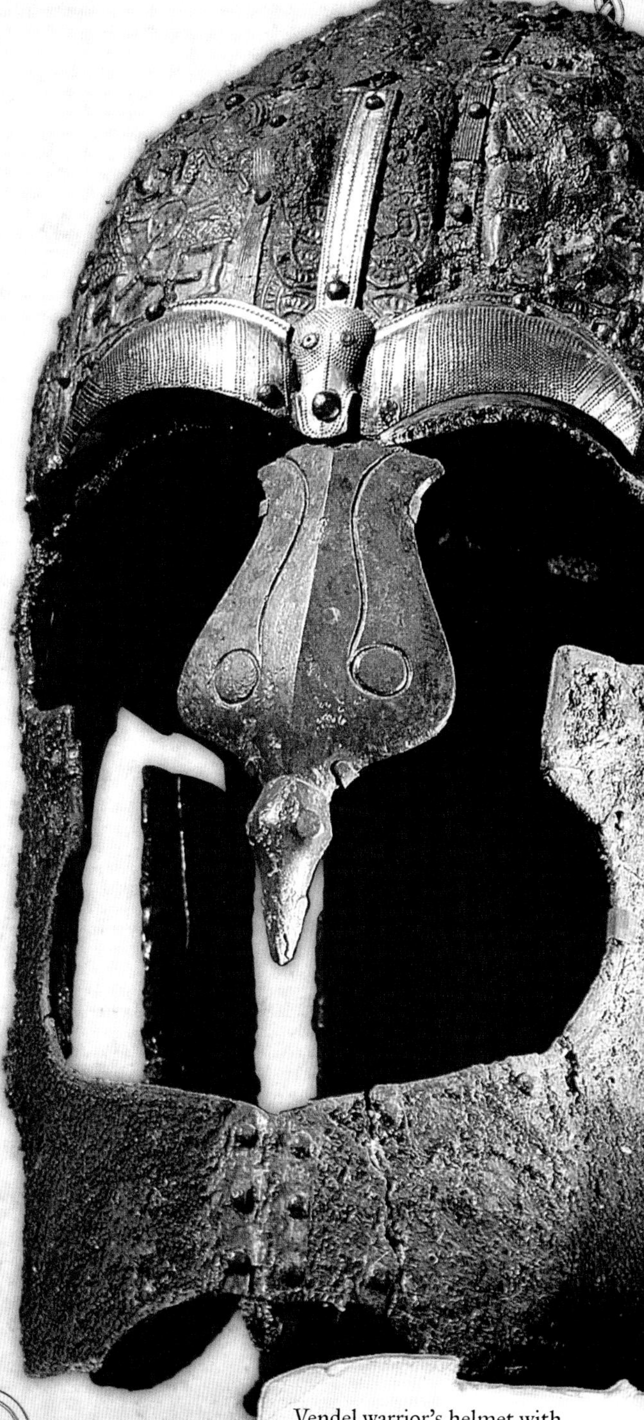

Vendel warrior's helmet with nose and cheek guards.

On the beach there stood, calling out sternly
A Viking messenger; he spoke these words.
Boastfully he spoke the sea-rovers' demands
To the earl, standing there on the shore ...
'It would be better for you
To buy off quickly this rush of spears with tax
Than that we – rough fighters as we are – should engage in battle.
What need for us to kill each other if you will just agree?'

But Byrhtnoth will not consent to this cowardly way out.

'Our riches will not come to you so easily.
Spear-point and sword's edge shall decide between us,
Grim war play indeed, before we give tribute.'

Byrhtnoth is killed during the ensuing battle.

According to William of Malmesbury's account a similar taunting preceded the battle of Stamford Bridge, again between the English and the extraordinary lone arrogant Viking who was holding the bridge single-handed. Flyting is a very ancient custom; even the ancient Greeks and Trojans did it. Today we call it 'Mind Games'.

VIKING FORTRESSES

In the homelands, the Vikings built formal strongholds such as the fortress at Fyrkat. This was a great round rigidly symmetrical fort in north Jutland, one of a series built after 980 during the turbulent reign of King Harald Bluetooth. The structure combined the functions of military camp or barracks, high-status manufacturing centre and administrative centre.

It was built on a reshaped ridge to a preconceived design. There was a timber-laced rampart of stone and turf enclosing a circular space 148 yards (136 meters) across. The outer face of the rampart was covered with tongue-and-groove timber to make scaling the wall impossible; attackers were then left between the unscalable wall and the surrounding ditch. The circular fort has a gateway at each compass point. Streets connect the gates, dividing the fort into quadrants, each with four bow-sided buildings arranged round a courtyard with a small rectangular building in the middle.

TRELLEBORG

Trelleborg is laid out very similarly to Fyrkat. Aggersborg, overlooking the Limfjord in north Denmark, is the biggest of the Danish forts, with an internal diameter of 262 yards (240 meters), and space for three times as many buildings as Fyrkat. These remarkable fortresses all appeared at the same time, and they formed part of a determined overall military strategy initiated by King Harald Bluetooth. Another Trelleborg-style fort, Borgring, was found in 2014 at Vallø near Køge on Zealand. Invisible on the ground, it was discovered by geophysical survey at a location which looked like a gap in the fortress system. The Trelleborg forts are the work of an oppressive monarch, a king bent on overmastering control – and succeeding in displaying it.

THE DANEVIRKE

The southern frontier of Denmark was defended by a set of linear earthworks running west to east across the neck of the Jutland peninsula. These are known as the Danevirke, which is first mentioned in the Danish chronicles as early as 808; in that year, we read, King Godred 'decided to fortify the border of his kingdom against Saxony with a rampart ... broken by a single gate through which wagons and horsemen would be able to enter and leave.' But the documents are deceptive. Tree-ring evidence shows that the Danevirke was created before 737. Perhaps Godred added one of the seven earthworks.

In England, there were *longphorts*, defended encampments where an army might overwinter. They were temporary sites, sometimes occupied only for short periods. The best-known was at Repton in Derbyshire, where the Great Army spent the winter of 873 – 874.

CHAPTER 8.

TRADING & RAIDING

The Scandinavians had already established trading contacts by sea with their neighbours before the Viking Age began. When the Viking Age started, with its distinctive flurry of destructive predatory raids, the trading continued alongside. The sight of a Viking sail must always have triggered a tremor of anxiety, at the very least, yet as often as not it would have been the sail of a merchantman hoping for business.

NORSE RED ALERT

Across northern Europe, coastal communities were vigilant. Charlemagne set up coastguards, forts and ships at all the main ports and river estuaries in order to ensure a quick response to a Viking attack. There was a similar reaction in England. The Anglo-Saxon Chronicle notes that in 896 a squadron of six Viking ships raiding the Channel coast of England was taken by surprise when a larger force of Anglo-Saxon vessels intercepted it while most of the crews were ashore. There was a battle during which the Vikings were defeated. Many were killed, and the rest were captured and subsequently executed. Two Viking ships escaped, one with just five survivors.

Viking assaults spread far and wide, to England, France, Spain, even into the Mediterranean. The most famous expedition to Spain was led by Bjorn and Hastein, who set out from the Loire estuary with 62 ships in 859. They went through the Straits of Gibraltar, and looted Algeciras. After attacks on the North African coast, they turned back to Spain and the Balearics. After overwintering in the Rhône Delta, they raided up the Rhône valley as far as Valence. Beaten back by the Franks, they moved across to Italy, sacking Pisa. Although only a third of the ships that had set off arrived back in the Loire again in 862, the surviving Viking adventurers must have become enormously wealthy after the expedition.

HARRYING THE BRITISH

The Anglo-Saxon Chronicle is one of the key contemporary sources for information about the Vikings. It is valuable for the precise detail it gives about events and dates. It is also the source of our image of the Vikings as marauders, pirates and extortionists. But there are also references to the violence of the response of those they attacked. King Alfred was not above slaughtering the entire crew of a captured Viking longship.

The attack on Lindisfarne in 793 is often taken as marking the beginning of the Viking Age in Britain, though there were certainly earlier attacks. King Offa needed to go to the defence of the people of Kent against attacks by pagan seamen in 792, and there were other disturbances along the English Channel coast too.

MEDIEVAL MONASTIC SPIN

The Anglo-Saxon Chronicle notes that in 789, in the reign of King Beorhtric of Wessex, men from three ships landed at Portland and killed the king's official when he rode out from Dorchester to investigate the reported illegal landing. The incidents noted in the Chronicle seem small in scale, and many will have gone unrecorded, but the cumulative unsettling effect on the English state of mind can only be imagined.

The scribes of the Anglo-Saxon Chronicle, often writing long after the event, understandably demonized the Vikings as rapacious, ruthless and violent interlopers. The chroniclers were Christian monks whose monasteries were under frequent Viking

A Viking raid.

attack. In the eyes of the monks, the heathen raiders saw only the bullion value of the venerated treasures they stole.

PLUNDERING LINDISFARNE

After 'terrible portents' appeared in the sky over Northumbria – exceptional lightning flashes and fiery dragons (probably Northern Lights) – the Vikings descended on England. They attacked on June 8, 793, when 'the ravages of heathen men miserably destroyed God's church on Lindisfarne, by plunder and slaughter.'

In 634, the monks had come from Iona in Scotland to bring Christianity to the Northumbrians. Lindisfarne was an important Christian focus, so, even though the Viking attack was little more than a hit-and-run affair, it had a powerful symbolic significance for the English. The raid was seen, both then and later, as a turning-point in English history.

Alcuin, an Anglo-Saxon monk who was then living at the court of Charlemagne, wrote an anguished letter to King Aethelred of Northumbria: 'never before has such terror appeared in Britain as we have now suffered ... Behold, the church of St Cuthbert spattered with the blood of the priests of God, despoiled of all its ornaments; a place more venerable than all in Britain is given as a prey to pagan peoples.'

The victims made much of the fact that the raiders were non-Christians. Alcuin saw the disaster as a visitation, a punishment meted out to the English for their wickedness. This same view was held by Gildas, another monk, 300 years before, only then the assailants were the English and those being punished for their wickedness were the Britons.

From the Vikings' point of view, the Lindisfarne raid was a success, and they were back the following year to attack another Northumbrian monastery, probably Jarrow, but this time the Viking leader was killed and there were no more attacks on Northumbria for a generation.

It was only two years after Lindisfarne that there was another attack, not in Northumbria but in Iona, and there were probably earlier attacks in the Northern Isles that we know nothing about because there are no chronicles to tell. Before long there were few monasteries round the coasts of Britain – indeed the coasts of northern Europe – that had not been subjected to a nightmare visitation from the Northmen.

THE EMERALD ISLE

The Vikings started raiding Ireland in the 790s. At first the forays were small, sporadic and confined to the coast, but by the 830s the assaults had intensified considerably. They were more frequent and they boldly penetrated inland along the rivers. One by one the great monasteries of Ireland were plundered. Their people were taken as well as their treasures, and some religious houses were pillaged many times.

An indication of the anxiety of the time is a note written in the margin of a book by a monk in an isolated monastery in south-west Ireland. He gave thanks to God for a stormy night;

Fierce and wild is the wind tonight,
It tosses the tresses of the sea to white;
On such a night I may take my ease;
Fierce Northmen only course the quiet seas.

The Irish monk was right to be nervous. On the island of Inchmarnock in south-west Scotland, an inscribed stone was found, the so-called Hostage Stone. The grey slab has four figures crudely scratched onto it. Three are Vikings wearing chain mail armour. The fourth is a monk they have captured. They are taking the poor man in a fetterlock (an early form of handcuff) to their ship, recognizably a Viking longship, fitted with oars and a single square sail. This was the constant, chilling threat hanging over the monasteries.

INCURSION AND CONTROL

In the 840s, bands of Viking raiders started to establish *longphorts*. These were defended ship-bases where the ships and crews could overwinter. Now raiders who had previously only appeared each summer, and might be bottled up in the Baltic by rough winter weather out in the North Sea, were now in Ireland all the time.

The Vikings were slowly establishing a stranglehold. One of the earliest bases, set up in 841 beside the Dubh-Linn on the River Liffey, became the capital of a Norse colony-kingdom and a trading centre. This was the forerunner of the modern capital, Dublin. In 902 the native Irish succeeded in expelling the Vikings from Dublin – they went to the Isle of Man, north-west England and Scotland – but Viking domination was regained 15 years later.

Nor was Dublin the only Viking settlement in Ireland. In the tenth century more followed: Arklow, Wicklow, Waterford, Wexford, Limerick and Cork. Yet on the whole Viking rule was restricted to the towns; most of rural Ireland remained outside direct Viking control.

In 980, the Irish defeated the Vikings at the Battle of Tara; after that the Vikings had to pay tribute to the Irish. The Irish were ready to tolerate a controlled and confined Viking presence in Ireland, because of the wealth that their towns generated.

The Battle of Clontarf in 1014 is often seen as the decisive confrontation between the Vikings and the Irish, because the Vikings were defeated; but in spite of that defeat King Sihtric Silkbeard ruled on in Dublin for another 20 years. In fact Dublin was still Norse-speaking when the Anglo-Norman conquerors arrived in 1170.

RAVAGING ENGLAND

In the 830s, there was renewed Viking attack on England. In 834, a large-scale Viking expedition descended on Frisia, on the Dutch coast, and sacked the town of Dorestad on the Rhine. After this success, the expedition turned to cross the southern North Sea. In 835, 'heathen men ravaged Sheppey' in East Kent. In 840 a force of Hampshire West Saxons beat off a Viking onslaught at Southampton, though in the same year a force of Dorset men was defeated at Portland.

In 841, there were Viking strikes on the coasts of Kent, East Anglia and Lincolnshire; the following year brought a new attack on Southampton. Three years later, the West Saxons defeated Viking raiders in a battle at the mouth of the River Parrett in the West Country.

The winter of 850 – 851 brought a significant intensification of the Viking attack. Instead of returning home for the winter, the Viking warriors set up camp on the Isle of Thanet. As soon as the spring weather allowed, they were able to resume their offensive; early in 851 they attacked and defeated the Mercians, though then they fought the West Saxons and were defeated.

In 854 – 855, another Viking force overwintered in England, this time on the Isle of Sheppey, which meant that a major onslaught was on the way. In the following spring, raiding resumed on the English coast.

In 860, King Aethelbald of Wessex died and was succeeded by his brother Aethelberht.

And in his reign a great pirate host landed and stormed Winchester [12 *miles inland*]. *Against the host fought ealdorman Osric with the men of Hampshire and ealdorman Aethelwulf with the men of Berkshire, and they put the host to flight, and had possession of the place of slaughter.*

Viking sword with double-edged blade.

CHAPTER 9.

THE GREAT HEATHEN ARMY

After that there was a period of relative quiet while the Vikings reconsidered their tactics. Eventually Viking leaders from Sweden, Norway and Denmark combined under a unified command and transformed their attack strategy from small-scale raiding to full-on invasion. Since the end of the eighth century their hit-and-run attacks had focussed on monasteries and plundering wealth. However the aim of The Great Army that landed in East Anglia in 865 was very different. Its purpose was to conquer England. The vast Viking force spent the winter of 865 in East Anglia, and then marched north to capture York in 866.

LEADERSHIP STRUGGLE

The Great Army's northern invasion was made easier by a leadership struggle among the defending Northumbrians. At the crucial moment when the Viking army descended, there were two rival kings, Osberht and Aelle. The next year, the Northumbrians regrouped and attacked the Vikings occupying York, but failed to dislodge them. Some Northumbrians got inside the city, but the Vikings slaughtered huge numbers both inside and outside the city. Amid the 'immense slaughter' both Northumbrian kings were killed.

The Northumbrian survivors made peace and the Vikings installed a puppet ruler, Egbert, as king of Northumbria. That winter, 867 – 868, the Great Army overwintered at Nottingham. In 869, it marched to Thetford and in the spring of 870 it successfully defeated the kingdom of East Anglia.

The Vikings were now in control of Northumbria, East Anglia, parts of Mercia, but none of Wessex. They now turned their attention to the conquest of Wessex; if they could gain Wessex, all England would be under Viking domination. By the end of 870, the Vikings had succeeded in capturing Reading, on the north-eastern border of Wessex.

KING ALFRED THE GREAT

871 brought a significant change. Alfred became king of Wessex. Several battles followed, but the Vikings were unable to break the West Saxon resistance. Acknowledging this, the Vikings made a peace treaty and turned their attention to the rest of England, in particular consolidating their hold on Mercia by conquering the unoccupied parts of it. Seven years into Alfred's reign came the Vikings' surprise attack on Chippenham. A contemporary chronicler described it –

> 878. *In this year, at Midwinter, after Twelfth Night, the [Viking] army stole itself away to Chippenham and harried the West Saxons' land, and settled there, and drove many of the people over sea, and of the remainder the greater portion they harried. And the people submitted to them, save the king, Alfred, and he with a little band withdrew to the woods and moor-fastnesses.*

Alfred was forced to flee for his life from Chippenham and hide in the marshes at Athelney. Several months of guerrilla warfare followed before the West Saxons were strong enough to confront the Vikings in open battle again.

> *At Easter Alfred, with a little band, made a fortress at Athelney, and from that work warred on the [Viking] army, with that portion of the men of Somerset that was nearest. In the seventh week after Easter he rode to Egbert's Stone, on the east of Selwood, and there came to meet him all the men from Somersetshire and Wiltshire and that part of Hampshire which remained ... One night after*

that [Alfred marched] to Edington, and there fought against all the army and put it to flight, and rode after it as far as the works and there sat fourteen nights. And then the army gave him hostages with great oaths that they would depart from his kingdom; and also promised him that their king would receive baptism; and they fulfilled their promise. Three weeks later, King Guthrum came to him [King Alfred] with thirty of his men, and the king received him there at baptism ... And [Guthrum] was twelve nights with the king, and he largely gifted him and his companions with money.

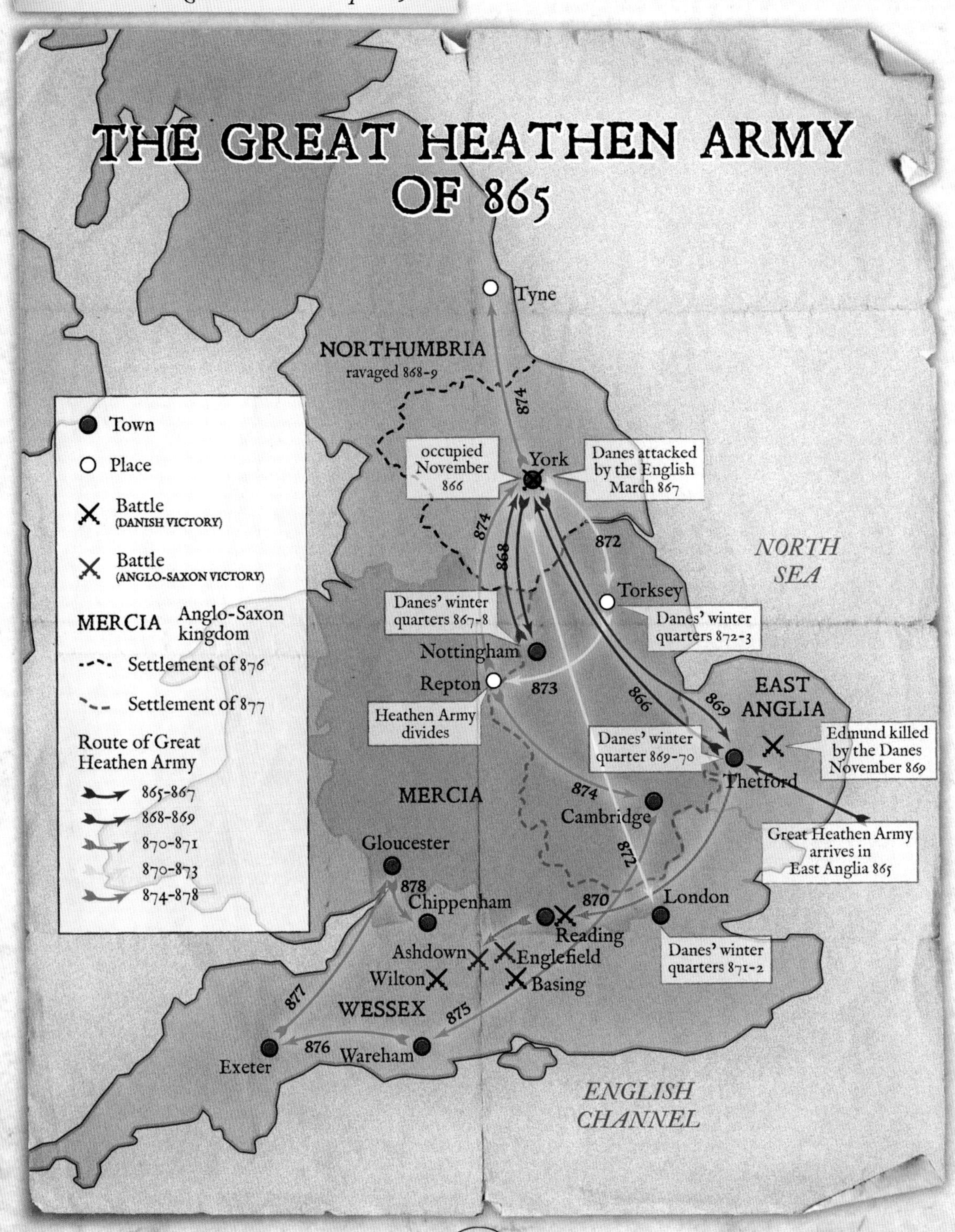

ESTABLISHING THE DANELAW

The Battle of Edington was a turning-point, another landmark in English history. The Vikings were defeated and their leader, Guthrum, was obliged to make a treaty with Alfred, agreeing to be baptized and agreeing to a division of England. Alfred was to take southern England and the lands west of Watling Street, while Guthrum was to have London, East Anglia and all the lands east of Watling Street; this Viking-controlled zone was to become known as the Danelaw.

King Alfred was nevertheless not content to let so much of England become a Danish colony and in 886 his warriors took London. The Viking army turned its attention to the kingdom of the Franks. Meanwhile other Viking raids along the English side of the Channel coast continued.

882. *King Alfred went out to sea with ships and fought against four ships' companies of Danish men, and captured two of the ships, and the men aboard were slain. And two ships' companies surrendered to him, and they were badly cut about and severely wounded before they surrendered.*

The treaty with Guthrum did not ensure a total long-term peace, and Alfred had to go on fending off Viking attacks.

885. *The [Viking] army separated into two. One part went east, the other to besiege the city of Rochester, but they [the people of Rochester] defended the city until King Alfred came without his force. Then the army went to their ships and were deprived of their horses and withdrew over sea. The same year King Alfred sent a naval force from Kent to East Anglia. As they came to the mouth of the Stour, they met sixteen ships of Vikings and fought against them and captured all the ships and slew the men. When they were returning homeward with the booty, a great naval force of Vikings met them and fought against them and the Danish gained the victory.*

RAIDING THE SOUTH COAST

In 892, a large fleet of Viking ships, 250 of them according to the chronicler, penetrated up the River Rother to find and destroy a new, half-built fort at Newenden. After this success, the fleet fell back to Appledore, where the Vikings made a winter camp which they were to use as a base for south coast raiding for several years.

King Alfred had set up a network of *burhs*, small fortified settlements which were very effective in defending the coastal settlements from attack and Viking plundering was strictly circumscribed. Appledore was nevertheless an invaluable base for the Vikings' expeditions, and it was used as a springboard for the 894 attack on Exeter, which was successfully besieged, though the people of Exeter held out long enough to be rescued by a relief force sent out by Alfred.

Returning along the coast to Appledore, the Viking fleet stopped to attack Chichester, but the local people soundly defeated them; the Vikings lost several ships in this raid.

In 896, six Viking ships attacked the Isle of Wight. Alfred sent nine Saxon ships to deal with them. Three Viking ships were engaged and defeated at sea. The other three ran aground and the skirmishing continued on land. The ships were refloated, but by this time so many Vikings had been killed that there were not enough left to crew the ships properly. As a result they were later driven onto the Sussex shore, where they and their crews were captured. The Vikings were taken to Winchester and sentenced by Alfred to be hanged.

EDMUND'S MARTYRDOM

The continual harrying by the Vikings was a major problem to the English, who were reduced to paying the raiders to go away. In 865, the first payment of Danegeld is recorded; the people of Kent paid the Vikings for the promise of peace. But the Vikings were dishonourable. 'Under cover of that peace and money, the army stole away inland by night and ravaged all of eastern Kent.'

The year 865 was pivotal for another reason. The Anglo-Saxon Chronicle records the historic event. 'In this year a Great Heathen Army came into England and took up winter quarters in East Anglia', whose ruler was King Edmund. Not much is known about him, because in the wake of his death the usurping Vikings destroyed the charters and chronicles that might have provided evidence of his reign. But, according to the Anglo-Saxon Chronicle, 'the [Viking] army rode across Mercia into East Anglia and took winter quarters at Thetford; and that winter King Edmund fought against them, and the Danish took the victory, and killed the king and conquered all that land.' Within a year of subduing East Anglia, the Great Army had moved on to invade Wessex.

The chronicle does not say whether Edmund died in battle or was executed afterwards, but the tradition took hold that Edmund was martyred. He met his death, it was said, at a place called Haegelisdun, which some people think is modern Hoxne, after refusing the Vikings' demand to renounce Christ. To punish him, the Vikings first beat him, then shot him with arrows, then beheaded him. This sounds like the triple death of sacrificial victims in old 'Celtic' Europe. It was a cruel death that the Vikings gave him. The decapitated head was 'thrown into a wood' where it lay undiscovered for a time. Those searching for it were led to it by a wolf, a Latin-speaking wolf who cried *'Hic, hic, hic'* ('Here, here, here').

Edmund was recognized as a martyr and the body, initially buried in a wooden chapel close to the place where he was killed, was put into a stone church at Beadoriceworth (now Bury St Edmunds) in the eleventh century, and then incorporated into an abbey complex. Some historians doubt whether Edmund was really killed in the way tradition has it, but it is telling that, within only a quarter of a century of his death, even the Vikings were honouring Edmund as a saint. If the cruelty and violence of the murder seem too excessive to be true, there was to be another, equally brutal and gratuitously cruel murder 150 years later – the martyrdom of Aelfheah, the Archbishop of Canterbury.

MOVING ON TO MERCIA

The Great Army's progress cannot be reconstructed in detail but by the 870s, through its exceptional violence and threat of violence, the Vikings gained control of most of eastern England.

In 867, the Danes reached the city of York. They overwintered at Repton in Mercia (the English Midlands) in 873 – 874, making a substantial D-shaped enclosure (excavated

by archaeologists Martin and Birthe Biddle) before once more heading off for the north and east. Repton was a significant choice. It was the historic burial-place of Mercian kings such as Wiglaf and St Wystan, and the Vikings were making a point by occupying it. When they arrived, they drove out the Mercian king, Burhred. After a reign lasting twenty-two years, he was forced to flee 'over sea'.

Repton is only 40 miles from Cheshire and the Wirral, yet it seems there was no Viking penetration there for another 20 years, which is surprising. The Anglo-Saxon Chronicle tells us that in 893 a band of Vikings occupied 'a deserted city in Wirral which is called Chester'. They included the remnants of a Viking force under Hástein which had recently been crushed by the West Saxon King Alfred at Buttington on the banks of the River Severn. The Mercians chased off these Viking refugees the following year, driving them into Wales. It may have been at this time that the dilapidated walls of Chester were repaired; in 907, Chester was officially listed as a fortified *burh*.

The occupation of a crumbling Roman city is an interesting re-run of what happened during the progress of the Anglo-Saxon

Aethelflaed, Lady of the Mercians, *c.* 872–918, daughter of Alfred the Great, charging into battle.

settlement 200 or more years before. The English had been through this 'squatter phase' already, re-inhabiting the Roman ruins.

A UNITED KINGDOM

In 874 the great army divided in two. In 876, the warriors led by Halfdan 'shared out the land of the Northumbrians and they proceeded to plough and support themselves'. Others, led by Guthrum, took land in Mercia in 877 and East Anglia in 879. Guthrum had previously tried to settle in Wessex but after his defeat by King Alfred he had been forced to agree to a frontier between the kingdom of Wessex and Viking territory, following the line of Watling Street.

This fixed the boundary between Wessex and Mercia, but it was not the end of Alfred's trouble with the Vikings. Towards the end of his reign new bands of Vikings raided the Channel coasts, on both the English and the French sides. Roundly defeated by the Franks in 891, these new invaders crossed to England and tried to seize land there. The English successfully resisted these onslaughts and the attackers finally disbanded, some settling in areas already under Viking control in East Anglia and Northumbria. King Alfred's old enemy, but now godson, Guthrum, was described by the chroniclers as 'the northern king whose baptismal name was Athelstan'; he died in 890 and the chroniclers imply that he was regarded as the first Viking king of East Anglia.

Viking aggression had the effect of welding the English kingdoms together. The underlying idea was that separately they were vulnerable, that they were 'better together', safer as a single unified nation. It was the Viking threat that created English nationhood.

CROSSING THE IRISH SEA

A major impact on the course of events in England following King Alfred's death in 899, was the expulsion of the Vikings from Dublin in 902. This led to the displacement of Vikings across the Irish Sea. The Welsh Annals record that in 903 a man with the Old Norse name Ingmunt (or Ingimund) seized a place called Maes Ros Melion on Anglesey. Unusually, we have information about Ingimund from another source, the Irish Three Fragments of Annals, which says that Ingimund and his followers were thrown out of Wales as well.

The outcasts followed the coastline of North Wales to the Wirral, where they asked the ruler for land to settle. The ruler there was Aethelflaed of Mercia, and she granted Ingimund the land he wanted – probably the northern half of the Wirral. It seems that by this stage there were Vikings living on one or even both sides of the Mersey estuary, and this may be why Aethelflaed allowed Ingimund to settle there; it was a territory that had already become a Viking colony.

Far from being grateful for this generous land grant to which he was not at all entitled, Ingimund was dissatisfied. He wanted more. He and his followers launched an attack on the city of Chester, hoping for a share of its wealth and strategic importance. The people of Chester fought the attackers off, it was recorded, by releasing swarms of bees and pouring boiling beer on them. Ingimund retreated.

SKIRMISHES & STAND-OFFS

This episode shows the sort of complex interplay between Vikings and Anglo-Saxons, between interlopers and sitting tenants, that went on all over England; interplay that was deeply unsatisfactory from both sides' point of view. There were skirmishes, there were stand-offs, and sometimes there were full-scale battles. The famous Battle of Brunanburgh took place in 937, probably in the Wirral. In this landmark confrontation, the English under King Aethelstan crushed a coalition army consisting of Scots, Dublin-based Vikings and others. Bromburgh, in the south-east of the Wirral, is the closest place-name match to Brunanburgh.

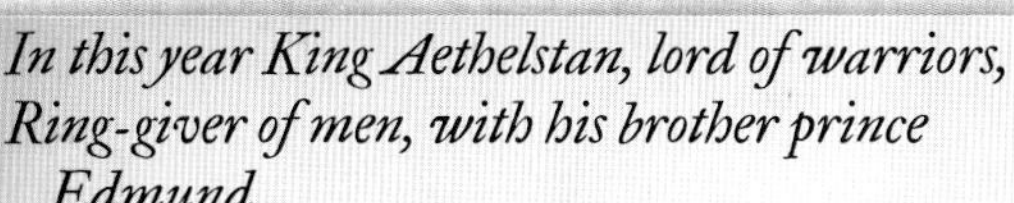

In this year King Aethelstan, lord of warriors,
Ring-giver of men, with his brother prince
Edmund,
Won undying glory with the edges of swords,
In warfare around Brunanburh.
With their hammered blades, the sons of
Edward
Clove the shield-wall and hacked the linden
bucklers ...

KING OVER ALL ENGLAND

After this major Viking defeat, control of the area by the English strengthened. There was another Viking raid from the Irish Sea on Cheshire in 980, but generally the Anglo-Saxons and the Viking incomers lived fairly peaceably together until the Norman Conquest.

By 900, the year after Alfred's death, there had been Vikings living in England for fifty years. The chroniclers described Alfred as 'king over all England except that part which was under Danish domination, and he ruled the kingdom twenty-eight and a half years.' But this glossed over the fact that the area under Danish domination was very large. The area of Danish settlement and Danish rule, known as the Danelaw, had become well-established. It included the kingdoms of York and East Anglia, with the area known as the Five Boroughs in between – the fortified towns of Leicester, Derby, Lincoln, Nottingham and Stamford.

Within the Danelaw, the Church had somehow survived, though many monasteries had been abandoned and their estates seized. King Alfred remembered nostalgically that there had once been a time 'before everything was ravaged and burnt', but it was very much his determined opposition to the Vikings that prevented them from completely overrunning England – and it was Alfred's successors, building on his achievement, who were able to turn the tide and create a unified Anglo-Saxon kingdom of England in the middle of the tenth century, but only after long-continued fighting, battle after battle. The last Viking king of York was Erik Bloodaxe, and he was defeated by the Anglo-Saxons in 954.

RAIDING WALES

The Welsh too were the victims of Viking attacks. The Welsh Annals tell us that there were raids on Gwynedd (an independent kingdom in north-west Wales) from 854 until 919; this might be seen as the first Viking Age in Wales. Then there was a lull lasting three decades. A second Viking Age started in 950, when many Welsh monasteries were raided. A third Viking Age came in the late eleventh century. The Welsh suffered every bit as much as the English. In 998 Morgeneu, the Bishop of St David's, was killed in a raid. The major objective in the later raids was the taking of captives, especially wealthy high-status captives, princes, chiefs and leading churchmen, with a view to ransom.

The annals say that between 970 and 972 'Godfrey, son of Harold, ravaged Anglesey, and through great cunning he subdued the whole island.' It is possible that the Vikings succeeded in setting up colonies or enclaves on Anglesey and the neighbouring mainland at that time.

Llanbedrgoch, a large walled and ditched enclosure established in north-east Anglesey before the Viking Age, may have been a settlement that was captured and taken over by Viking colonists. Five skeletons were found buried in the enclosure ditch, dating from the late tenth century. Two of the skeletons were of men, with their wrists tied. There were also a young woman of 20, a youth of 17 and a child of 10. They were related. When they were found in 1994 they were at first assumed to be victims of the Vikings' brutality in their quest for wealth by way of slavery – five visible victims among the thousands who remain archaeologically and historically invisible. But recent forensic analysis shows something different – the men had spent their early years in Scandinavia; so these were not Welsh victims of violence, they were *Viking* victims.

CHAPTER 10.

VIKING RAIDS ON THE FRANKISH EMPIRE

In parallel to the raids on England, the Frankish empire, Charlemagne's domain, was also attacked. An early successful raid on Frisia was led by King Godfred of Denmark, in 810. But the Carolingian defence system was well organized and a subsequent attack on the Normandy coast in 820 was beaten off. The big Viking attacks on the Franks began in earnest in 834 and went on for a generation. In 841 Rouen was attacked. Then the Vikings set up a raiding base at Noirmoutier at the mouth of the Loire, the first on the European mainland outside Denmark. From there, in 844, they penetrated up the Garonne. In 845 Paris was looted.

PLUNDERING PARIS

The Frankish empire was seriously threatened by this intensifying onslaught. More and more Danegeld was paid in the hope of making the Vikings go away. In the 860s, Vikings regularly raided northern France. The monk Ermentarius of Noirmoutier recorded the events :

> *The number of ships grows and the endless stream of Vikings never ceases. Everywhere Christians are the victims of massacre, burning and plundering as the Vikings conquer all in their path and no-one resists them ... an innumerable fleet sailed up the Seine and the evil grows in the whole region. Rouen is laid waste, plundered and burned; Paris, Beauvais and Meaux taken, Melun's strong fortress levelled to the ground, Chartres occupied, Evreux and Bayeux plundered and every town besieged.*

Ermentarius' account of the Viking plundering of Paris on Easter Day, March 28, 845 says that the Vikings gained little joy from their 'heavy-laden ships', because most of those who took part fell ill and died on the voyage home of a mysterious illness that drove them blind and mad. Ermentarius comments with satisfaction that this shows God's judgement on their evil deeds. But how could he have known what happened to the Viking raiders after they left the region? There must be a suspicion that he made it up. How much more did he invent?

RESOLUTE DEFENSE

The Vikings' foray up the Seine and their attack on Paris should not be doubted, but great concerted expeditions of the kind Ermentarius describes were fairly uncommon. Most of the Viking raids consisted of no more than a hundred men, and they were uncoordinated and opportunistic. This made them harder to predict and the uncertainty must in itself have engendered fear among the victim communities.

The raiders seem to have had very little loyalty to their nominal rulers back in Scandinavia. This created another problem; there was no possibility of negotiating terms for a mediated peace. The Frankish king Charles the Bald, for instance, could not make a formal protest to the King of Denmark in order to get the expedition called off. Instead, he was forced to pay off the Viking raiders themselves (7,000 pounds of silver) to leave the ruins of Paris to smoulder in peace.

The Franks fought back. The key to Charles the Bald's defences for the Seine was a fortified bridge, *Pont de l'Arche*, begun in 862. It took eight years to complete, but it successfully blocked the Vikings' invasion attempt in 876 and kept them out until they destroyed it in 885.

BLOOD MONEY

From the point of view of their victims, it must have been some consolation that the Vikings also attacked one another. When Charlemagne's heirs fought each other over the legacy of his empire, they all hired armies of Viking mercenaries to fight for them, so Vikings were fighting Vikings. They could be bought. In England they were given substantial bribes to go away and leave the English in peace, though unfortunately it required repeated bribes. On the European mainland, it became the custom to reward a Viking army with gifts of silver or even land in return for protection from other Viking groups. The system was similar to a gangland protection racket.

If we have any doubts about the word of Ermentarius, other sources seem to corroborate his description of Viking campaigning in what is now northern France. According to the Anglo-Saxon Chronicle, after being halted and turned back by King Alfred, the Viking army in England turned its attention to France, campaigning there in 880 – 90, first penetrating 40 miles up the River Somme to Amiens, remaining there for a year, then in 886 penetrating up the Seine to overwinter in Paris. From Paris, they roamed ever-deeper into the kingdom of the Franks. By 890, they were roaming westwards, towards the borders of the Franks. The Bretons stopped them from entering Brittany, 'and drove them out into a river, and drowned many'.

King Odo of France at the battle of Montfaucon, 888, during which he defeated the Vikings.

CHAPTER 11.
RENEWED ATTACKS ON ENGLAND

A second wave of raids on England began in 980. There were Viking attacks on Thanet in Kent, Southampton on the south coast and Cheshire on the Irish Sea. In the following year, these raids extended to the coast of Devon and Cornwall. Then, in 982, Dorset was attacked and London was set on fire. These new raiders were different men with a different ambition. The first wave of Viking raiders had ultimately wanted land on which to settle. This second wave did not want land – it wanted treasure. England was wealthy and so an attractive target.

EXTORTION AND BLACKMAIL

The first of a new series of Danegelds was paid by the English in 991; the Vikings, led by Olaf Tryggvason, later king of Norway, took £10,000 in Danegeld. The sums needed to buy off the Vikings went up and up. By 1002 the payment had gone up to £24,000, by 1012 it had risen to £48,000. The silver hoards found in Scandinavia offer ample evidence of the enormous affluence of Anglo-Saxon England.

The severity of the Viking attacks made paying Danegeld seem worthwhile. In 994 the chroniclers say a fleet of ninety-four ships under Anlaf (Olaf) and Sweyn went up the Thames to London. [Sweyn is an anglicized form of the Scandinavian Sven or Sveinn; they are all the same name.]

They intended to set [London] on fire, but they suffered greater loss and injury than they ever thought possible that any garrison would inflict on them. The Holy Mother of God manifested her clemency to the garrison and delivered them from their foes. They went away, doing as much harm as any host was capable of doing in burning, harrying and slaughter, both along the coast and in Essex, Kent, Sussex and Hampshire ... and continued to do unspeakable damage. Then the king agreed to send to them tribute and supplies, if they would desist from harrying.

SWEYN FORKBEARD

In 994 Danegeld was (again) paid to Olaf, who had returned with Sweyn Forkbeard, the King of Denmark. After this, Olaf concerned himself mainly with home affairs in Norway, while Sweyn took up the lucrative looting operation. It was a handing-on of the protection racket. The situation was complicated by the fact that some Vikings were ready to fight for the English – as always for cash. In 1012, Thorkell the Tall, with his forty-five ships, entered the pay of King Aethelred and helped to save the English king from the attacks of Sweyn Forkbeard the following year.

Meanwhile the raids on English communities continued relentlessly. In 997, the Vikings raided Devon and Cornwall.

They entered the estuary of the Tamar until they came to Lydford. There they burned and slew everything they met and burnt to the ground Ordwulf's church at Tavistock, carrying off an indescribable amount of plunder with them to the ships.

CNUT THE GREAT

Sweyn arrived with his fleet in the Humber in 1013 and was accepted as king by the Danelaw, over the northern kingdoms of England. When Sweyn died in 1014, his son Cnut was chosen to be king of England, all England, after the death of Aethelred, which came in 1016. [Canute is an anglicized form of the

Scandinavian Cnut or Knut; they are all the same name.] Then began the reign of Cnut the Great, which went on until his death in 1035. Cnut's rule in England as a strong Viking king brought a major advantage to the English, who now had someone on the throne who could do more than just defend England against attack – he could actually avert it. Cnut was powerful enough in the Viking homelands to be able to prevent raids on England by maverick bands of Vikings from the other side of the North Sea.

The Anglo-Saxon monarchy was restored under Edward the Confessor, but the Vikings across the North Sea still hankered after a lion's share of England's wealth. They made four more attempts to regain control.

BATTLE OF STAMFORD BRIDGE

The first expedition came in 1066, when Harald Hardrada the king of Norway and earl Tostig invaded with a great army, sailing 360 shiploads of warriors into the Humber and marching them to York. They were confronted by King Harold of England at Stamford Bridge.

That day a very stubborn battle was fought by both sides. There were slain Harald Hardrada and earl Tostig, and the remaining Norwegians were put to flight, while the English fiercely assailed their rear until some of them reached their ships. Some were drowned, others burnt to death. There were few survivors and the English had possession of the place of slaughter.

Viking invaders sailing up the river Humber, East Anglia in the tenth century.

The English king was magnanimous in victory. He spared the lives of Olaf, the king of Norway's son, their bishop, and all the others who were left aboard the ships. They had to go ashore and swear oaths to King Harold that they would for ever maintain peace and friendship with England. Then Harold let them sail home.

WILLIAM THE CONQUEROR

The second expedition came in 1069, when a Danish royal fleet sailed into the Humber to support the English rebellion against King William I and the Norman conquerors. The third came the following year when Sveinn Estridsson, the king of Denmark, came with a fleet; he was bought off by William. Finally, another Cnut, Sveinn Estridsson's son and successor, planned another abortive invasion. These final onslaughts marked the end of the Viking harrying of England, which had gone on for 300 years.

DEMONIZING THE INVADERS

Is it possible that the incidents were exaggerated? Viking raids certainly happened, but analysis of the records suggests that Viking raids were but one part of the general pattern of violence that prevailed in the eighth and ninth centuries, as kings, princes, chieftains and local lords fought each other for supremacy.

The Irish Annals tell of 113 attacks on monasteries between 795 and 820. Of these, only 26 were carried out by Vikings; 87 were carried out by Irish kings – or even monks from rival monasteries. The Vikings may have been singled out because they were non-Christian, or maybe even because they were outsiders. It was possible to vilify Vikings, accuse them of sacrilege, vandalizing the beautiful and the sacred, and picking on the weak and defenceless. The Vikings evidently saw themselves very differently. They saw themselves as heroic adventurers, driven by a warrior ideology.

In England generally, there is surprisingly little direct archaeological evidence of Viking violence. The bishop's throne from North Elmham shows signs of burning. An ingot mould found at Whitby could have been used for melting down loot. A stone from Lindisfarne shows warriors waving axes, possibly Viking raiders. The monasteries at Jarrow and Monkwearmouth were both burnt down at some stage, perhaps by Vikings. It is not a long list, and the evidence could be interpreted non-violently.

CHURCHYARD GRAVES

It was thought at one time that a scene of a Viking massacre had been found at East Harling in Norfolk. Pits filled with bones were associated with an eighth century coin hoard. But a non-violent explanation is available. The bone-pits are now thought to be evidence of a medieval churchyard clearance; medieval pottery was found in some of the pits.

Another potential massacre site was found at Repton in Derbyshire, the place where the Viking Great Army overwintered in 873 – 74. Just outside the fortified enclosure there was a two-chambered mortuary chapel containing the remains of 250 people, mostly men, and dating from the ninth century, the time of the Viking occupation of the site.

A mound was heaped over the charnel house. When the stone building was discovered in the seventeenth century, it was said that in the midst of the bones was the skeleton of a giant, though this had disappeared by the time of the excavation by Martin and Birthe Biddle in the 1970s and 1980s.

The central burial was probably that of a Viking chief or king. The rest of the bones were probably battle victims of the Viking army initially buried elsewhere, then later gathered for reburial at the ancient Mercian royal centre, the place where Mercian kings were buried. Most of the bones belong to males aged between 15 and 45. They are the bones of massively robust, non-local males with Scandinavian characteristics. It was a Viking war-grave.

CHAPTER 12.

MURDERING AN ARCHBISHOP

However they saw themselves, many of the Viking raiders were guilty of many crimes. The record of events, however explained or excused, is a record of acts of aggression against unwilling victims. They stole, they burnt, they destroyed, they abducted and they killed. It is the unbridled, almost gleeful, violence and murderous cruelty of the Vikings that sticks in our collective memory.

That cruelty is exemplified by the murder of the Archbishop of Canterbury in 1012. Aelfheah, also spelt Alphege, but in any case pronounced 'Alfie', was Bishop of Winchester when he helped ealdorman Aethelweard negotiate a peace treaty with King Olaf Tryggvason after a Viking raid in 994. Olaf was paid Danegeld, and in return he undertook never to raid or fight the English again. He also converted to Christianity. It was Bishop Aelfheah who baptized him.

Aelfheah's luck took a turn for the worse when he became Archbishop of Canterbury. He travelled to Rome to receive the pallium, the symbol of his new status, from the Pope, but he was robbed during the journey.

In September 1011, Vikings laid siege to Canterbury and, once inside, sacked the city. The cathedral was plundered and burned and Aelfheah himself was taken prisoner. The raiders went back to their ships, taking Aelfheah with them. He was held captive for seven months. The Anglo-Saxon Chronicle gives an account of his death.

The raiding army became much stirred up against the bishop because he did not want to offer them any money, and forbade that anything might be granted in return for him. Also they were very drunk. Then they seized the bishop, led him to their mead-hall on the Saturday in the octave of Easter and then pelted him there with bones and the heads of cattle. One of them struck him on the head with the butt of an axe, so that with the blow he sank down and his holy blood fell on the earth and sent forth his holy soul to God's kingdom.

FINDING GLORY IN GOD

Aelfheah was the first Archbishop of Canterbury to die a violent death, and it was considered shocking at the time. Thorkell the Tall tried to rescue Aelfheah from the mob that was about to kill him, by offering them everything he owned except his ship in exchange for Aelfheah's life. None of the surviving versions of the Anglo-Saxon Chronicle mentions this, but the chroniclers were not interested in giving any credit to a 'good Viking'.

Canonized, Aelfheah became a key saint in Canterbury's mythic story. He was first buried in St Paul's Cathedral, but in 1023 King Cnut organized an elaborate ceremony in which the body was returned to Canterbury for reburial. Thorkell the Tall was appalled at the brutality of his fellow-Vikings and following the murder switched sides to support King Aethelred.

Aelfheah was venerated, especially at Canterbury, as the first martyred archbishop and it was heavily symbolic that Thomas Becket prayed to his murdered predecessor immediately before his own assassination, when he was Archbishop of Canterbury, in December 1170.

Viking sword with straight, double-edged blade.

CHAPTER 13.

MASSACRE AND MASS EXECUTION

The violence was not all one way, though. Sometimes the victims of Viking raids managed to wreak revenge. The largest-scale example of this was the St Brice's Day Massacre, which took place on November 13, 1002.

England had been subjected to repeated Viking raids, every year from 997 to 1001. On top of this provocation, the English king, Aethelred, was told that there was a conspiracy to assassinate him and all his councillors. The Danes already living in England would turn traitor; they 'would faithlessly take his life, then all his councillors, and possess his kingdom afterwards'. Aethelred consequently 'ordered slain all the Danish men who were in England'.

ST BRICE'S DAY MASSACRE

There is no formal record of the number of people killed in the massacre, but it is believed to have been considerable. Amongst those killed was Gunhilde, the sister of King Sweyn of Denmark. It is thought that her husband, Pallig Tokesen, who was the Danish ealdorman of Devon, was also among those killed. According to one version of events, Tokesen's defection, joining the raiders attacking the Channel coast of England, was one of the factors that provoked the massacre.

Aethelred reflected on the massacre two years later in a royal charter which explained the need to rebuild St Frideswide's Church in Oxford, which subsequently became Oxford Cathedral. He said it would be well known that he decreed 'that all the Danes who had sprung up in this island, sprouting like cockle [weeds] among the wheat, were to be destroyed by a most just extermination, and thus this decree was to be put into effect even as far as death'.

He went on to describe what happened in Oxford, 'Those Danes who dwelt in the afore-mentioned town, striving to escape death, entered this sanctuary of Christ, having broken by force the doors and bolts, and resolved to make refuge and defence for themselves therein against the people of the town. But when all the people in pursuit forced by necessity to drive them out, and could not, they set fire to the planks and burnt, as it seems, this church with its ornaments and its books.'

RETALIATION AND REPRISAL

Aethelred tried to blame the terrified Danish citizens for the fire, but the wording he used – 'as it seems' – shows uncertainty about who started the fire. It may have been the townspeople who did it in their efforts to flush the Danes out of the church.

People died elsewhere in Oxford too. When a garden was excavated at St John's College in 2008, the skeletons of about 36 young men aged between 16 and 25 were found. It is possible that they too were victims of the St Brice's Day Massacre. On the other hand some recent forensic analysis suggests that the young men were Viking warriors who were not resident in England, in other words captured raiders who were executed. Such retaliatory reprisals had also happened elsewhere.

The St Brice's Day Massacre could probably not have extended into the Danelaw (to the north of Oxford), because the Danish population were too strong there, so some historians think the massacre may have been confined to border towns like Oxford. It had a strong political motive, exploiting ethnic hatred, but it had a very negative result in prompting Sweyn's invasion of England in 1003.

The Viking mass grave at Ridgeway Hill, Weymouth, Dorset.

MASS GRAVE

In the tenth century, there was a Viking raid on Weymouth in Dorset. It looks as if the crew of one raiding longship fell into the hands of the natives, who exacted summary retribution. A mass grave discovered in 2009 on Ridgeway Hill near Weymouth tells us that 54 Vikings were executed there following capture. Most of them were young, between 18 and 25, but one, perhaps their leader, was over 50. The oddest thing about them is that they were in poor health.

Many of the young men suffered from infections and physical impairments of one form or another. Some had brucellosis, probably through drinking infected milk. Forensic analysis of the executed men's teeth showed that they came from Scandinavia – one of them from north of the Arctic Circle. This was not an elite group of Viking warriors and perhaps their poor physical condition helps to explain how they came to be captured.

The location of the mass grave, beside a main road and on a parish boundary, was a common site for an execution in those times. The captives were forced to strip before being killed, all at the same time, with a large and very sharp weapon, probably a sword. They were beheaded, but not cleanly, and many suffered multiple blows to vertebrae, jaws and skulls.

One man had his hands sliced through, probably when he instinctively tried to defend himself against the swinging sword. The mass execution was a bloodbath. The bodies were thrown into a disused Roman quarry, to save digging a burial pit, and three of the heads were not buried; they were perhaps kept as souvenirs or impaled on stakes at the execution site.

The archaeology of the Ridgeway Hill Viking mass grave can nevertheless be interpreted in more than one way. It may show us that the native Anglo-Saxons were just as brutal as the Viking raiders – when they were given the opportunity to take revenge. It may alternatively show us how the leadership of a Viking expedition dealt with a backsliding crew that failed to measure up to the standards expected of them. This may have been the crew of a ship that let down a Viking fleet in some way, perhaps even betrayed fellow-Vikings by changing sides. One thing is certain: the Ridgeway Hill mass execution proves the savagery of the times.

PART 3.

VIKING MYTHS, RELIGION & BELIEFS

CHAPTER 14.

THE LAND OF ICE AND FIRE

Like the ancient Greeks and Romans, the Vikings worshipped a whole pantheon of gods, and it was their paganism that particularly struck contemporary witnesses. The monks who recorded the Viking raids repeatedly labelled the raiders with either the Latin name *pagani* (pagans) or the Germanic equivalent *haethena* (heathen). These labels were really little more than terms of abuse and vituperation hurled by Christians at non-Christians, and they tell us little about what the Vikings actually believed.

The Vikings appear to have had no word for 'religion', but rather thought more in terms of ideals, customs and traditional practices. It may be that what was seen in the thirteenth century as Viking religion was partly a construct that had been assembled by Christians in order to build a strategy for converting Vikings to Christianity. Christians did not invent the Viking religion, but rather codified and expressed it in a way that made comparison with other European beliefs easier. Even so, the sagas allow us to reconstruct it with some confidence.

The Norns, divine female beings who ruled over the fate of gods and men.

THE COSMOS AND CREATION

The cosmos had formed from a great void known as Ginnungagap. Gods and giants emerged as primal beings in a land of cold, fire, ice and mist. From the start there were murderous disputes, and the worlds were eventually formed out of the body parts of a slain giant. The first human beings were called Askr and Embla – interesting that their names start with the same letters as Adam and Eve – and they were made by the gods from logs of driftwood washed up on the shore.

There are many narratives, telling different parts of the elaborate creation story, including one to explain the origin of the dwarves, who lived under rocks and in the mountains, and the elves, who were the spirits of the countryside and woodland.

ASGARD AND VALHALLA

The gods lived in a divine world or kingdom called Asgard. There were two families of gods, the Aesir and the Vanir. Existing parallel with Asgard was Midgard, the Middle Place, which was the inspiration for Tolkien's Middle-Earth, and this is where people lived. Asgard was a divine replica of the human world, an open landscape dotted with stately halls with outbuildings, each the feudal home of a god and his retinue. There were about fourteen of these halls, but the most famous of them by far was Valhöll, the hall of the chief god, Odin. Rather oddly, there were also temples in Asgard, where the gods and goddesses worshipped. A peculiarity of the Viking belief system is that the gods themselves worshipped something, though it is not known who or what.

Giants lived in Jötunheim, or Giant World and beings with other, more demonic powers lived in Utgard, the Outer Place.

SPIRITS OF THE UNDERWORLD

There was also an underworld, which seems to have been subdivided just like Dante's Inferno into nine gradations, and this was called Hel. The similarity to the medieval Christian idea of an underworld, and the similarity of the name and structure suggests a borrowing in one direction or the other. Hel, Hell. Too much of a coincidence? Hel was a destination for the dead, but only one of many destinations. Some of the dead went to Hel, but some went to Odin's hall and some went to the water-world. But quite what determined where people went after death remains unclear.

THE TREE OF LIFE

This whole elaborate cosmos was held together by the great world-ash-tree, Yggdrasil, though it is not clear how the worlds were arranged within the structure of the tree. The tree was nevertheless seen as linking and connecting the different parts of the cosmos. Travellers were able to move among them by following the tree roots, or by following sacred rivers and lakes. They could cross over the rainbow bridge, called Bifröst. They could also cross by way of the all-important sea, the home of the Midgard Serpent, a dragon whose coils encircled the world.

THE GUARDIANS OF TIME

The different landscapes had their guardians, who carried out specific functions and had specific duties. There were three otherworldly women, the Norns, who governed time: past, present and future. Certain animals moved around the world-ash-tree: an eagle, a squirrel, a dragon. The gods possessed their own specific familiar animals. On top of all these, there were dozens of supernatural beings: ogres, spirits, trolls, wolves and hounds. There were also the deified powers of the earth itself and the streams, stones, air and mist.

The Vikings lived in an unimaginably complex cosmos that was populated by a huge number of invisible creatures and forces. But they evidently did not think of this as 'supernature' in the modern sense, but as an extension of nature itself, and just as real.

Odin sits enthroned, flanked by his ravens Huginn and Muninn, and the wolves Geri and Freki.

CHAPTER 15.

ODIN – FATHER OF THE BATTLE-SLAIN

Most of what we know about Viking mythology and Viking religion comes from documents written just after the Viking Age ended, the poems of the *Poetic Edda* and the Icelander Snorri Sturluson's thirteenth century *Prose Edda* account of them. The Vikings' chief god was Odin. Snorri defined his place and role.

> *Odin is the highest and oldest of the gods; he rules all things, and however powerful the other gods are they all serve him as children serve their father ... Odin is called All-father, because he is the father of all the gods; he is also called Valfather because his chosen sons are all those who die in battle. Valhöll is for them.*

GOD OF WISDOM

The word *valr*, the first syllable of the words Valfather and Valhöll (better known in the nineteenth century as Valhalla) means 'the slain', and more specifically 'those slain in battle'.

Odin had many aspects and many other names. He was 'god of the hanged' and 'helmeted one'. He had special dedicated animals and birds (wolves and ravens), which fed on the corpses of the slain. The wolves were named Geri and Freki. 'Geri and Freki the battle-accustomed father of hosts feeds, but on wine alone splendidly weaponed Odin ever lives.'

Odin had two special ravens, Huginn and Muninn (Thought and Memory), which embodied his function as the god of wisdom. Odin's son, Tyr*, had one hand bitten off by the monstrous grey wolf, Fenrir, who is destined to be the death of Odin.

A whole range of prophesies in the *Poetic Edda* and the *Prose Edda* tells us that this will be Odin's fate in the last battle of the gods and men against monsters and giants – The Battle of Ragnarok.

[* Tyr is a personal name that is common in Denmark but very rare elsewhere in Scandinavia, implying that in detail myths and beliefs varied from place to place.]

Since Snorri Sturluson was writing after the great age of the Vikings was over, there is a possibility that some of the detail may not be authentically Viking. It is reassuring to find some early Viking Age images that corroborate some of it. Snorri describes Odin's eight-legged horse Sleipnir; the name crops up in several of the Edda poems and there are some Gotland stones showing a figure riding an eight-legged horse.

THE WORLD SERPENT

The story of Thor's fishing expedition to catch the World Serpent, accompanied by the giant Hymir, is found in three Icelandic texts, and it similarly appears in Viking sculpture – a long way from Iceland. A carving in St Mary's Church at Gosforth in Cumbria shows two figures in a boat, one of them (presumably Thor) fishing with a huge hook, which he is using to catch the World Serpent, which inhabits the ocean girdling all lands. Other carvings from Gosforth and elsewhere depict the Battle of Ragnarok, which was prophesied to take place between the gods and giants at the end of the world, the battle that has yet to happen.

Some of these mythological scenes and incidents found their way into Christian iconography by a back-door route. The Battle of Ragnarok and Thor's struggle with the serpent could be illicitly identified with the Biblical struggle between Good and Evil or more specifically Christ's struggle with the Devil. It is a kind of mythological smuggling.

The Gosforth Cross is an unusually tall and slender carved stone cross standing in a churchyard. It is covered in elaborate interlace designs and figurative sculpture which includes major Christian scenes like the Crucifixion, but also several that are identifiably pagan and Viking: Valkyrie figures, the slaying of Fenrir at the Battle of Ragnarok and the bound figure of the treacherous god Loki. No doubt medieval Christians persuaded themselves that Loki was Satan, the treacherous and disgraced fallen angel. The Gosforth Cross is an extraordinary mixture of Christian and Viking images telling of a tenth century phase of transition and conversion. Where it was possible, old ideas were carried forward and assimilated; people were naturally reluctant to shed their traditions.

HAMMER OF THE GODS

The situation regarding Odin is complicated further by something the eleventh century Anglo-Saxon writer Aelfric says. While Snorri makes Odin the highest god, Aelfric says the god Thor is the equal of the Roman Jupiter. Adam of Bremen describes the images of the gods in the temple at Uppsala in Sweden; one of them is Odin's, and another is Thor's – the most powerful of the gods.

In the *Prose Edda*, Thor has a predominantly protective role, though he is vulnerable without his hammer. Thor was evidently a very popular god. Many of the place-names given to new settlements incorporate his name, such as Thorsness (Thor's headland), and sometimes people gave their children names that included the name of Thor, such as Thorstein and Thorgrim.

People wore amulets that invoked Thor's protection; they were often pendants in the form of Thor's hammer. Often these were simple iron 'T' shapes, but some were more elaborate and made of silver. The wearing of amulets was perhaps a reaction to a perceived threat from Christianity. Before encounters with Christians were common, there would have been no need to assert a pagan identity. The idea of threat as an aid to sharpening identity is one to return to later.

PANTHEON OF THE GODS

Besides Odin, the Vikings had an entire pantheon of lesser gods and goddesses. Odin's wife, Frigg was prominent. There was also Idun, who kept apples that preserved the youth of the gods. There was a trio of deities linked with fertility, especially in Sweden: Frey, his sister Freyja and their father Njord. Warriors who died heroically in battle expected to be gathered up from the battlefield by Valkyries and welcomed into Odin's hall with cups of wine. There the fallen warriors would feast and drink with Odin while they waited to take their part in the great Battle of Ragnarok at the world's end.

GODDESS OF FERTILITY

In Norse mythology, Freyja is the owner of the magic necklace Brisingamen and wears a cloak of falcon feathers. Women did not take part in battles, but they had an equivalent expectation that they would be received into the otherworld and are welcomed there by Freyja. A talisman in the form of a goddess in a long robe and holding out a drinking horn is probably Freyja. In Egil's Saga, the daughter of Egil anticipates imminent death. She says, 'I have not eaten and shall not until I am with Freyja.'

SIGURD AND BRYNHILD

As in ancient Greek mythology, Viking myths show the lives of human beings entangled with the destinies of the gods. Valkyries became involved with mortal warriors, as did Brynhild in the famous legend of Sigurd. Brynhild's long sleep behind a wall of flames was the punishment she was given by Odin for awarding victory to a mortal warrior against his instructions. Sigurd himself is a hero of remarkable stature, so much so that he must be regarded as a demi-god.

The Sigurd legend was an enormously popular one, and this can be gauged from the coverage given to it in the Edda poems. Around half of the Eddic poems are about the myths of the gods. Nearly all of the rest deal with Sigurd. The stonemasons who carved mythic scenes took great delight in the Sigurd story, and their favourite episode was Sigurd slaying the serpent Fafnir.

THE TEMPLE OF THE GODS

The eleventh century German observer, Adam of Bremen, described the heathen temple at Old Uppsala. This has not been corroborated by archaeology, but may even so be a true account.

That nation [Sweden] has a most famous temple which is called Uppsala, not far from the town of Sigtuna or Birka. In that temple which is fitted out in gold, the people honour the statues of three gods. The most powerful of them, Thor, has his seat in the centre of a triple throne. On either side Wodan [Odin] and Fricco [Frey] take their places. Thor, they say, has dominion over the air. He is the one who governs thunder and lightning, winds and pouring rain, fine weather and fertility. The next is Wodan, which is to say 'Fury'. He wages war and gives a man courage in the face of the enemy. The third is Fricco, distributing peace and sensual delight to mortals. His image they portray with a huge erect phallus. Wodan, on the other hand, they sculpt in armour, as our armourers usually portray Mars. And Thor with his sceptre looks very like Jupiter.

They have priests appointed to offer the people sacrifices. If plague or famine is approaching the sacrifice is to the idol Thor; if war, to Wodan; if a marriage is to be solemnized, to Fricco. In addition every nine years a communal celebration involving all the Swedish provinces is held at Uppsala. No-one is exempt from it. Kings and people, one and all, send their gifts to Uppsala. What is crueller than any penalty – those who have already turned to Christianity have to buy themselves out of these ceremonies.

The sacrifice is like this. Of every living creature that is male, nine heads are offered, with whose blood it is the custom to placate the gods. The bodies are hung in the grove near the temple. To the pagans that grove is so sacred that each individual tree is thought divine by virtue of the creatures sacrificed. There they hang dogs and horses side by side

with. A certain Christian informed me he had seen seventy-two miscellaneous bodies suspended there.

Note 1. Near this temple is a huge tree, its branches spreading far and wide. It is always green, winter and summer alike. There is also a well there where they have the practice of holding pagan sacrifices. A living man is plunged into it. If he does not surface again, the people's desires will be fulfilled.

Note 2. A gold chain surrounds the temple, hanging from the gables of the building. It shines far afield to those who approach it since the shrine is set on a plain, and has hills round about it in the form of an amphitheatre.

Note 3. These feasts and sacrifices continue for nine days. Each day they offer a man with the rest of the beasts, so that in nine days that makes seventy-two creatures offered up. This sacrifice takes place about the spring equinox.

Maeshowe, part of the Orkney World Heritage Site, is the finest chambered tomb in north-west Europe.

CHAPTER 16.

VIKING HEROIC IDEALS

The heroic life depended on certain ideals, including the obligations of one social group to another and the rights and rewards that were their due in return. Loyalty was an important heroic value.

A sense of adventure was an essential element in the Viking heroic cult. Wealth and leisure would also have been necessary, the prerogatives of the upper classes. The literature of the time was produced for those upper classes, and so it is their values that we know most about. But not all Vikings were heroic adventurers. Many Scandinavians were too poor to lead a life of heroic adventure. There was an alternative life-style, for the non-heroic, the non-adventurous.

One aspect of this non-heroic life was the everyday dangers of travel, and the circumspection and caution travellers needed to show in order to be safe. There were codes of behaviour that had to be followed if a traveller wanted hospitality; a traveller should expect to pay for his board and lodging with pleasant and interesting conversation, with news and gossip – not bad advice for a house-guest even today.

Out in the field no man
should move
A foot beyond his weapons.
For a man never knows,
out on the trackways,
When he may need his spear.

Peer into all the crannies and
corners
Before you step inside,
For you cannot know where false
friends
May lurk in wait for you ...

When he sits to eat he needs a wash,
A towel, and a hearty welcome.
Good humour, if he can manage it,
Conversation and time to respond.

If we thought Vikings caroused into the night, drinking to excess, the habits of ordinary people were very different.

A man should not hold on to the ale cup,
But drink moderately from it.
Spare of speech he should be, or silent.
No man will accuse you of ill manners
For going too early to bed.

The heroic view of death in battle was complemented by an alternative, non-heroic view.

Better living than not living.
Only the living hold wealth.
I saw a fire blaze up in a rich man's house,
But death stood outside the door.

A cripple can ride, a man with one arm can
herd sheep.
The deaf can fight well enough.
Better blind than burnt on the pyre.
What good is a corpse to anyone?

As is often found in peasant societies where learning is uncommon, the Vikings were suspicious of clever people. They believed it was possible to know too much, to be too clever, too wise.

Medium wise a man ought to be,
Never too wise.
The men who have the richest lives
Are those who know just enough.

Gilt-bronze weather vane.

Medium wise a man ought to be,
Never too wise.
For a wise man's heart is rarely glad,
A really wise man's, that is.

Medium wise a man ought to be,
Never too wise.
No-one should know his fate in advance;
His fate will be freer of care.

Another trait of these societies is a streak of misogyny, which seems to go with male chauvinism and poor education.

In woman's words let no man trust.
Nor what a wife may say,
For their hearts are formed on a whirling wheel
And fickleness is fixed in their breasts.

Side by side with the epic, mythic ideal of the hero was a more moderate, indeed for us a more recognizable, domesticated, approach to life. Apart from the warrior class, the Vikings were not so very different from ourselves. One Viking poem is a list of homilies, useful scraps of advice, tips for getting by in everyday life.

Loving a woman whose heart is false
Is like driving an unshod horse over slippery ice,
A mettled two-year-old, not fully broken;
Or like handling a rudderless ship in a fierce gale.

Sweet talk and gifts offered
Will win a wench's favour.
Praise the lovely creature's looks.
To win you must woo.

Another man's love you never must mock.
Never mock another man for what is common to all.
It turns men of sense into idiots,
Love is mighty over all.

Don't say it's been a good day till sunset.
Don't say she's a good wife till she's buried.
Don't say the ice is safe till you've crossed it.

Longhouse reconstruction of everyday life, L'Anse aux Meadows, Canada.

CHAPTER 17.

RUNE-STONES AND STANDING STONES

Rune-stones belong to the pagan Viking culture, but the use of them was taken over and expanded as Christianity took over. The Malar valley in central Sweden was at the core of this process; several thousand inscribed stones were erected in this valley alone in the eleventh and twelfth centuries. A typical rune-stone has a cross in the middle and an inscription in a kind of meandering strap round it, asking for God to aid the soul of the dead person, and also declaring who raised the monument.

DRAGON'S HEAD BOULDERS

Rune-stones were only roughly shaped and dressed boulders. Even the surface that carried the inscription was left fairly uneven. The runic inscription was carved round the edge of one of the stone's broad sides, between two parallel lines. These lines might be straight or curved, but they often followed the irregular edges of the boulder, and took the appearance of a strap or serpent; sometimes the ends were given dragons' heads. Inside the inscription there was often a symbolic image of some kind. It might be a cross or a mythical beast like a dragon. King Harald's monument at Jelling has a fine drawing of a great beast battling with a snake. Some rune-stones have several symbolic images.

WHILE MAN LIVES ON

Rune-stones were sometimes placed by bridges or causeways. At Salna, Uppland, in Sweden, a pillar 10 feet (3 meters) high was raised by a stone bridge. Some of the inscription has been lost, and unfortunately the stone was moved in the nineteenth century;

Oystaein and Iorund and Biorn, [brothers, set up this stone to] ... their father. God help his spirit and soul, and forgive him his offences and sins. Ever will stand, while man lives on. This strong-built broad bridge, to the good man's memory. Boys made it for their father. There can be no better way-monument.

A similar memorial was erected at Arby, also in Uppland. An inscribed boulder marked the track leading to a bridge over a river;

Nasi and his brothers raised this stone
In memory of their good father Iarl and
Made a bridge to God's glory.

Another, at Nas, in the same province, commemorated the making of some causeways.

Lifstaein caused to be made, for the benefit of his own soul and the souls of his wife Ingirun and his sons Iarund and Nikolas and Ludin, these causeways. He owned the farm at Torsholma and had the right to call up a ship's crew from Rolsta.

A FALLEN WARRIOR

Other rune-stones are simple memorials, though often telling a potent story –

Ingifast had this stone cut in memory of his father Sigvid. He fell in Holmgard, a ship's captain with his crew.

Holmgard is Novgorod, which is 125 miles from the Baltic. Presumably Sigvid died in some sort of land battle, with all of his men, yet he was still remembered as the captain of a substantial warship, to judge from the word used for warship, *skaeith*.

Another memorial commemorates a man who fought in England.

Griotgard, Aeinridi, sons,
Made [this] for their valiant father.
Gudvaer was west in England.

He shared tribute.
Cities in Saxland [Anglo-Saxon land, England?]
Like a man he stormed.

The inscriptions read like memorials to war heroes. There is no hint here that these were opportunistic raids on defenceless civilians.

Øybiorn put up this stone for Skoerdir.
He met his death in England in the army.

Yet some of those who were commemorated died fighting in the homelands.

Thorulf erected this stone, Svein's retainer, in memory of Erik his comrade who met his death when fighting-men besieged Hedeby and he was a ship's captain, a very good man.

The exact meaning of the inscriptions is sometimes hard to reach. The word translated here as 'comrade' might mean 'business partner' or 'member of the same fighting unit', in other words 'comrade-in-arms'. So it is not just the runes that are ambiguous, the vocabulary is ambiguous too.

LAYING RUNE-STONES

Viking rune-stones were not confined to the homelands. A few runic inscriptions have been found in Britain and Ireland, sometimes in places where we do not expect to find a Viking presence. One was in St Paul's churchyard in London. This was part of a burial monument, though it does not give the name or deeds of the dead man, only the names of the men who raised the monument; *Ginna and Toki had this stone laid down.*

In the wall of a medieval church tower in Winchester there is a recycled block of stone, originally from a Viking tomb; it is badly damaged, but there are enough surviving 'twigs' to show that it was also a runic inscription.

Rune-stone on Adelso Island, Stockholm, Sweden.

CHAPTER 18.

VIKING BURIAL & COMMEMORATION

ON A CUMBRIAN HILLTOP

In 2004 a Viking cemetery was found at Cumwhitton, near Carlisle, Cumbria, when a metal detectorist turned up a fine tenth century oval Viking brooch. These usually come in pairs associated with the burial of women. The Cumwhitton oval brooch is very similar to the pair found in a ninth century woman's grave in Phoenix Park, Dublin.

Excavation at Cumwhitton revealed not one grave but several, including a cluster of five close together on a hilltop. The men all had weapons buried with them, either spears or swords in scabbards. One burial even had an axe and a shield. Another man had spurs, but also a necklace and three silver rings, unusual in a male burial. The women had brooches, a pair of shears and an antler or bone comb.

The most interesting aspect of the Cumwhitton grave-goods is that they came from different places. The buckles and strap-ends were locally made, the spurs and textiles came from elsewhere in Britain. The design of one of the inlaid sword hilts comes from northern Britain, another is Frankish: the axehead and the oval brooches came from Scandinavia.

A pair of tenth-century gold brooches, Denmark.

The orientation of the graves, heads to the west, suggests that the people might have been Christians. The small number and close-knit arrangement suggests that the graves represent two generations of one family of Viking incomers. What happened? Did this kinship group settle in the Eden valley for three or four decades and then move on? The kinship between the grave-goods and those in a Christian context at Workington in Cumbria implies that the Cumwhitton Vikings may have been in the process of assimilating into the local community.

SUNDAY BEST

As well as brooches, whalebone plaques were sometimes buried as grave-goods; they show a veneration for the fertility goddess Freyja, and were often placed in the graves of women. Women were also buried with keys, to show that they managed household spending and had access to domestic stores. Weapons and sometimes tools were buried with men; the weapons were sometimes broken or bent, 'killing' them so that they could enter the otherworld. There were also metal dress-fastenings such as pins, buckles and strap-ends, which imply that corpses were buried fully dressed, in fact dressed in what centuries later would be called 'Sunday-best'.

LYING BURIED IN THE WEST

An exceptionally well furnished grave was found at Ardvouray on the west coast of Barra in the Western Isles. The body was accompanied by a pair of oval brooches, a ringed pin, an iron buckle, a comb, a drinking-horn, a knife, a whetstone, a carding-comb, a weaving-sword and a pair of shears.

This was the grave of a high-status woman in Viking dress, a pure Viking burial, suggesting that the lady was a first-generation colonist. She was buried beside a standing stone that was much older, so her community decided to bury her at a place that was already a landmark, an established pre-Viking sacred site.

This was a community of colonists who accepted pre-existing holy places and were perhaps trying to embed themselves in a British belief system.

Viking picture stone with runic writing, Sweden.

CHAPTER 19.

VIKING SHIP BURIALS

Vikings are associated above all with ship burials, though these were reserved for chieftains and kings: ships were very expensive. In the poem *Beowulf*, the mythical King Skjold arrived in Denmark by ship and when he died he departed by ship. He was laid out in his ship along with his weapons and quantities of treasure. This is a poetic version of what was by the beginning of the Viking Age already a well-established tradition for burying dead chiefs.

Archaeology has revealed that in the Viking Age some chiefs were buried in their ships, some were burned before burial, some partly burned. The practice is known from all over the Viking homelands and also from areas that were colonized such as Orkney, Shetland and Brittany.

THE GOKSTAD LONGSHIP

The most famous ship burial is the Gokstad ship, which was found under a burial mound on Gokstad Farm in Sandefjord, Norway, in 1879 – 80. That winter, the farmer's two sons were digging the frozen soil when they uncovered the bow of a boat with its painter. Nicolay Nicolayson, the President of the Society for the Preservation of Ancient Norwegian Monuments, got to hear about the discovery and arrived at the site in February 1880.

He persuaded the farmer's sons to stop digging and began his own excavation there the following month. The burial mound was 165 feet (50 meters) across and, although ploughed down, still 16 feet (5 meters) high. Nicolayson and his team dug into the mound from the side and on the second day they were startled to unearth the prow of a full-sized longship.

PAINSTAKING RESTORATION

The Gokstad ship was 75 feet (23 meters) long with a beam of 17 feet (5.2 meters), and clinker-built, mainly of oak. There were sixteen tapered planks on each side, overlapping each other by 1.2 inches (3 cm) and secured with iron rivets. The two uppermost strakes, along with the top of the stem and stern posts, had stuck out of the clay material of the mound, and they had disintegrated.

The ship was painstakingly restored, and the missing pieces replaced in modern timber. The crossbeams had ledges cut into them, 1 inch (2.5 cm) wide, to make a seating for a deck that could be fitted in removable sections. Chests probably containing the 32 oarsmen's possessions were placed on the deck as seats for the oarsmen; when the ship was under sail, the chests were probably stowed under the decking as ballast.

The hull shape is rather flat, and would have been best suited to calm water conditions in the fjords and inshore waters. Under strong wind in open water, the ship would have become difficult to steer. To counter this loss of control, there was very likely some sort of reefing system for taking in sail. A piece of the Gokstad ship's sail survived. It was made of a white woollen cloth with red stripes sewn onto it.

THE ROYAL SKELETON

At the time the ship was buried, 32 shields were fixed to each side of the ship, a pair for each oarsman on board, and they were painted alternately yellow and black. The skeleton of a strongly-built man in his 40s was found on a bed inside a wooden burial chamber covered with birch bark; its ceiling had traces of silk interwoven with gold threads – the cloth of gold prized by medieval kings as a sign of their royal status.

The skeleton showed signs of injuries: cuts to the legs that must have been battle wounds. The man's identity is not known, but a possibility is that he was the local chieftain, Olaf Geirstad-Alf, who according to the *Heimskringla* died around the time when the ship was built, in 890. Some of the grave-goods buried with him, silver, gold and weapons, were taken in antiquity by robbers. But they left behind three small boats, a tent, a sledge, riding gear, twelve horses, eight dogs, two goshawks and two peacocks.

THE OSEBERG SHIP

The Oseberg ship was discovered in a burial mound at the Oseberg Farm near Tønsberg in Norway and excavated in 1904 – 05 by the Norwegian Haakon Shetelig and the Swedish Gabriel Gustafson. The burial chamber has been tree-ring dated to 834, but the ship is at least 30 years older.

The Oseberg ship deserves its fame as the finest surviving relic of the Viking Age. It was clinker-built and made of oak, like the Gokstad ship, though 6.5 feet (2 meters) shorter. It had 30 oarsmen and an estimated sail area of 107 square yards (90 square meters). Its fittings included a broad steering oar, an iron anchor, a gangplank and a bailer. This time the bow and stern posts were preserved intact, and beautifully decorated with elegant, complicated interlaced patterns in 'gripping beast' style. Oseberg was very lightly built indeed and clearly meant for use only in sheltered inshore waters. It was unsuitable for ocean-going because of its low freeboard; a modern replica sank twice because moderate waves were able to lap over the gunwales.

Gokstad Viking ship excavation, 1880.

RICH RESTING PLACE

Given the grace and delicacy of the Oseberg ship, it seems appropriate that it was used for the burial of two ladies, one in her 60s, one in her 50s. Possibly one was sacrificed in order to keep the other company in death. The richness of the burial shows that at least one of them was a very high status lady. One wore a fine red woollen dress with an up-market lozenge twill pattern, and a fine white linen veil. The other had a plainer blue woollen dress with a wool veil, which perhaps indicates lower status.

The identity of the two women is not known, but it is possible that the higher-ranking lady is Queen Åse, the mother of Halfdan the Black and grandmother of Harald Fair-Hair. Recent forensic tests suggest that both women lived in Agder in Norway, which was the home of Queen Åse. The younger woman's DNA is thought by one scientist to show that she came from Iran, but this has been challenged by other scientists who think the sample was contaminated.

THE BUDDHA BUCKET

Once again, grave robbers had removed the richest grave-goods, but they left much of interest and value, including four elaborately decorated sleighs and a richly-carved wooden cart with four wheels – the only complete Viking cart to have survived.

There were also bedposts, wooden chests and the so-called Buddha bucket, a wooden bucket with brass fittings; the handle mounting is in the shape of a figure sitting cross-legged. It has been compared to the Buddha sitting in the lotus position, but the character of the piece is pure Celtic.

The face is one that is often seen in iron age Celtic art, oval, bald, with almond-shaped eyes and prominent brow-ridge. The cross-legged posture shows that it is the iron age god Cernunnos. A similar face is seen on a bowl handle from a Viking grave at Miklebostad in Norway – and that certainly came from Ireland. The Buddha bucket was most likely collected in Britain or Ireland.

BURYING THE BODIES

An account of the Danes written in about 1200 recounts a law made by King Frode about the burial of warriors. The head of a family was to be buried with his horse and weapons. The bodies of ten captains might be burned together in one ship, but the body of a commander had to be burned on its own on a pyre in a ship. A king or an earl who fell in battle had to be burned in his own ship.

Although much in this account by Saxo deals with legendary Denmark, the details about the burial procedure are corroborated by archaeology, even to the size of the ship corresponding with the status of the individual buried in it. There is even corroboration from the Arab author ibn Fadlan's account of a princely Viking burial, which says that poorer Vikings were buried in small boats.

The Buddha bucket, a brass and enamel figure sitting with crossed legs on the bucket handle.

The best-known ship burials, Oseberg and Gokstad, are naturally the ones that contain big longships, but balancing these are the very large numbers of burials in small boats, usually clinker-built rowing-boats. There are no burials in big trading vessels, which implies that wealthy merchants were not entitled to ship burial.

STANDING BOLDLY

Another type of aristocratic burial involved wagons, chambers or occasionally sledges. The chamber graves are associated with horses, so each of these is connected in some way with transport.

There are also the Gotland picture stones, which are like rune-stones but covered with images rather than runes. In some ways the picture stones are ship burials on the cheap, as they always have images of ships on them.

The ships usually have, among the human figures portrayed, one who is given prominence. It is thought that this figure represents the dead person. Usually he sits in the bow of the ship, often holding a weapon in his hand, which calls to mind the rune-stone inscription, 'He who stood boldly in the bow of the ship now lies buried in the west.'

CHRISTIAN TRANSFUSION

The Vikings seem to have absorbed Christianity relatively easily. Perhaps Christ was accepted as one more god to place alongside the many gods they already had. The Christians too had a history of assimilating sacred places and traditions from other religions; it is possible that the Christians tried to equate the various pagan gods the Vikings introduced with Christian saints.

Some mutual assimilation went on. Viking colonists were ready to bury their dead in Christian burial grounds; archaeology has uncovered furnished graves (graves with pagan grave-goods) in Christian graveyards. Similarly, the early Christian burials in Scandinavia took place in pagan burial grounds, but later, during the tenth century, churches and churchyards start to appear.

There is not a great deal of evidence of conversion, but there is some. The Anglo-Saxon Chronicle famously describes the conversion to Christianity of the Viking leader Guthrum after his defeat by King Alfred in 878. Most of the evidence points to rapid conversion to Christianity of all the settlers in England shortly after this, except in Cumbria. The first Christian king of Dublin died in retreat on Iona in 980. The first Viking bishopric was established in Orkney in 1050.

THE HOGBACK TOMBS

The Vikings colonized Strathclyde, the dark age kingdom that focused on the Firth of Clyde and had the natural fortress of Dumbarton Rock as its capital. The Viking kings of Strathclyde were buried at Govan, a few miles up the Clyde. The Old Parish Church at Govan contains a remarkable collection of Viking sculpture, in fact one of the most important concentrations of Viking sculpture in the whole of Britain.

It includes some intricately carved high-status hogback tombstones, which are thought to have been developed from the Anglo-Saxon tradition of decorated recumbent slab tombs. The hogback tombs represent bow-sided longhouses with pitched roofs, perhaps specifically the palatial mead-halls of the kings who were buried beneath.

The Govan hogbacks are believed to be the tombs of the Viking kings of Strathclyde. When Guthfrith, the king of Dublin, was expelled from Northumbria by Aethelstan in 927, he fled to Strathclyde before returning to Dublin. The kings of Dublin and Strathclyde fought alongside the Scots against Aethelstan shortly afterwards, in the 930s, notably at the Battle of Brunanburgh.

CHAPTER 20.

VIKING RELIGIOUS SITES

SUMMER HOME OF KINGS

At Fugledegard on the western shore of Lake Tissø in Zealand, Denmark, stood a royal residential complex. Ploughing in 1976 produced a huge tenth century gold neck-ring, 12 inches (30 cm) in diameter and weighing nearly 4.4 lbs (2 kg); it ranks as one of the biggest gold finds in Denmark. This discovery led to a thorough investigation of the area and what emerged were the remains of a substantial royal residence, called Kalmagården. The residence is very similar to others in southern Scandinavia, such as Old Lejre in central Zealand and Jarrestad in Scania. Perhaps Kalmagården was a seasonal residence for the royal family based at Old Lejre.

ROYAL RITUALS

There were several ritual sites, all of them within a kilometre of the royal residence. From time to time during the nineteenth and twentieth centuries, various objects were picked out of the lake: axes, spears, swords and jewellery.

A small number of objects might represent casual accidental losses, but the large number suggests deliberate deposition. It was a very ancient practice. There are examples from all over Europe of rivers, lakes and marshes where offerings of precious objects were deposited, and they date from the iron age, over two thousand years ago, or even the bronze age, over three thousand years ago.

So this lake deposit in Lake Tissø may have continued an ancient religious practice. This takes on a new significance when we realise that the lake's name comes either from the god Tyr or from the word 'Ti', an Old Danish word meaning God. So the name may mean 'Tyr's Lake' or 'God's Lake'.

SACRIFICIAL OFFERINGS

A tool chest containing a template for tenth century metal box fittings was found in the River Halleby, and this river forms the southern edge of the special precinct, an area extending over 123 acres (50 hectares). To the west, the precinct was bounded by the Maderne, a marshy area. A large number of horse bones has been found there, which may indicate the sacrifice of horses. This too was an ancient religious practice dating from hundreds of years before the Viking Age.

On a hilltop a few hundred yards west of the royal residence there were some clay pits. This was where the clay was dug to build the royal complex, but also in this area were more sacrificed objects including jewellery and glass beads, implying that the building work was accompanied by rituals.

UNCOVERING THE PAGAN CULT

In the royal residence itself, there were several cult buildings, where cult meals were eaten. Wells were found too in the marketplace. The large number of animal skulls and limb bones of animals in them suggests that they too may have been used for sacrificial offerings. The layering of the well deposits show that this practice went on for quite a long time in the ninth and tenth centuries.

These are only the remains that have so far been found at Lake Tissø, but there are almost certainly more waiting to be discovered in this unusual complex. What has been found so far shows a deliberate organization of the landscape for religious purposes, in particular for sacrificial offerings to different gods and activities of a more social nature. It is a fascinating site, and all the more so for being laid out so late, immediately before the Vikings were converted to Christianity.

BREATHING IN THE LAND

Lake Tissø is just one religious ceremonial focus, on the island of Zealand in Denmark. But there were many others in the Scandinavian homelands, such as Borg in Lofoten, Uppsala in Uppland, Uppåkra in Scania, Gudme in Funen and Lejre in Zealand. Some survive in place-names. *Vi* means a pagan religious site, *Ullevi* means a pagan religious site dedicated to Ull. *Torslunda* means Thor's grove and *Fröslunda* means Frey's grove. These names are seen in Sweden. Another common topographic name is *Helgafell*, meaning holy mountain. The Vikings clearly invested the landscape of their homelands with strong spiritual significance.

GHOST SHIP BURIALS

In Jutland, Denmark, at Lindholm Høje, there is a remarkable Viking burial ground. The ship burials for chiefs and kings, in which a full-sized real wooden ship is used as a tomb, are well-known. The graves at Lindholm Høje are made in the shape of a ship, each marked with a kerb made of rocks planted in the ground.

The burial ground contains about 200 of these, each one a kind of ghost-ship, just as in neolithic Britain the stone circle was a ghost-roundhouse. The ship was heavily symbolic. The wealth of the Vikings was dependent on voyages by sea and river, whether for raiding or for trading, and those voyages in turn were dependent on ships.

VIKING SKAEITHS

Ships were central to the Vikings' secular culture, their way of life. However, the ship was also a powerful symbol of the great voyage beyond the grave, the final voyage into the unknown. An inscription on an early tenth century rune-stone at Stevns on Zealand indicates that the Vikings thought of these stone settings as real ships. A woman called Ragnhild made a grave-mound and *skaeith* in memory of her husband Gunnulf.

Lindholm Høje Viking cemetery, Älborg, Denmark.

A *skaeith* is a stone ship and the rune-stone is thought to have represented its prow. As with the real ship burials, there are large and small stone ships, and the size difference may reflect the different social status of the dead. It is reasonable to assume so, because the largest stone setting in the shape of a ship is 328 yards (300 meters) long and it was built at Jelling, the major royal centre. The real ship burials were buried under mounds, but the stone ships were left open to the sky, as permanent features of the landscape.

WEARING THOR'S HAMMER

At Birka in Sweden there is a Viking cemetery which consists of a great many low burial mounds. The grave-goods inside these mounds reflect Birka's importance as a trading centre. One of the richest burials at Birka is that of a woman who was buried inside a small rectangular wooden chamber about 7 feet (2.2 meters) long.

At her feet, in the south-east corner, was placed an array of grave-goods including a bronze bowl, a casket containing a comb and a glass linen-smoother, a drinking glass, a wine jug imported from the Rhineland and two buckets. In the north-east corner was a whalebone plaque.

The woman's body was fully dressed, with all her brooches and beads in place. She was laid out on her back west-to-east just as in a Christian burial, but there is little doubt that this was a pagan burial, partly because of the presence of grave-goods, and one of them was an iron ring with Thor's hammer pendants, and she wore this potent symbol round her neck.

ROYAL BURIAL MOUNDS

At Uppsala, also in Sweden, there were different types of burial, perhaps more recognizable. These were burials beneath large round mounds or barrows, the same sort as were built in Britain in the late neolithic and early bronze age, though these Uppsala mounds date from the fifth and sixth centuries. Uppsala, with its ancient royal burial mounds, became a famous focus for pagan worship in the Viking Age. No doubt the antiquity of the great royal burial mounds provided validation – a genuine royal seal of approval.

THE TEMPLE OF BLÓT

In the Viking Age a temple stood close beside the royal mounds, though when the Vikings converted to Christianity the temple was replaced by a church. Adam of Bremen described the temple at Old Uppsala in detail, including its temple-hall, used perhaps for communal meals, perhaps for sacrifice (the Viking word for this was *blót*). These animal sacrifices were violent acts, more violent than was necessary just to kill, and it seems that worshippers liked to see an impressive spray of blood.

ADAM OF BREMEN'S TEMPLE

At Götavi in Sweden, a special sacrificial platform made of packed stones was built. It was rectangular and made of nine rows of stones; nine was a number with mystical power. Scholars have been skeptical about Adam of Bremen's account of the Uppsala temple, because nothing like it has been found by archaeologists, but recently the remains of a huge hall 109 yards (100 meters) long have come to light; it was in use from 600 onwards and burnt down in about 900.

Its purpose is not yet known; perhaps it is Adam's temple.

THE TEMPLE AT UPPÅKRA

Temples probably stood at many of the sites now occupied by churches, and all trace of them was destroyed when the churches were built, so evidence of the temples of the Vikings are bound to be hard to find. The remains of one were found by archaeologists in 2004 at the old royal centre of Uppåkra, near Lund in Scania. This temple was a small building, 43 feet (13 meters) long by 23 feet (7 meters) wide, but very strongly built of oak logs standing upright side by side in a foundation trench. Like the houses, it was bow-sided and had a central hearth. It had three doors, each flanked by a pair of stout posts.

What made it different from a house was the array of four massive wooden columns marking the corners of a square round the hearth. The post-holes were dug 6.5 feet (2 meters) deep, so they must have risen to a considerable height, probably supporting a tall square tower or lantern that rose well above the main pitched roof and probably served as a means of lighting the interior from above. If the roof was steeply pitched, the temple would have looked quite like a stave church; it is reasonable to guess that the architecture of the medieval stave churches would have borrowed quite a lot from the architecture of the temples they replaced. Uppåkra was in use for several hundred years, falling out of use in the tenth century.

THE SANCTITY OF THE LAND

We can now be certain that the Vikings had built shrines and temples, though they also worshipped out in the landscape too, and had a well-developed sense of the sanctity of the land. Norse folk tales speak of the *landvaettir*, the 'land-spirits' who were the spirits of the place. Some Vikings at least had an acute sense of the specialness of certain places. Snorri tells us a tale of an Icelander called Hrolf Redbeard.

He took all Holmsland between the Rivers Fiska and Ranga and he lived at Fors [the Waterfall]. His children were Thorstein Rednose, who lived there after him, and Thora and Asa and Helga ...

Thorstein Rednose was a great man for sacrificing. He sacrificed to the Waterfall; all the left-overs had to be taken and thrown into it. He could also see into the future. When his sheep were taken from the common fold he used to count up to two thousand of them and then all the rest would jump out over the wall. In autumn he could see which of them could not survive the winter, and he had them slaughtered.

The last autumn of his life he sat at the common fold and said, 'It's up to you to slaughter the sheep you pick out. Now I am going to die – or perhaps all the sheep are – or perhaps both.' On the night he died, all the sheep were plunged into the Waterfall.

THE NAME OF THE DEAD

This strange tale shows how a particular landmark could become woven into every aspect of a Viking's life. What exactly happened to the sheep is ambiguous. Were they deliberately thrown into the waterfall, sacrificed by Thorstein's family to mark his death? Or did the sheep jump in of their own accord? This is the sort of mystery that surrounds special places.

Cattle die, kin die,
The man dies too.
One thing I know that never dies:
The good name of the dead.

(*Above and left*) Viking broad-sword with double-edged blade.

PART 4.

VIKING SOCIAL NETWORK

CHAPTER 21.

VIKING HIERARCHY AND EVERYDAY LIFE

Viking society was hierarchical, though less rigidly hierarchical than other European societies of the time. It was possible for people to move from one social class to another. At the top of the hierarchy were powerful rulers who controlled the land and the wealth. At the very top were the kings and the earls, and in Viking society they were the real movers and shakers. They did not behave like modern constitutional monarchs; instead they were powerful instigators of action, innovators, agents of change.

THE KINGS & EARLS

During the Viking Age, political and military power came to be concentrated in fewer and fewer hands. This is demonstrated above all by the emergence of Cnut the Great in the eleventh century as the ruler of a Northern Empire.

In the later middle ages, after the Viking Age had come to an end, the earls were subordinate to the kings, but in the Viking Age the earls were sometimes independent rulers in their own right, not answerable to anybody.

In Cambridgeshire around the year 900 there was an Earl Sihtric who issued his own coins, and several English Midland towns were ruled by earls. One of the most powerful earldoms was the earldom of Orkney. The kings and earls were supported by bands of aristocrats or regional chieftains, the *jarls*, who led military expeditions.

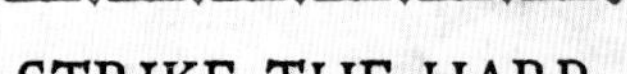

STRIKE THE HARP

Aristocrats were not only interested in fighting. There were other accomplishments that a gentleman was expected to acquire. Just after the Viking Age ended, a young man called Kali, whose father had migrated back to Norway after living in Orkney, composed this verse about himself. Sometimes this verse is attributed to Earl Rognvald I of Orkney.

Artful I am at chess;
Nine special skills I have;
Not likely to forget runes;
Often at book or smithy;
I know the art of skiing.
I shoot and row well enough;
Two more I keep in mind;
Strike the harp, write down a verse.

WALKING ON OARS

Prowess in sport was an accomplishment that was considered important for aristocrats. There were rowing races, which would have had a clear practical purpose, given that in a successful raiding foray the speed of a longship's arrival and departure was of the essence.

In the sagas we hear of an extraordinary skill of King Olaf Tryggvason's: his ability to walk on the oars all the way down one side of a longship and up the other, even when the ship was being rowed at speed. It was said that he could do this without getting his feet wet and while juggling with three swords!

King Olaf's phenomenal oar-stepping skill would have had no practical application: it was accomplishment for the sake of accomplishment. There is something laddish about the Viking aristocrat culture.

LOCAL COUNCILLORS

The armies the aristocrats led into battle were manned by freemen, the *karlar*, or *karls*. The *karls* were the middle class: the farmers, merchants and small landowners, and they were allowed to carry weapons. They were

also entitled to attend assemblies at which they could vote and contribute to decision-making; administrative and legal issues were settled at these local assemblies.

Many Vikings did not fight at all, or went on one or two raids when young. Only a relatively small number of men were 'professional' warriors. The Great Army which arrived in East Anglia in 865 and was defeated by King Alfred in 878 was manned by warriors who must have seen continuous military service in England across a period of 15 years – but this length of service was exceptional.

BLOODSHED AND SLAVERY

At the bottom of Viking society was the slave class. The slaves, the *thraell*, had no legal rights. Slaves were nevertheless an important economic commodity, and it has been said that the Vikings were the greatest slave-traders of their time. The Vikings were in hot pursuit of movable wealth, and that included slaves.

Entries in the Irish Annals routinely record plunder and bloodshed as elements of Viking raids, and occasionally they mention the taking of prisoners. The raiders sometimes timed their raids on monasteries so that they fell on major feast days, which meant that there would be a lot of people in the monastery, ripe for capture and possible enslavement.

In the raid of 821, 'a great number of women' were snatched from the Howth peninsula north of Dublin and taken away into captivity. Again in 836, Viking raiders in County Meath 'carried off many prisoners, and killed many, and led away very many captives.' In 895, exactly a hundred years after the first raid, even the number of prisoners taken is given in the annals – 710, following a raid on Armagh. In 871, Ivar and Olaf, the kings of Dublin, came back from Strathclyde with 'a great prey of Angles, Britons and Picts'.

BECOMING A FREE MAN

Slaves might be freed, and for this there was a prescribed legal process that had to be followed. The slave's owner had first to agree to the freedom and the slave had to buy him off. Then there was a feast of the 'freedom-ale', given by the freed slave. This was a formal event, to which the freed slave had to invite his former master and at least five other people.

The master and his wife had to sit in high seats representing their authority as heads of the household. If for some reason they did not attend the freedom-ale, the seats were left empty to represent them.

The freed man had to slaughter a sheep to validate the freedom and cut off its head; the master had then to take the neck-ransom, the final installment of the money with which the slave was buying his freedom, from the sacrificed sheep's neck.

GANG-RAPE OF A SLAVE GIRL

There is little evidence of Viking slavery in the archaeological record, apart from the slave-collar found in Dublin. Some of the slaves were doubtless retained as workers or servants, while many would have been traded on. Some were sacrificed.

The tenth century Arab writer ibn Fadlan described the funeral of a Viking chieftain in Russia; during the ceremony a drugged slave girl was gang-raped and then murdered. If true, the story corroborates the Vikings' reputation as brutal and barbaric.

AFTERLIFE COMPANIONS

Some Viking graves include a second burial, which again suggests a murdered servant or slave, killed and buried in order to accompany his master in the afterlife. In the Isle of Man a young man was buried under a mound; above him was buried the body of a young woman who was killed with a sword blow to the back of the head while she was kneeling down – an execution.

WOMEN OF THE HEARTH

Women were generally treated as subservient, though the quantity and quality of grave-goods in some female burials shows that women could achieve high status and on a personal level were highly valued and loved. In the absence of male heirs, they were able to inherit fortunes. Sagas may not always represent a specific historical reality, but the behaviour of some of the women characters in the sagas suggests that women could be major political players.

A Viking selling a slave girl to a Persian merchant.

PURSUIT OF POWER

The most outstanding of these was Ragnhild, who was a daughter of Erik Bloodaxe. She engineered the death of her husband, Earl Arnfinn, and married his successor, his brother Havard. Then she persuaded one nephew, Einar, to kill Havard, then another nephew to kill Einar, before she married Earl Ljot, the brother of Arnfinn and Havard. Ragnhild wielded no power in her own right, but was in a position to scheme and murder to formidable effect.

VIKING CLASS BARRIERS

Viking society was strongly bound by class divisions and differences. A Viking poem of unknown date quoted by Snorri has a narrative with characters from different classes. The children's names indicate which class they belong to. The boys in the low-class family are Drumbr (rotten log) and Kleggi (horsefly). In the middle-class family the boys are Smidr (craftsman) and Bondi (yeoman) and the girls are Ristill (slender) and Svarri (serious). The children in a third family have princely names.

UNDER VIKING JURISDICTION

As the English saw it, the Vikings did things differently from the Anglo-Saxons. Documents from the reign of King Edgar (959 – 975) refer to rights and laws operating 'among the Danes' as 'they best decide upon'. A little later, in the reign of Aethelred II (978 – 1016), documents use the phrase 'under the Danes' laws' – hence the name 'Danelaw' to describe the large tracts of England that fell under Viking jurisdiction.

In some instances, the difference was only a variation in vocabulary. For example, in the Viking-run areas of England the landscape was divided up into administrative areas known as *wapentakes*; these were similar to the Anglo-Saxon *hundreds*.

THE THING ABOUT A NAME

Each *wapentake* held its own regular meeting at special meeting-places. In different places this has been called different things, but *thing* is the commonest Viking word for the assembly that the Anglo-Saxons called a *moot*; thing-haugr (assembly-mound), mot-haugr (meeting mound), spell-haugr (speech-mound), thing-vellir (assembly field). This last name is found across Scandinavia and most famously in Iceland, where it was the place of national assembly until 1798.

The 'mound' that crops up in some of the place-names above was a physical feature, a built mound, often with concentric terraces. The best known of these is the Tynwald on the Isle of Man, which is still the focus of ceremonial outdoor meetings. There was once such a mound at Govan in Strathclyde, but it has been destroyed.

The 'thing' finds its way into a variety of place-names: Tynwald (Isle of Man), Tingwall (Shetland), Tinwald (Dumfriesshire), Dingwall (Ross-shire) and Thingwall (Wirral).

Silver penny of Aethelred II.

THE BLOODLINE OF KINGS

Things were at the very heart of Viking society, meetings at which changes in the law might be discussed. Even kingship might be discussed. In the Scandinavian homelands, the crown by tradition passed along the royal bloodline, from father to son to grandson, but it was not automatic. Any candidate for the throne had to be acceptable to the assembly of free men; he had to be accepted by acclamation at their *things*. So there was a limitation on kings. Their power was not absolute. The law constrained them. Custom constrained them.

DISRESPECTING THE LOCALS

The eleventh century king of Norway, Olaf Haraldsson, tried to force Christianity on the people of Norway, who forced him out; he fled the country and was killed at the Battle of Stiklestad in 1030. Olaf's son Magnus set about taking revenge on his father's enemies, attempting to steal the properties of those who had been killed. This was in breach of custom, and Magnus's courtiers used the court poet, Sigvat Thordarson, to give the king the necessary advice on kingship.

Court poets, rather like jesters or fools in other countries, were often called in to perform this role. What Sigvat came up with was *The Plain-Speaking Verses*. The lines are ornate and courteous, but their thrust is clear. 'The two Olafs respected the possessions of men' (*but you don't* is implied).

You must not be angry, my king,
At your advisers' plain speech.
The freedom you give us to speak
Will lead to your honour, my prince ...
Who urges you, prince
Firm in your hatreds,
To back away from the promises you made?
Who urges you, battle-joiner,
To slaughter your servants' cattle? ...
No-one before can have advised
A young prince to act so.
Your men are weary of this plundering.
Your army grows restless, my king.

After this formal but polite rebuke, and its repetition by other courtiers, King Magnus changed his strategy, calling a conference that led to the formulation of a new legal code.

A KING'S WILD ANGER

Diplomacy too had its democratic side. In the middle ages, diplomacy was conducted by kings and their generally aristocratic agents and appointees. In the Viking Age, ordinary people were able to participate. Snorri tells of a peace treaty arranged between the kings of Denmark and Norway, Sveinn Estridsson and Harald Sigurdsson, because the ordinary people of the two countries were tired of the hostility that existed between the two countries.

'Both sides, Norwegians and Danes alike, wanted to conclude an agreement and peace treaty. They asked their kings to accept and the exchanges appeared to be leading towards a settlement. A peace conference was arranged, to be attended by King Harald and King Sveinn at the Gotaalv River. When spring came, each of the kings called up a huge army and fleet for this expedition. The kings met and discussed at length the terms of settlement. Their people complained of the losses they had suffered from the raids, and the thieving and killing.'

Snorri went on to quote verse from the Viking Age;

Those who never cease
From quarrelling are slow
To accept arbitration.
The princes grow in arrogance.
If there's to be a settlement
There's danger in the kings' wild anger.
Men skilled in arbitration
Weigh up both sides of the case.
It's important to tell both kings
Just what is wanted here.

Thereafter, experienced negotiators concluded a settlement. Harald should have Norway and Sveinn should have Denmark as far as the ancient boundary between the two countries. Neither side should pay reparations. Cross-border raiding should cease. The agreement,

formally bound by oaths, should last as long as they were both kings.

Oaths were very important to the Vikings, which is perhaps surprising as they were notorious for breaking sworn agreements. Possibly they considered oaths to one another, among Vikings, as binding, but not promises made to outsiders. Vikings who broke their word to other Vikings were held in contempt, as is clear from a (now-lost) runic inscription from Söderby;

Ørikr and his kin [raised this stone in memory of] his brother Helgi. And Sassur killed him and [committed] a contemptible act. He betrayed his comrade. God help Helgi's soul.

A fragmentary tenth century runic inscription on the Isle of Man records another betrayal;

Rosketil betrayed under trust a man bound to him by oaths.

A standing stone on the island of Bornholm carries another denunciation of betrayal.

Asvaldi raised this stone in memory of his brother. A noble warrior shamefully killed. Skogi betrayed an innocent man.

TREACHERY

The penalty in each case was an eternal denunciation that lasted as long as the rune-stone stood. The name of the betrayer was carved in stone for all to see, and vilified for ever. There might be other penalties too. Eadric Streona was the Anglo-Saxon ealdorman of Mercia. Eadric acquired a reputation for treachery. The Anglo-Saxon Chronicle entry for 1015 shows him as a turncoat during a Viking attack on England.

Ealdorman Eadric gathered his levies, as did Prince Edmund in the north. The ealdorman planned to betray the prince, and they parted without a fight, retiring in the face of the enemy. Ealdorman Eadric lured forty ships away from allegiance to the king and then went over to Cnut.

The Anglo-Saxon Chronicle entry a year later continued the vilification of Eadric.

Ealdorman Eadric did as he had often done before – he began a flight amongst the people of Hertfordshire, and so betrayed his lord the king.

EADRIC'S REWARD

Cnut became king of England the following year and decided to do something about the dangerously unreliable ealdorman.

As yet [Cnut] was in the prime of youth, yet he had the power of indescribable shrewdness. He loved those who, as he had heard, had fought faithfully and without deceit on Edmund's side. And those he knew to be faithless and who in time of war swung to either side in treacherous tergiversation he held in such contempt that one day he ordered many of the English leaders to be killed for such disloyalty as this. Among them was Eadric. He had fled from battle.

When he asked for some reward for this behaviour – as though he had done it to ensure Cnut's victory, the king said rather sadly, 'Can someone like you who have treacherously let down your own lord be capable of being true to me? I will return you your reward, one so appropriate that this craftiness of yours will give you little pleasure in the future.'

Calling earl Eric, he said, 'This fellow here, pay what we owe him. I mean, make sure he does not betray us. Kill him.' Eric lost no time, brought out his double-headed axe and with a mighty blow lopped off his head. By this example fighting-men might be loyal to their kings.

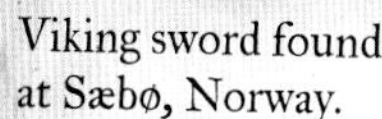

Viking sword found at Sæbø, Norway.

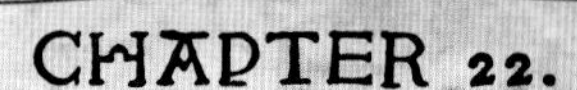

CHAPTER 22.

THE VIKING LEGAL SYSTEM

Contrary to their enduring image, the Vikings were a legal-minded people. The sagas show this, though unfortunately there are no surviving legal codes from the Viking Age. Much depended on oral transmission, custom and precedent.

HAKON'S HOMICIDE LAW

The *Saga of Hakon the Good* tells us that Hakon 'was a very knowledgeable man and paid great attention to legislation. He set up the Gulathing Law with the advice of Thorleif the Wise and the Frostathing Law with the advice of Earl Sigurd ... but the Heidsaevis Law had already been established by Halfdan the Black.'

It may be that Hakon established these law codes, or amended them. Probably local assemblies had developed laws long before, but they needed to be adjusted for the sake of consistency across the kingdom, and be adapted to the needs of a Christian society. Sometimes in the framing of laws there was a reference back to Viking Age practice, as in Norway in the 1260s;

Most men's kin have suffered through homicides ... It seems appropriate to insist that the law of Olaf the Saint should be observed just as he ordained it, though hitherto it has not been the case because of men's greed. Whoever kills a man without cause shall forfeit property and legal protection. Wheresoever he be found let him be declared an outlaw for whom no compensation can be accepted, either by king or kin.

THE LAW OF THE LAND

In the middle ages, Scandinavian kings could look back to the Viking Age as a time of more orderly behaviour, a time of lower crime rates. The sagas record how laws were established in Viking Age Iceland:

When Iceland had been widely settled, a Norwegian first brought law into this country from Norway. He was called Ulfliot, so Teit told me, and this was known as Ulfliot's law ... When he came back to Iceland the Althing was set up, and ever since then there has been a single law in this land. At the beginning of that heathen law it says that men should not have ships with animal figure-heads at sea, but if they have them they must unship them before they come in sight of land, and not sail near the land with figure-heads with jaws gaping or grinning muzzles, which would terrify the land-spirits ... Everyone had to pay a temple tax just as they now pay tithes to the church.

From early on the Icelanders had a sophisticated legal system based on the participation of its farmers. The great assembly for the whole of Iceland, the Althing, was held each summer at Thingvellir, and there every aspect of the law was decided and recorded. Its elected presiding officer was called the lawspeaker. Formal speeches before the assembly were made at the Law Rock.

Viking sword with strong, single-edged blade.

One of the issues discussed was the calendar, which the Icelanders realised was slightly out of phase with the solar cycle. The 52-week year of twelve 30-day months was too short, making summer move a little earlier each year. A man called Thorstein spoke at the Law Rock, proposing that they added an extra week every seven years. This impressed everyone and was put into immediate effect.

LEGALIZED ADOPTION

In the homelands there were clear laws regarding social structure, even on social mobility. Adoption had to be formal, open and public because it might entail a change of social status. Adoption meant adoption into the social class of the adopting family. There were prescribed ceremonies to make this change legal.

Three measures of ale must be brewed and a three-year-old ox slaughtered, the skin flayed from the right hind-leg of the ox above the knee-joint and a shoe made of it. The father shall make the child to be legitimized put his foot into the shoe, then take his sons who are not yet of age onto his lap, while those who are of age shall also put their feet into the shoe. Then the child to be legitimized shall be taken to the bosom of the man and woman of the house ... Consent must be given by those who are nearest in line to the one who wants to bring the man into the family.

Reforging a broken sword, twelfth century wood carving, Hylestad Stave Church, Norway.

CHAPTER 23.

MILITARY PLANNING & ORGANIZATION

RING-FORT ENCAMPMENTS

Military organization was highly developed in the homelands, to judge from the Danish ring-forts built in the 980s. The forts at Trelleborg, Fyrkat and Aggersborg were built to a common symmetrical plan, though varying in detail, and there were forts at Nonnebakken and Borgeby that were less regular.

All the forts were ringed by earth ramparts topped by timber palisades and their size strongly implies that they were designed to contain garrisons. Together with Jelling, where there were buildings of comparable size and date, the forts created a network of royal centres capable of controlling and defending the Danish kingdom.

The function of the ring-forts would have been similar to that of the contemporary network of *burhs* in late Anglo-Saxon England or the contemporary network of towns in the Frankish empire. The centralized planning involved shows a very different side of the Viking culture from the apparent impetuousness of the raids as experienced by the victims.

VIKING NAVAL LEVIES

How labour was managed is not so easy to detect. In the centuries after the Viking Age there was a system of ship levies in Denmark, Norway and Sweden. The king in each country had the right to summon a fleet for the defence of the realm and the kingdom was divided up into units assessed as able to provide specific numbers of ships and men to work them, along with standard military gear and provisions. The levy could be invoked for defence, and it could also be activated for offensive warfare.

THE CINQUE PORTS

A very similar system operated in medieval England, where the Cinque Ports were put under an obligation to provide specific numbers of ships and men for the king's use. Even inland communities were required to provide men and expenses for ship service. Eventually this levy system was replaced by the creation of a national fleet, the Royal Navy, to reduce the king's dependence on the loyalty of certain ports. This at any rate was the system in place, both in England and in Scandinavia immediately after the Viking Age.

FORENSIC EVIDENCE

Some historians think the levy system was in place during the Viking Age, others believe a different system was in operation. The variance in opinion has been caused by recent forensic evidence from Trelleborg that shows the Danish king was using foreign mercenaries. If he had a levy system in place, he would have no need for hired fighters. If there was no levy system, the forays across the North Sea to attack Britain may be seen as old-style raiding parties, rather than part of a formal national strategy.

THE NATIONAL WAR FLEET

On the whole it seems likely that several different approaches were in play: that there *were* levies, but supplemented by hiring mercenaries. The Vikings were certainly wealthy enough to do this. Ideas of levies for military service would also have been imported to the homelands by, for example Hakon the Good, who was brought up at the court of King Athelstan, where he picked up ways of governing from the English; his approach to kingship was more Anglo-Saxon than Norwegian.

There were certainly ship levies in Anglo-Saxon England. They are mentioned in the Anglo-Saxon Chronicle for 1008. There are also references to the levy in skaldic poetry written in Norway in the late tenth century. Overall, it would appear likely that in the Viking homelands in the tenth century there was a national war fleet maintained by a system of ship levies. Documents show that it existed in Denmark in 1085, and the likelihood is that the levy system was set up at least a century earlier by Harald Bluetooth, perhaps at the same time as the system of ring-forts.

The Three Swords monument, Hafrsfjord, Norway.

CHAPTER 24.

VIKING DOMESTIC HOUSING

HEROES AT HOME

The Vikings felt much the same as we all do about hearth and home. It was an Englishman, John Payne, who in 1822 wrote 'Be it ever so humble, there's no place like home', but the song could as easily have been written by a Viking. This is a Viking poem on the same theme;

A house of your own, however mean, is good.
All men are heroes at home;
Though you have but two goats and your best room is rope-thatched,
Still it is better than begging.

A VIKING LONG HOUSE

The typical town house was humble indeed, a post-and-wattle structure with a reed-thatched roof and a single door, roughly rectangular and about 20 feet (6 meters) by 50 feet (15 meters). In the fortified town of Hedeby in Jutland, rectangular houses of varying sizes and varying distances from the street were arranged informally, with their long axes at right angles to the street; the doors were in the short sides, facing the street. The main sign of central authority is the regulated size of the building plots.

In rural areas, the typical farmhouse was rectangular with the long sides slightly bowed. At the Braaid on the Isle of Man, a native round house built in the pre-Viking period was replaced by a house of classic imported Viking design, massive, rectangular with bowed sides.

THE FARMSTEAD AT STÖNG

The standard Viking hall-house was developed in Iceland, partly to adapt to the harsh winter conditions there, partly to accommodate the lack of suitable building materials. One of the fertile valleys settled with several farmsteads, Thjórsárdalur, was overwhelmed by ash during a major eruption of Mount Hekla. The Pompeii effect has ensured that one of these farmsteads, Stöng, was perfectly preserved.

After it was excavated in 1939, Stöng was carefully reconstructed with massive turf walls built on stone footings. The living rooms were dry-lined with timber panels, but leaving a ventilation space between the wood and the turf; this Viking house had cavity walls.

The main room, which was a 40-feet-long (12 meters) aisled hall, had a long hearth at its centre and narrow benches on each side. Opening out of one end, on the same axis, was a second but smaller living room on a similar design. Two other rooms opened from the back of the main hall. One was a dairy, the other a toilet.

The farm's outbuildings included a byre, a barn and a forge. Long after the original excavation a further discovery was made: a small family chapel with some Christian burials.

In some places there were true longhouses, with accommodation for people at one end and byres for cattle at the other, but in Scotland this arrangement was rare, and by the time of the Viking colonization phase it was becoming rare in Scandinavia as well. There were strong similarities between the houses in Scotland and those built 'back home' in Norway.

CARVED ANIMAL HEADS

Chiefs and kings naturally lived on a grander scale. The fine timber longhouse reconstructed at the Viking Centre at Ribe in Denmark, and based on an original that was built in about 980, gives a good idea of what a tenth century chief's house would have looked like. In plan, it was a bow-sided

Reconstruction of a Viking fortress, Trelleborg, Denmark.

rectangle. The huge roof, steeply pitched to each side, high in the middle and dropping at each end, looks like a capsized ship.

The standardized houses found in the Danish fortresses all had this same distinctive look, which is why this house type is becoming known as a Trelleborg house. The ends of the ridge roof were probably decorated with projecting animal heads, to judge from the house-shaped Cammin casket, an early eleventh century reliquary destroyed in the Second World War.

The main door, in the middle of one of the long sides, was probably also developed into a focal feature. The entrance to the hall at Lejre in Zealand in Denmark will have had carved flanking pillars and a carved wooden gable above it.

The chief's residence at Borg in Lofoten, northern Norway was a large and impressive building 88 yards (80 meters) long. It has been reconstructed with a lofty pitched roof and gablet ends and inside it is divided into five rooms, one of which is a roomy ceremonial hall. Halls like these were the setting for important social events such as feasts, where eating, drinking, music, dancing and the recitation of poetry were important elements.

A BANQUET OF CONSEQUENCES

Feasts and banquets were staged with care; they were occasions when social rank was confirmed and friendships and alliances too might be reinforced. The funeral ode for Erik Bloodaxe, written in 954, visualized King Erik's reception at a feast at Valhöll.

The preparations had to be right, the orders of precedence had to be correct. Everybody had to behave in the prescribed manner. To get it wrong could cause great offence that could lead to injury or death. This was true even if there was no time for preparation; even impromptu entertaining had to be done correctly.

BAD HOSTING

The *Saga of Egil Skalla-Grimsson* was written in the thirteenth century, though we know that Egil lived in the tenth. Egil arrived unannounced with a troupe of followers at the home of Armod Skaeg, a wealthy farmer, and they were disappointed by their reception. The farmer's daughter whispered a message to Egil from her mother, recommending him not to eat too much of the food offered as better food was on its way. The girl was struck by her father for what he saw as impropriety.

Tables were set out in the hall and plenty of strong beer was served to Egil and his men. Armod goaded them into drinking, which was taken as a further insult. The next morning Egil confronted Armod, intending to kill him, but he relented for the sake of the wife and daughter and contented himself with cutting off his beard and poking out one of his eyes. This was the penalty for bad hosting.

DRINKING HORNS

Grave-goods from wealthy burials include large wooden buckets, which were probably used for decanting beer into smaller vessels like jugs, which were in turn used to fill the guests' drinking-horns. Drinking-horns evidently had a ceremonial function as well as a practical one. Guests were probably presented with a horn of beer by way of welcome. There are pictures from the eighth to eleventh centuries showing Valkyries offering drinking-horns to men on horseback, warriors slain on the battlefield being welcomed to Valhöll.

Viking battle axe-head.

CHAPTER 25.

VIKING TOWNS AND SETTLEMENTS

Town life was non-agricultural, revolving round trade and manufacturing. The craftsmen and craftswomen based there depended on the population of the surrounding area supplying raw materials. Sometimes these were bought by the sale of products manufactured in the town.

The craft industries were engaged mainly in producing large volumes of low-value artifacts, like combs and pins and leather goods. Often the raw materials came from nearby, but were occasionally far-travelled, like jet from eastern England, whalebone from Norway and amber from the Baltic.

Some Vikings, presumably those of high-status, had a taste for ostentation. To meet this taste, some brooches were surprisingly large, sometimes too large and heavy to be of practical use. Some weighed over 1.3 lbs (600 grams) and had pins 20 inches (50 cm) long; it is hard to imagine how such a brooch could be worn.

END OF THE WORLD OCEAN

Hedeby was an important trading town in Denmark, close to the southern border with the Saxons, though now it is on the German side of the border. Hedeby was the Danes' name for their town; their Saxon neighbours called it Slesvig.

An Arab merchant from the Caliphate of Cordoba wrote, 'Slesvig is a large town at the very end of the world ocean.' He also said that both men and women wore eye make-up; that they practised infanticide; that the women were free to divorce their husbands; that their singing was the most dreadful thing you ever heard, like the growling of dogs.

He visited the place in about 950, when it was a thriving and evidently colourful trading centre, between Saxons and Danes, between Western Europe and Scandinavia, between North Sea and Baltic. Today Hedeby is a peaceful patchwork of fields. Then it was busy, urban, rich and coveted; it was held sometimes by Danes, sometimes by Swedes, sometimes by Saxons.

DEFENDED BY RAMPARTS

Hedeby was surrounded by a roughly semicircular tenth century rampart with an outer ditch on the southern side, which was the direction of greatest threat. To the south-west was a further rampart, then beyond that the Danevirke, the system of earthworks defending Denmark's southern border. On the east side, Hedeby had a waterfront on a bay of the Schlei fjord, which gave access to the Baltic Sea. Hedeby was at a key location.

The sea route to the Baltic round the north of Jutland was dangerous. Even in the nineteenth century, many ships were wrecked along Jutland's north-west coast. A safer route was overland, across the narrowest part of the peninsula.

FAR-REACHING TRADERS

Merchants travelled by water as far as Hollingstedt on the River Treene in the west, then went the few miles overland to reach the head of navigation of the Schlei inlet of the Baltic in the east. It was at this point on the Schlei that Hedeby grew up in the eighth century as a waterfront village.

The first settlement was the South Settlement, and finds there include stone imported from the Rhineland, coins from Frisia and amber from the Baltic, showing how busy and far-reaching trading was in the eighth century. At the start of the ninth

century a second settlement grew up, the North Settlement, which was not walled but protected instead by a small fort.

CREATING A STREET GRID

In the late ninth century both were abandoned and by this time a Central Settlement had become established beside a stream. As the Central Settlement grew the stream was diverted into a planked conduit and jetties were built out into the harbour. The reorganization involved creating a regular street grid with closely-packed houses.

The organization of this urban engineering shows a strong civic authority. But Hedeby was too low-lying and the rising water level meant that it became waterlogged and harder to live in. House timbers tended to rot and the average life of a house was only thirty years.

INVASION AND ABANDONMENT

In the cemeteries there is one high-status burial, probably a king's, in a chamber underneath a ship. Ultimately it was not the rising water that finished Hedeby but fire. Harald Hardrada from Norway attacked just before 1050, setting fire to the town. Then in 1066, while a thwarted Hardrada was attempting to invade England instead, Hedeby was raided by the Slavs. Then the site was abandoned; the people of Hedeby moved north to occupy the site of modern Schleswig.

Viking coins and jewellery found at Birka, Sweden, 830 – 50.

THE TRADING HUB OF BIRKA

Birka, in Sweden, was a similar waterfront town to Hedeby. Now it is a peaceful, empty place where bare rocks are thinly covered with pasture and birch trees. It is not entirely deserted – in summer it is visited by archaeologists and tourists – but it is no longer a town.

It was founded in around 750 on Bjorko (meaning Birch Island) on Lake Malar, an important route centre not far west of the site of Stockholm. The development of Birka as a trading hub was prompted by the presence of a royal estate on the nearby island of Adelso. Birka was run by an agent of the king of Sweden and had its own assembly.

ASSEMBLY AND HILLFORT

By the tenth century, about a thousand people lived at Birka. Like the rest of Scandinavia, Birka has risen in relation to the sea, and the shape of its coastline has changed. The town site is overlooked by a small hillfort, and in the ninth century the town was enclosed by an arc-shaped rampart, running from the fort down to the lakeshore. The rampart encloses an area of soil darkened and enriched by fires, charcoal and organic remains left after 200 years of occupation.

The town consisted of small rectangular houses and workshops, built on plots that were defined by ditches. The manufacturing that went on at Birka produced iron, bronze, textiles, furs and bone- and antler-carving. Finds of weights show that merchants were there too.

WINTER FUR TRADING

In winter, furs were delivered across the ice on sledges. In summer, ships moored on the waterfront. Iron was one of Birka's exports, but furs were the main source of its wealth, and some at least were shipped to Hedeby for onward shipment to Western Europe; others went across the Baltic to begin the long journey south to the Caliphate. A silver hoard buried at Birka during the final years of the town's existence in the 970s included Arabic coins.

Birka was abandoned in favour of Sigtuna, partly because of the gradual rise in land level, partly because of declining long-distance trade. There was always a short overland haul of ships to the south-east to reach the Baltic, but as the land rose this got longer.

THE NATURAL HARBOUR

Kaupang was a third trading town in the Scandinavian homelands. It stood on a natural harbour just to the west of the entrance to the Oslofjord. It too is marked by a patch of darkened soil, but a smaller area than at Birka. There were houses and workshops close to a waterfront where there were stone jetties.

The main industrial activities were metalworking and the carving of soapstone vessels. Fragments of imported pottery from the Rhineland together with coins show that Kaupang was active from the late eighth century through most of the ninth century. As well as its long-distance trade, Kaupang was an important market focus for Norwegian merchant seamen, who sailed there with cargoes of skins, furs, down, walrus-hide rope and ivory.

The grave-goods found in Kaupang's burial grounds show that the town's main connections were with the south, especially with the Rhineland. There were only a few trinkets from Britain. In the middle years of the Viking Age, Norway appears to have been without a major trading town of its own, even though there was some trade with Britain, Ireland and Iceland.

VIKING YORK

In England the great Viking town was York. In 866 the Danes captured a flourishing and well-established Anglo-Saxon town. It already had trading links with Frisia; now contacts with Scandinavia were opened. By 1000, York was 'filled with the treasure of merchants, chiefly of the Danish race.'

There was an industrial and commercial sector between the Rivers Ouse and Foss. Some of the walls of the old Roman fortress were still in place and kept in repair. The area of the fortress contained the Anglo-Saxon minster, and it may have contained the Viking palace too.

Tenth century workshops have been uncovered in Coppergate and Hungate (both Viking names). Both pagan and Christian burials have been discovered, near the church of St Mary Bishophill Junior.

BUILDING VIKING DUBLIN

The main Viking town in Ireland was Dublin, which the Vikings developed initially in the ninth century as an overwintering base. Soon they were manufacturing and trading from it and it flourished, mainly because of its commanding location on the Irish Sea; there were routes north to the Hebrides, Orkney and Shetland, and east to Wales and Chester, which gave Vikings access to Anglo-Saxon traders.

Viking Dublin had an early earth rampart which was replaced with a stone wall in the late Viking Age. Ireland functioned differently from other colonized areas. The Vikings seem not to have colonized Irish rural areas; instead they colonized the towns: not just Dublin, but Wexford, Waterford, Cork and Limerick. They too became major Viking trading centres.

A silver penny of the Viking kingdom of York.

VIKING NEW TOWNS

In the late Viking Age, the developing interest of the Scandinavian kings in expanding trade led to the building of new towns. These were to function as markets, but also as administrative and religious centres.

Birka, as already mentioned, was replaced by Sigtuna, which had a mint and a bishop's seat. Schleswig similarly replaced Hedeby. Viborg, Alborg, Arhus and Roskilde were all set up in Denmark; Trondheim and Oslo were set up in Norway. Lund in Skåne, southern Sweden, was founded by Cnut as a Scandinavian new town.

The early eleventh century town plan, which included rectangular houses of different sizes and some large bow-sided houses, was cleared for redevelopment. The main change in this redevelopment was the building of a substantial stave-church.

BORROWED TECHNIQUES

Town houses were mainly rectangular with walls lightly built of posts and wattles, made by weaving thin wooden rods between upright stakes driven into the ground. Inside, life revolved round a central hearth, which is where food was cooked and which provided heat and light. The raised platforms on each side were used as seats by day and beds by night.

Some of the houses found at York and Waterford had cellars, and these were probably merchants' houses. The 'Viking' houses at Dublin, York and Hedeby were significantly different from one another. The Dublin houses were built using Irish carpentry techniques, while the sunken houses at York owe something to Anglo-Saxon house design. Both were different from houses at Hedeby, back in the homelands.

Viking colonists probably routinely borrowed from local building techniques – another aspect of the assimilation process.

CHAPTER 26.

VIKING DIET AND NUTRITION

The Vikings ate two meals a day, one in the morning, one in the evening, and the preparation of these meals was one of the major tasks assigned to women; the other was making clothing for the family.

TRADING FOOD

A staple food was fish, which throughout the homelands, and many of the colonies, could be caught locally, but it was also traded long distances where necessary. There were considerable variations in diet according to what was available, but foodstuffs were also transported.

Rye found in Denmark is thought to have been imported from Russia. A walnut in the Oseberg ship burial came from further to the south. The food buried with the queen in the Oseberg ship gives a good indication of the diet of the rich: oxen, wheat, oats, cress, apples, hazelnuts, herbs and spices. At other sites, there is evidence that people were eating a range of wild fruits – cherries, plums, sloes and berries.

BAKING DAILY BREAD

They were also eating cabbages, onions, peas, garlic, and making bread that sometimes included dried peas and pine bark, which suggests a serious shortage of grain. Dough was kneaded in wooden bowls, then baked in the embers of the household fire in the long-handled pans that have been found in a number of women's graves.

Baking must have happened every day, as unleavened barley bread would have needed to be eaten while hot; when cooled down it became rock-hard and inedible. At Hedeby and Lund there were proper bread ovens, so it is likely that in the bigger towns there were professional bakers.

EATING MEAT

The Vikings were meat-eaters. They ate mutton, lamb, beef, veal, pork, goat and horse-meat. Domesticated animals also provided them with wool, hides, milk, cheese – and transport. There were wild animals too, which provided them with more meat: deer, elk, wild boar and bear. In the north of Scandinavia there were reindeer, whales and seals. Wildfowl, hares and seabirds were also on the menu. On the farms there were chickens and geese. The Vikings also kept dogs and cats; dogs for hunting, cats for ratting, though probably both were kept as pets.

FISHING AND COOKING

Fish were a vital part of the Viking diet, and fishing was a major activity. Many settlements have been found with nets, hooks and sinkers, showing how important fishing was. People living in the towns were supplied with fish; evidence of substantial fish consumption has come from York, Lund, Birka and Hedeby.

The citizens of York were eating cod, haddock and herring caught in the North Sea, as well as locally caught eels. Fish and meat were eaten fresh, but also preserved (by drying or smoking) to provide winter food and to supply the crews of ships.

In most houses, women cooked on the long open central hearths. Cauldrons made of soapstone or iron were hung over the fire, either on a chain from a roof-beam or from a tripod. Other pots and bowls were heated among the embers. Common foods prepared in this way would be meat stew, broth and porridge. Spits were used for roasting meat.

MILK AND ALCOHOL

Milk was either drunk or turned into cheese or butter. Honey was the base for fermenting mead. Malted barley was used to make beer and hops (found at Hedeby) were added for flavour.

Wines fermented from fruits were known to the Vikings, and imported from the Rhineland, but would only have been available to the rich. Wine barrels were found at Hedeby. The Vikings knew nothing about distilling, so there were no spirits.

They believed in moderation, in both drinking and eating.

The glutton, unless he keeps himself in check,
Will eat himself to death.

Shark meat drying, Reykjavik, Iceland. A local Viking traditional delicacy.

CHAPTER 27.

TRADE, BARTER AND CURRENCY

BARTERING WITH BULLION

Trade was often carried out by barter, especially where easily measured commodities were involved, such as beads, textiles or furs. Bullion was used too; metal was valued according to weight, and the Vikings seem to have adopted bullion as a kind of currency following their contact with the coin-using Caliphate. The bullion usually came in the form of silver ingots and hack-silver (pieces of cut silver from dismantled manufactured objects). Recently there have been many finds of bullion thanks to the widespread activities of metal detectorists.

VIKING COINAGE

Islamic coins started arriving in Scandinavia as bullion, and gradually the advantage of a coinage-based economy became apparent. An important next step was the design and manufacture of Viking coins. These were minted in the ninth century at the major homeland trading centres of Ribe and Hedeby. But the major Viking coinage development was in England, where it was stimulated by the existence of West Saxon coinage, prompting the minting of Viking coins in East Anglia, Mercia and Northumbria.

The first Viking ruler in England to mint his own coins was Guthrum, baptized as Athelstan in 878; he established his own kingdom in East Anglia and issued coins under his new Christian name. The Viking kings of York similarly issued their own coins.

REMEMBERING ST EDMUND

A fine silver penny found in the Cuerdale hoard in Lancashire was minted in about 900 by the Scandinavian kings of East Anglia. It has a cross on one side and it commemorates St Edmund, the last Anglo-Saxon king of East Anglia, killed by Viking warriors of the Great Army in 870; the minting of this coin was a tactful gesture of reconciliation.

ARM-RING MONEY

Another kind of currency was arm-rings. These were used for currency, display and decoration – some of them were beautiful and elaborate pieces of craftsmanship, often with animal-head

St Edmund silver penny.

terminals. They were an essential part of the Viking custom of ring-giving. The arm-ring was a personal ornament, usually made of silver, occasionally gold. Some were manufactured to conform to standard weights, multiples of the Viking ounce. They were referred to as ring-money and they might enter trade as bullion.

ARM-RING GIVERS

Ring-giving indicated the generosity of the giver. Ring-wearing showed status, wealth, achievement. Rings were not given as a matter of course, so someone wearing many arm-rings must have been regarded as highly valued and appreciated. In this, as in many other ways, the Vikings were like the Anglo-Saxons, who also had the custom of ring-giving. The Anglo-Saxon Chronicle describes the West Saxon army defeating an invading army of Vikings from Ireland in 936 –

Here King Athelstan, leader of warriors,
Ring-giver to his men, and also his brother,
The prince Edmund, fought and won
Life-long battle-glory with the swords' edges
At Brunanburh. They split the shield-wall,
Slashed lime-wood shields with forged swords.

The Cuerdale Viking silver hoard.

Chapter 28.

Carvers & Craftsmen

It was in the Viking towns that the craftsmen gathered. Merchants drew in the raw materials, and were probably also customers for many of the manufactured goods. Some of the crafts were the equivalent of heavy industry, the metalworking or smithing which used substantial quantities of iron to make cooking pots and cauldrons.

Other crafts were the equivalent of light industries, using small quantities of raw materials and huge amounts of skilled labour, like the manufacture of jewellery. Copper and copper alloy were used to make pins with decorative heads; some had dragon heads, which seem to have been everywhere – not just on the prows of ships, like those found in the Scheldt estuary, but on bed-posts.

The craft industries were diverse and, at Hedeby, generally scattered across the town, though blacksmiths tended to be located at the edge, probably because of the risk of fire.

Amber and Jet

Amber was a distinctive Baltic material that had been exported and exploited long before the Viking Age. Amber was exported across Europe as early as the bronze age, two thousand years before. Its distinctive colour, translucence and texture made it very attractive. Raw amber, very much a Baltic homeland resource, was taken to Hedeby to be turned into jewellery items such as beads and pendants, or gaming pieces.

Jet was another distinctive raw material, though this time the source was in England, at Whitby; it was exported across the North Sea to Norway, where it was carved into small amulets.

Deer Antler Combs

Combs were made out of deer-antler, a material that was shed naturally and could be collected. The method of comb manufacture was quite elaborate. Two long plates were cut to make the back of the comb, then a row of rectangular plates was riveted between them; the teeth were then cut into the row of rectangular plates.

Glass Bead Making

Glass beads were made by bead-makers out of ready-made glass. This was often in the form of small cubes which were intended for use as mosaics, or broken drinking vessels. Ordinary beads were made in single colours, but the technique was available to decorate them with trails of different colours of glass or make multi-coloured beads.

Imported Crystal

A necklace from Birka with a prevailing yellow colour was made of a mixture of yellow, green, black glass beads attached to a small disc brooch. Another necklace, perhaps higher-status, and with a prevailing scarlet colour, was made of imported crystal and cornelian and hung with amulets and baubles gathered during the course of raid or trade.

Necklaces might be complete loops like modern necklaces, or they might be worn as festoons strung between two brooches. The most exotic necklace of all, found in the homelands, consists of a strings of spherical crystal pendants set in decorative silver bezel clasps; it was probably made in Gotland in south-west Sweden, but using a design borrowed from Slav jewellery.

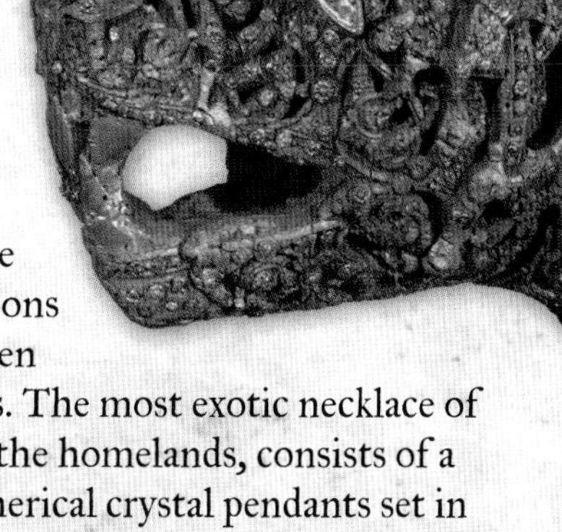

Animal-head post from the Oseberg ship.

SOAPSTONE AND SCHIST

Soapstone quarrying became an important activity in Norway, where the making of soapstone vessels was a major industry. Soapstone was a popular material because it was soft and easily worked; it was found in Norway and exported to Hedeby in Denmark, and also to Iceland. Another significant rock type was a hard metamorphic rock called schist. This came from Eidsborg in Telemark, and it was greatly valued as a whetstone.

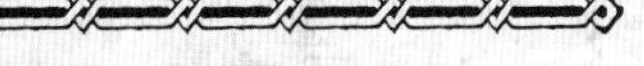

BRONZE CASTING

Bronze-casting was a highly specialized industry. The bronze smiths made mass-produced cheap brooches, but there was also a market for finely made ornaments. Usually a well-made piece was created in a two-piece clay mould that had been built round a wax model.

The mould was heated and the molten wax poured off; then the molten bronze was poured into the cavity. Once the bronze had cooled down and solidified, the clay mould was broken away to yield the finished bronze piece.

Cheap brooches might be made by pouring bronze into carved stone or antler moulds that could be used any number of times.

THE BAGHDAD BRAZIER

Not all the bronze objects found at Viking sites were Viking-made, though. An incredibly ornate brazier, a perforated rectangular box on legs and with a long handle sticking out of one side, was found in Sweden but was made in Baghdad. It was probably bought in Baghdad by a Viking merchant, who took it home with him on one of his trading trips.

Viking glass beads, Sweden.

Much of the material found in the Viking homelands originated elsewhere. In the early Viking Age, it was fashionable in Norway to wear brooches that were adapted from pieces of metalwork brought home from Britain and Ireland by raiders: they were trophies.

ORNAMENTAL BROOCHES

Viking women normally wore a pair of decorative oval brooches, a standard design that was in use from Iceland to Ukraine. They wore a third brooch to fasten the shawl or cloak at the front, and this was usually a trefoil shape or a disc with ornamental wings, known as 'equal-armed'. In the tenth century large disc brooches became fashionable, often with a matching but much smaller disc brooch to fasten the neck of the chemise. So women might wear as many as four brooches at once, as well as strings of beads.

EASTERN TRADE ROUTE

The route from the Baltic to Baghdad would have begun by travelling along the Volga River to Bulgar, an important market where fur-traders met silver merchants; it was also one of the western end-points of the Silk Road from China.

From Bulgar, the route went on to Itil, the main town of the Khazars, which took traders to the Caspian Sea. Then there was a camel-train from Gorgan on the southern shore of the Caspian Sea to Baghdad.

A disadvantage of this Volga route was that the Viking traders had to pay tribute twice, to the Bulgars and the Khazars, but there were huge advantages as the route led to the heart of the silver supplies of the Caliphate.

Furs, wax, weapons and honey were traded in exchange for Arabic silver. Viking merchants travelled fully equipped with their own small pairs of scales, to check the weight

Viking bronze matrix used in the manufacture of helmets, Uppland, Sweden.

of the silver they were buying or exchanging.

In the tenth century the Vikings used this eastern route less frequently and it is not clear why. There may have been political difficulties, but the underlying problem seems to have been that the great silver mines of the Eastern Caliphate were becoming exhausted and new sources were coming on stream closer to home, near the Harz Mountains in Germany.

BURIED TREASURE

The Vikings left behind a number of hoards. They were collections of bullion buried in the ground for safekeeping until the owner could return. If for some reason the owner was unable to return, the hoard remained in the ground until it was dug up centuries later – as treasure.

The hoards consist of a great variety of things. There are ingots, coins, brooches, rings, pendants, some complete, some broken up into pieces. Over a thousand hoards of silver treasure have been found in Scandinavia, and a few of gold. Above all they give us the evidence that some Vikings became very rich, whether by trading or by raiding.

THE CUERDALE HOARD

Some hoards have been found in the Viking colonies. The Cuerdale hoard, found near Preston in 1840, consisted of a lead chest full of silver: 7,500 coins and a thousand other objects including ornaments and ingots weighing a total of 88 lbs (40 kg). This is everyone's idea of treasure.

The coins, minted in Northumbria and East Anglia, indicate that the hoard was buried in about 910, a time of conflict and disturbance. The Viking leaders of Dublin had been expelled from Ireland and were roaming through Wales and Lancashire, looking for land to settle. Meanwhile near Wolverhampton a Northumbrian Viking army was defeated in battle by the Anglo-Saxons. The hoard was evidently buried for safekeeping against this turbulent background.

THE GALLOWAY HOARD

Viking hoards show us not only what the Vikings made, but also what they bought when they traded, and what they stole when they raided. In October 2014, Derek McLennan, a committed metal detectorist, discovered the most significant hoard of Viking treasure found in modern times. It was in Dumfries and Galloway in Scotland, on a site that is being kept secret to prevent illegal treasure-hunters from robbing it.

The hoard was found only two spade-depths down. It consisted of an unusual cross made of solid silver, dozens of silver arm-rings and some silver ingots. When that hoard was dug out, it was found that there was a *second* hoard of even higher quality underneath, and it included a silver Carolingian jar with engraved decoration, 6 inches (15 cm) high and the biggest ever found, complete with its lid in place.

It was manufactured about a hundred years before the hoard was buried, perhaps in the tenth century. It was wrapped in cloth and buried upside down. A gold ingot, a folded sheet of silver, five latticework brooches, an Irish penannular brooch and some exotic beads were all crammed inside – a mini-treasure hoard in itself. There was also a beautiful gold pin in the shape of a bird, possibly made by Anglo-Saxons.

The hoard is remarkable for the range of material it contains – gold, silver, enamel, glass, textiles – and also for the geographic range of its origins. The silver ingots and bracelets are typical of the Irish Sea region, the Carolingian jar came from the kingdom of the Franks, the glass beads were traded from central Europe and the enamelled cross and the gold pin came from the Anglo-Saxons.

The hoard shows the sort of range we find in rich burials in the Viking homelands, yet this was found in Scotland. We are still finding out more about the Vikings, and finding that there is more to learn.

CHAPTER 29.

VIKING ARTISTIC STYLES

DARK RESTLESS PATTERNS

The art of the Vikings is as vigorous and animated as their lives, full of incident and adventure. Although styles changed through the 300 years of the Viking Age, restless dense patterning remained a constant trait.

The patterns were sometimes made out of swirling vegetation, but equally often out of stylized animals, distorted sometimes out of all recognition. These themes were firmly rooted in the pre-Viking era, and can be seen in Scandinavian art of the fifth century. But the Vikings were also open to new influences from all over Western Europe. With conversion to Christianity, Scandinavia was swept along with the new European fashion for Romanesque art and architecture.

THE OSEBERG TAPESTRY

There is not very much fine art in the Viking culture, or at least not much that has survived. Nearly all the artwork is ornament applied to everyday functional objects, often lavishly and sometimes completely transforming them into something magical. One piece of fine art that allows a glimpse of what may have been lost is the Oseberg tapestry, which has been painstakingly reconstructed – an impressive work of art.

THE BROA-OSEBERG STYLE

Most of the Vikings' woodwork has perished. It is, even so, possible to detect six artistic phases.

The earliest phase was the Broa-Oseberg style (750 – 850), which is represented by the contents of the Oseberg ship burial with its fine carved prow and the goods buried in a man's grave at Broa on Gotland.

The Broa grave produced some decorated bridle-mounts, with stylized small-headed animals, lots of curving tendrils, and the 'gripping beast'. The main feature of the gripping beast is that its paws are clutching other animals, or the decorative border, or itself. The woodcarvings on the Oseberg ship were of an outstanding quality, clearly a royal commission.

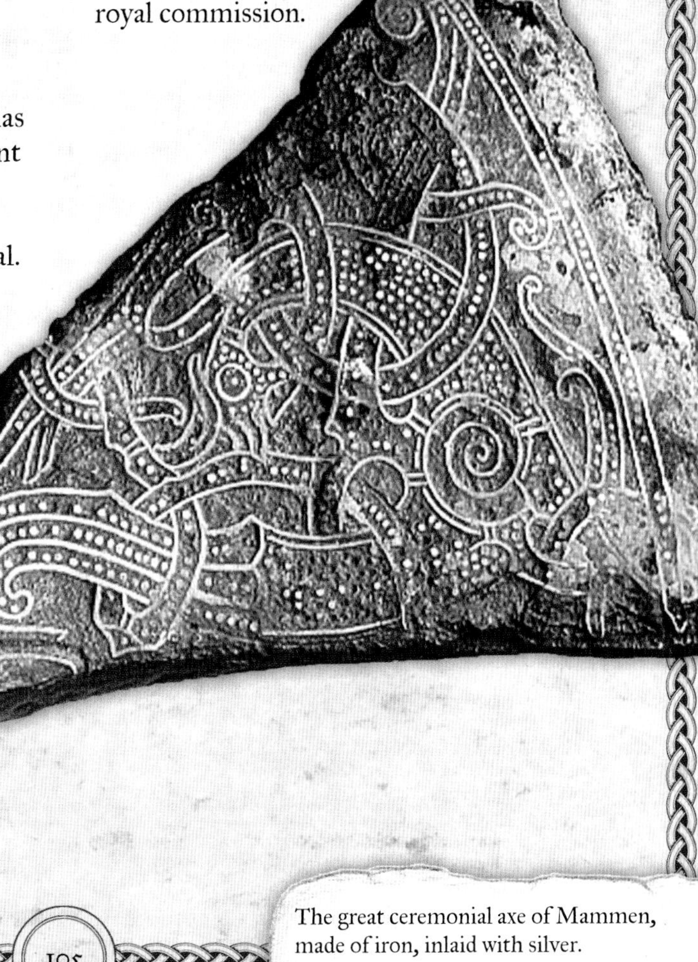

The great ceremonial axe of Mammen, made of iron, inlaid with silver.

BORRE-JELLINGE STYLES

The Borre (840 – 975) and Jellinge (890 – 990) styles were more or less contemporary with each other. A Swedish pendant from the Vårby hoard buried in 940 shows the new Borre-style gripping beast, which has a ribbon-like body and a mask-like head seen from in front; as before, it has powerful joints and gripping paws. This motif was developed in circular openwork silver-gilt brooches.

The Jellinge style also has gripping beasts, but seen in profile. The style is named from the silver cup found in the North Mound at the royal site of Jelling, in the burial chamber of King Gorm (959). The cup is decorated with two interlocked ribbon-shaped animals, each S-shaped, so the design makes an elaborate interlaced figure-of-eight design. Viking settlers introduced the Jellinge style to England, where it was preferred to the Borre style.

MAMMEN STYLE

The Mammen style (950 – 1010) grew out of the Jellinge style and is not always easy to distinguish from it. Some see it as a transition only between the Jellinge and Ringerike styles. One difference is the introduction of plant-based designs: vine scrolls and acanthus leaves were common in

Urnes Stave Church, Norway.

Western European art in the ninth and tenth centuries, so it is not surprising that tendrils and leaves began to appear in Viking art.

There is a remarkable axe, from a man's grave at Mammen (dated 970), which has designs inlaid with silver wire on both sides. There is a bird design on one side, a plant design on the other. Harald Bluetooth's massive rune-stone at Jelling is well-known for its runic inscription and crucifixion, but also for the great beast image that features on one side; this is a lion-like animal in Mammen style.

RINGERIKE STYLE

The Ringerike style (990 – 1090) flourished at a time when the practice of raising stone monuments was spreading. Its distinctive leaf-based style was developed from the Mammen plant motifs. The tendrils are now elongated and regularly cross over each other as they curl. Once again this was an inspiration borrowed from Western European art.

URNES STYLE

The Urnes style (1040 – 1140) is the final Viking style, which developed out of Ringerike. It is an extreme development of interlacing tendrils, and makes use of the interplay between curving lines of different widths. The most wonderful example of Urnes art is to be seen on the false door and other carved timbers built into the wall of the Urnes stave-church.

They show attenuated curving-limbed beasts intertwined with interlaced tendrils, endlessly curving and recurving. The high relief decoration of the blind portal forms a border round an inner panel, the door, which has lower-relief decoration in similar style.

The boundary between the two is a relatively tall but narrow rounded arch. From its date we might expect that it would be a Romanesque arch, but it is something more exotic, a horseshoe arch: the curve is more than a semicircle, extending downwards by a third of its radius.

This beautiful arch style was invented by the Visigoths by the seventh century and widely adopted in Moorish Spain, from where it spread right across the Islamic world. Perhaps the Vikings saw it in the Middle East and took it home from there. The Vikings were magpies, picking things up everywhere.

The existing building of Urnes church dates from the twelfth century, but the door and other carvings from an earlier building were fortunately saved and recycled. The Urnes carvings are a unique architectural survival, but we can be sure that the style will have been used at many other churches of the time. The style survives mainly on the rune-stones, but also on some small objects like the little silver brooch found at Lindholm Høje in Jutland.

Eleventh century manuscripts and twelfth century ecclesiastical artwork in Britain and Ireland show a Late Viking style, one that still incorporates interlacing and animal heads. Perhaps the greatest piece of colonial Viking art of all is the magnificent Cross of Cong, which was made in Ireland in the early twelfth century, in Urnes style.

We can even see the Urnes style in England, in the stone pilasters of the South Door of the Church of St Mary and St David, Kilpeck, Herefordshire. The Kilpeck carvings are often described as Norman, but the pilasters are more Urnes-style Viking than Norman.

Viking sword with double-edged blade and notched decoration.

CHAPTER 30.

SHIPS & NAVIGATION

A WORLD OF WATER

The Scandinavian homelands were fragmented and separated by stretches of water, so communication within the homelands was necessarily by water. Writing in the eleventh century, Adam of Bremen described a journey overland from Scania (then part of Denmark, though now in southern Sweden) to Sigtuna in Sweden as taking a month overland, but only five days by boat.

Ships were an essential part of the homeland culture, and had been for hundreds of years before the Viking Age. Prehistoric boats are known from archaeology and from drawings on rocks, but it is only from around AD 100 – 200 that ships similar in design to the Viking longship appeared.

THE NYDAM BOAT

The earliest near-ancestor of the Viking longship is the Nydam boat, discovered in 1863 at Nydam in south Jutland. The Nydam boat was made from oaks felled in 310 – 320, and was 79 feet (24 meters) long. Each side was built of five wide overlapping strakes, rising from a wide bottom plank. It was steered by means of a large oar hung over the side. Along the top of the hull, and lashed to the gunwales, there would originally have been wooden pins, lashed in position to hold fifteen pairs of oars.

Where the Nydam boat differed from the fully developed Viking ship was that it was for rowing only; there was neither mast nor sail. Re-excavation of the site in 1997 produced a couple of timber posts with crude bearded faces, probably ancestors of the Vikings' dragon-head prows.

The Nydam boat is useful in showing what the Viking longship developed from, and also in showing the sort of ship that the Anglo-Saxons would have used when they crossed the North Sea to colonize England – only 200 years before the Viking raids on the coastline of Britain began. Interestingly, even raiding by Scandinavians started before the Viking Age. Gregory of Tours describes the Danes raiding the Frankish coasts in 520.

REFINING SHIP DESIGN

Ships and ship technology were in place from the very beginning of the Viking period and they developed rapidly once the Vikings started looking further afield for wealth, whether by sea, especially across the North Sea, or along the major rivers of Europe, especially the Rivers Dnieper and Volga. Once wealth and prosperity depended on raid and trade, the refinement of ship technology became even more essential.

Sea-roving stimulated major developments in ship design. Viking ships were up to 99 feet (30 meters) long and clinker-built; their hulls were made of overlapping planks supported by internal ribs. They were relatively light, shallow-draught, flexible, and they could travel close inshore in shallow water, they could negotiate even quite shallow rivers, and they could be dragged up onto beaches relatively easily too.

Having low freeboard (low sides), it was easy for crews to jump over the sides and run quickly up a beach to engage the enemy, and just as easy to jump back on board and be away again. Speed was essential for success.

THE ENDLESS VOYAGE

Several full-size ships are known from their preservation in ship-burials, where they doubled as tombs for chiefs, kings or queens and a means of transport in the afterlife; the Vikings probably assumed their leaders would go on voyaging and plundering endlessly in the afterlife. Some smaller boat-graves have

been found in the Isle of Man and Scotland. The surviving ships vary in shape, reflecting changes in ship design during the Viking Age, and in size, reflecting differences in status.

The Gokstad ship was built in the 890s, a sleek, elegant ship 75 feet (23 meters) long, that might have been used for warfare or trade.

SKULDELEV 2

The smaller, lighter, shallower-draught ships were good for taking close inshore. But there were also bigger and heavier ships, which could cope with rough weather on the high seas.

One of the very biggest ships was Skuldelev 2, which was built at Dublin though found in Denmark. It was 99 feet (30 meters) long.

These great ships had large crews, who were also fighting men, and they had the capacity to be rowed as well as sailed; they were always fitted with a central mast and a single large square sail. They might be used for carrying people or cargo. In the later part of the Viking Age there were two distinct types of sea-going ships: the long narrow warships carrying large crews but with little space for anything else, and the deeper, broader cargo ships with higher freeboard that could carry substantial cargoes.

ROSKILDE 6

Roskilde 6, discovered as a wreck, is a true late Viking longship, in other words a purpose-built warship, and with a reconstructed length of 122 feet (37 meters) and a beam of 13 feet (4 meters) it is the largest ship to have been discovered so far from the Viking Age; it is also among the largest to be described in the documents. It was discovered and excavated in 1996 – 97 in the channel leading to the harbour of one of Denmark's earliest towns, the royal centre of Roskilde.

The ship had been deliberately scuttled and partly broken up, probably around 1040 – 45. It is not only the largest but the oldest of ten ships to be found in Roskilde Fjord, and it came to light, appropriately, when work began to extend the Viking Ship Museum. A well-preserved section of the ship's bottom and all 105 feet (32 meters) of the keel were found, allowing reconstruction.

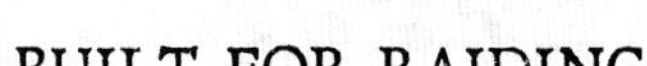

BUILT FOR RAIDING

The timber has been tree-ring dated to between 1018 and 1032 and the spacing of the rings corresponds so closely with those of the Oseberg and Gokstad ships that the timber must similarly have come from the Oslo area of Norway. The reconstructed hull has a very shallow draught; Roskilde 6 could float in waters that were only 33 inches (84 cm) deep: thigh-deep. In spite of her great size, the ship could be taken very close inshore, ideal for raiding.

The keel was oak. The floor timbers were carefully selected so that the wood fibres went in exactly the right direction; this made it possible to have very thin timbers and as a result a very light hull. Roskilde 6 was almost certainly a royal ship, built either for the use of the king in person, or at his command for service in the nation's ship-levy. Roskilde 6 may have been ordered by King Cnut; this was the type of ship Cnut used to conquer his neighbours and build a sea-empire.

SKULDELEV 2 AND HEDEBY 1

Two other longships have been discovered, Skuldelev 2 and Hedeby 1, showing very similar features to Roskilde 6, sharing in particular the length, narrowness and shallow draught; at 99 feet (30 meters), they are slightly shorter. They would have been powered by thirty pairs of oars, while Roskilde 6 was powered by forty. Writing in the thirteenth century, Snorri describes longships belonging to earls and kings as having from thirty to sixty pairs of oars. Was he exaggerating, or were there really longships with sixty pairs of oars?

Skuldelev 2, an ocean-going warship. Viking Ship Museum, Roskilde, Denmark.

QUAYSIDE TRADING POSTS

Trading posts developed at many sites along the northern Europe coastline, and their numbers increased through time. Large-scale industrial production took place at many of them. It was during the Viking Age that modern harbours with proper built quays appeared for the first time in Scandinavia.

KNARRS AND HAFSKIPS

We tend to think of the Viking longship as the universal Viking vessel, but it was a different sort of ship that was used to make open-sea voyages to Iceland and Greenland, the *knarr* or *hafskip*, or 'sea-ship'. One major difference between the two was that the longship was fitted with oars and rowlocks and had a low freeboard, while the *knarr* was powered by sail alone and had a high freeboard and no oars except the steering-oar.

SKULDELEV 1

Skuldelev 1 is the best surviving example of a *knarr*. This is one of the wrecks from the Skuldelev blockade, a group of ships scuttled to block the sea-inlet. Like its contemporary, Roskilde 6, it was built in Norway, this time in the Sogne Fjord. The hull is mostly slow-growing pine, but the keel is made of oak. It was quite a small ship, about 53 feet (16 meters) long, able to carry 27 short tons (24 metric tonnes) of cargo, and it is known that other merchant ships were bigger than this. One of the ships found in the harbour at Hedeby could have carried almost twice as much cargo.

Skuldelev 1 was probably fitted with a single large square sail, like its modern reconstruction, Ottar, built in 2000. It would have been a very useful, practical sort of vessel, that could be sailed by a crew of just 5 – 8 men. What happened during the Viking Age is that ship design developed so that larger and larger cargo vessels, carrying larger and larger quantities of cargo, could be made without increasing the size of the crew in proportion. Trading became more efficient.

PIRACY AND DAMAGE LIMITATION

The *knarr* was probably also occasionally used as a military transport. Piracy, ironically, must have been problem for the *knarr*. How this problem was dealt with is not known, but it may be that when valuable cargoes were being transported there was an escort vessel that was more manoeuvrable and carried armed men.

Both types of ship, the longship and the *knarr*, had a limited life span. They could be, and were, frequently repaired. Skuldelev 1 and Roskilde 6 both ended up in Roskilde Fjord, perhaps at the same time. Most of the navigation was in quiet waters like these, the Baltic coastline and the intricate shores of the Danish and Norwegian coastlines.

NAUTICAL CONNECTIONS

Many Scandinavian place-names have a connection with ships. Some start with the word for ship (*skib*, *skep*, *snekke*) or end with the word for hauling ships overland (*drag*, d*raet*). These names are commonest in the Viking homelands, Norway, Sweden and Denmark, but they are also found in Finland and, tellingly, Orkney and Shetland.

COASTAL BLOCKADES

At several places, ships were deliberately sunk to prevent approaching enemy squadrons from getting too close inshore or entering harbours or trading stations. The ships of the Roskilde blockade were varied; there were two longships, one larger than the other, a small fishing or ferry boat and two merchant ships, again of different sizes.

Blockades of this kind were not a Viking invention – some examples are known from the iron age. Some blockades consist of complex underwater constructions of piles and horizontal timbers; others consisted of old, worn-out ships that were filled with stones and deliberately scuttled in shallow water. Complementing the blockades, there were coastguard stations on coastal hills; signals were relayed from these stations by means of beacon fires.

THE MARITIME LANDSCAPE

The area round Ladby on the island of Funen, Denmark, is a good example of a Viking maritime landscape. Ladby itself is where the Ladby ship was found. This was a beautiful ship 72 feet (22 meters) long that was rowed by up to 32 rowers, an ideal craft for working these waters. It was dragged out of the water in about 925 and used for a Viking burial.

Ladby stands on a headland overlooking a winding sea inlet, Kertinge Fjord. The bay at the head of the fjord, Kertinge Nor, could be reached by water up the Fjord, and smaller vessels might be dragged overland to it from Odense Fjord to the north-west as well. This explains the place-name Draeby, the town where goods were transhipped.

Roskilde Fjord on the larger island of Zealand was another of these maritime landscapes. It was part of a network of sea inlets penetrating the island from the north and ending at Roskilde and Lejre.

Roskilde's history before the eleventh century is shadowy, but it can be assumed it was an important place earlier if, as Adam of Bremen tells us, it was chosen to be the burial place of Harald Bluetooth, who died in about 980.

Lejre is believed to be the location of Heorot, the royal hall described in the poem *Beowulf*. The twelfth century Danish scholar Saxo Grammaticus believed that Lejre was the home of the Danish royal dynasty of the Scyldings. These memories or traditions are supported by archaeological investigations, which show activity there in the early Viking Age.

THE ROSKILDE BLOCKADE

The Roskilde Fjord is very important for us today because it has yielded up the remains of an unusually large number of shipwrecks, both from the Viking Age and from the medieval period. There is a narrow stretch of the fjord, halfway between Roskilde and the sea, where a fleet of Viking ships was deliberately sunk in the eleventh century, presumably to prevent enemies from penetrating to Roskilde.

It seems likely that this was linked with the desperate power struggle between Sveinn Estridsson and Harald Hardrada in the middle of the eleventh century. The blockade of Viking ships was discovered in 1957 – 59, and five of the ships were excavated shortly afterwards. Two of them were built of Danish timber, two had been built in Norway and one had been built in Ireland, indicating the huge reach of the Viking sea-empire.

UNION OF LAND AND SEA

The ship was the ultimate Viking archetype, and it is not surprising that Vikings made their high-status monuments in the form of a ship. Countless stone ships were built as burial monuments, and once built they would have reminded everyone who saw them of the importance of ships and seafaring in the culture. Often those stone ships were created close to the shore, so that they created a visual unity between land and sea. But this was not always the case. Some stone ships were built a long way inland. The biggest

Wood and stone ship's anchor.

stone settings in the form of ships were created at Jelling.

Precisely how the Vikings thought about their ships or the sea is hard to tell. But there are clues. There is a rune-stone in Sweden which says that a man called Öleifr 'ploughed his *barth* to the east and died in the lands of the Lombards'. A *barth* is a type of warship with a distinctive prow design. In this inscription the sea is thought of as being a field that can be ploughed, cultivated – and harvested. The ship is the plough.

THE DANGERS OF VOYAGING

The wave beats the high benches.
The keel cleaves the wave.
The ugly sea will break the beautiful ship.

The sea is seen as threatening and dangerous, full of monsters. The skalds' poems have descriptions of ships struggling against the waves, with the boat as man's best weapon against the elements. In Viking mythology, the sea was also the home of the Midgard Serpent. Hurled there by Odin, it will not arise again, the poet promises, until the world ends.

We know about the successful voyages to Iceland, Greenland and Vinland, but we know little about the unsuccessful voyages, the ships that sailed off the map never to be heard of again. An eleventh century rune-stone on Bornholm relates what must have happened to many Viking adventurers.

Sasser raised this stone in memory of his father Halvard; he drowned at sea with all his crew.

THE SEA STALLION

The first modern replica of a Skuldelev ship, the *Saga Siglar*, demonstrated its seaworthy qualities by sailing round the world in 1984 – 86, but in the end it sank in the Mediterranean.

Skuldelev 2 was a warship built in Ireland in 1040. It was an impressive 99 feet (30 meters) long, and a replica longship called the *Sea Stallion of Glendalough* was completed in 2004, using authentic Viking shipbuilding techniques.

Building the hull took 27,000 man-hours and a total of fourteen mature oak trees 3 feet (1 meter) in diameter. Its seaworthiness was proved when it successfully sailed across the North Sea and back in 2007 – 08.

One reason this ship, like all the Vikings' ships, was so successful is that the trees were split with axes, not saws. Sawing would have been quicker, but there were advantages in splitting. Splitting maintains the integrity of the grain of the wood fibre instead of cutting across it, which is what sawing does.

The hulls were clinker-built, with the planks overlapping so that any unevenness in the edge did not compromise the structure. Splitting and the clinker-built construction meant that individual timbers and hulls as a whole were both stronger and lighter than the ships of later centuries.

KING OLAF'S LONGSHIP

Snorri described how in about the year 1000 King Olaf Tryggvason ordered the building of a longship. It was to be huge, and it was to be called *Ormen den Lange*, the *Long Serpent*. A shipwright called Thorberg Skafhug was taken on to create the stern and the prow, while others were ordered to fetch the timber and assemble the rest of the ship.

When the moment came to add the topmost timbers of the hull, the strakes, Thorberg had to return home on some urgent errand. The ship was finished without him and the king went to inspect it with his courtiers. They all said they had never seen such a fine ship. The next morning the strakes on one side of the hull were found hacked to pieces.

The king was angry and demanded to know who the vandal was. Thorberg admitted that he had done it. The king ordered him to make good the damage. When he had, everyone could see that his work was much better, so the king asked him to replace the strakes on the other side in the same way.

Oseberg Viking longship 815 – 820 AD.
Viking Ship Museum, Oslo, Norway.

The story shows the level of pride master-shipwrights took in their work. The skalds too took pride in the ships' speed, efficiency and beauty, continually praising them. The poetry contains endless numbers of similes for ships, often comparing them to living things – falcons, swans, dogs, wolves and horses, and ships were usually named after animals: the *Serpent*, the *Bison*, the *Crane*, the *Reindeer*.

IN PRAISE OF QUEEN EMMA

The enormous importance given to ships was demonstrated in the elaborate and inventive artwork lavished on their windvanes, carved gunwales, prows and dragons' heads. The finished appearance of the ships was described in a book written in about 1040 in honour of Queen Emma, the remarkable lady who was married first to King Aethelred (the Unready) and then to King Cnut. It was called the *Encomium Emmae Reginae*, In Praise of Queen Emma. The manuscript, which was written shortly after the death of Cnut, vividly describes the invasion fleets assembled for the conquest of England by Sweyn Forkbeard in 1013 and Cnut in 1016.

FORKBEARD'S FLEET

On one side lions moulded of gold were to be seen on the ships ... birds on the tops of the masts indicated by their movement the winds as they blew, or dragons of various kinds poured fire from their nostrils. The royal vessel excelled the others in beauty as much as the king preceded the soldiers in honour of his proper dignity.

THE FLEET OF KING CNUT

So great was the ornamentation of the ships that the eyes of the beholders were dazzled. The flashing of arms shone in one place, in another the flame of suspended shields. Gold shone from the prows, silver flashed too. So great was the magnificence of the fleet that the ships alone would have terrified the enemy.

GILDED ENGRAVED COPPER

These descriptions are consistent with the archaeological remains so there is no reason to doubt them. The gilded weathervanes may sound lavish, but gilded copper weathervanes have survived from the Viking Age. Heggen Church in Norway has an eleventh century weathervane made of gilded engraved copper. The shields suspended from the gunwales are known from depictions of longships, and so are the monstrous moulded figures.

THE INVASION FLEET

The size of the invasion and raiding fleets varied enormously. According to the Anglo-Saxon Chronicle, London was attacked in September 994 by 94 ships, commanded by Sweyn and Olaf. It is possible that the numbers are exaggerated, and it is hard to imagine any Saxon who was there troubling to count 94 ships. Even so, it seems fair to accept that there were a great many ships. This shows a high level of commitment on the part of the Vikings, and a very substantial investment of time and capital.

THE ULTIMATE ICON

Viking society was founded on ships. They were used for transport, for trade, for warfare, for burial, for communal identity. The Vikings made toy ships for their children. They even made their houses look like upturned ships. In the so-called 'Trelleborg House' the curving walls of the long sides are strongly reminiscent of the shape of a longship.

The square formations of such houses in the forts suggest to some historians that they may have been designed so that each hall accommodated the crew of a ship, a captain and his oarsmen. Maybe the *skibsfreden*, the special code of law applying to ships on long voyages, also applied in these halls.

Ships in their turn shaped the Vikings' perception of the world around them. They saw the world from the sea. They were acutely conscious of the value of certain coastlines in providing them with shelter, refuge and opportunities for commerce, and allowed the physical landscape of the coasts to guide the evolving pattern of settlement across north-west Europe.

CHAPTER 31

LANGUAGE, LITERATURE & RUNES

VIKING DIALECTS

The Vikings spoke Old Norse, a northern branch of the Germanic language family. Their language was therefore related to German, Dutch and English. The more distinctively Scandinavian form of this language is found in runic inscriptions from AD 600 onwards, in other words, not long before the first Viking raids, and it was surprisingly uniform across Scandinavia at that early stage.

During the Viking Age itself clearly distinct dialects developed. There was Old East Norse, which was spoken in Denmark and Sweden, and Old West Norse, which was spoken in Norway and Iceland. Because the raiders came from different parts of Scandinavia, the different dialects found their way into Britain and Ireland, Old East Norse especially in eastern England, Old West Norse in north-west England, Ireland and Scotland.

TALKING TO VIKINGS

It is not clear how well the Vikings and, for example, the English could understand one another. A near-contemporary comment suggests that they *were* indeed able to understand each other; 'Back then, the language spoken in England was the same as that spoken in Norway.' There was certainly a substantial common vocabulary, or words that sounded very similar and meant the same thing, for instance;

Old Norse	*Old English*	*Middle English*
stein	stän	stone
geit	gät	goat
staup	stëap	steep
-lauss	-leas	-less
skip	scip*	ship
bryggja	brycg**	bridge

*pronounced ship
**pronounced bridge

Having many words in common means that Vikings and Anglo-Saxons could probably make one another understand. Some Old Norse words were borrowed by the Anglo-Saxons and became English words; *they*, *them* and *their* are Old Norse words.

THE EPIC POEM OF BEOWULF

The Vikings and Anglo-Saxons probably had a body of literature in common too. The poem *Beowulf*, which was not recognized as a great masterpiece of Anglo-Saxon literature until the early nineteenth century, tells a doubly strange story. Beowulf is a hero of a Swedish tribe called the Geats. He goes to the aid of Hrothgar, the king of the Danes whose mead hall in Heorot is under attack by a monster called Grendel. After destroying Grendel, Beowulf returns to Geatland and becomes king of the Geats.

The poem was written some time between the eighth century and the eleventh century, but it describes events that took place in about 500, after the Angles and Saxons had begun their migration to England. The poem

may have originated in southern Scandinavia and been taken to England by people who were Geats, from the area round Göteborg in south-west Sweden.

THE ROYAL HALL OF HEOROT

Lejre in Denmark is believed to be the Heorot of the poem, and archaeologists have found a hall there that was built in about 550, the time of Beowulf. The general view now is that both the people and the places in *Beowulf* are based on a historical reality.

Beowulf, the great Anglo-Saxon poem, is not really Anglo-Saxon in origin; it is set in Scandinavia. It refers back to a phase of history that predates the Anglo-Saxons' arrival in England and represents a harking-back to ancient ancestral roots, an almost mythic time before England was born. It also represents a piece of story-telling that predates the Viking Age, yet it is about an important Viking royal palace.

It is likely that this same story, and probably many others like it that have not survived, would have been recited in the Danish mead halls too, and probably at Lejre itself, the place where much of the action took place. The Anglo-Saxons knew *Beowulf* and the Vikings would have known a version of the story too.

Runic stone with inscription, Arhus, Denmark.

READING THE RUNES

Runes are an alphabet made of straight lines, well-suited for and in fact designed for carving on stone or wood. Curving lines were avoided as they were harder to carve. Runes originated somewhere within the Roman Empire, as some of the symbols in the early script closely resemble Roman letters.

They were devised before the Viking Age began, in about 200, and were in use as late as 1500. By 700 there was a runic alphabet of twenty-four characters, though later this was reduced to only sixteen characters, representing a limited range of sounds. The result is that runic writing does not represent pronunciation very closely.

THE DEEDS OF THE DEAD

Rune-stones were high-status memorials, consisting of large freestanding natural boulders covered with inscriptions. They were very public statements and intended to be widely understood, even though literacy was probably uncommon among Vikings generally. And we do not know how many Vikings could read or write runes. The rune-stones often commemorated warriors or their achievements.

One example reads: 'Grjotgard and Einridi raised a stone in memory of their father Gudver who was west in England and shared payment.' Another is a monument to Skerdir, who 'died in England in the retinue'. Another is a monument to Hefnir, the son of Thorstein, who 'went to England as a young warrior, then died grievously at home'. Another is an epitaph, arranged in verse, again to a warrior: 'He was the most respected of men, who lost [his] life in England.'

THE JELLING STONES

Perhaps the best-known rune-stones are the Jelling Stones, erected by King Harald Bluetooth to commemorate his parents. The inscription on one of them reads, 'King Harald ordered these memorials to be made after Gorm, his father, and Thyra, his mother. The Harald who won the whole of Denmark and Norway and turned the Danes to Christianity.' As well as honouring his parents, the inscription tells us exactly how Harald himself wanted to be remembered by posterity.

A group of about thirty rune-stones in central Sweden tell us about a particular expedition to the east by a group of aristocratic adventurers in the first half of the eleventh century. The commander of the fleet was Yngvar, who later had a saga written about him, *Yngvar the Far-travelled*. According to the inscriptions, some members of this expedition reached the Middle East, and some must have survived the return journey too, or the tale could not have been told. Inscriptions tell fragments of the story.

- *Thialfi and Holmlaug had all these stones erected in memory of Banki their son, who had a ship of his own and steered it eastwards in Yngvar's force. May God help Banki's soul. Aeskil cut [these runes].*
- *Andvert and Kiti and Kar and Blesi and Diarf erected this stone in memory of Gunnlaeif, their father. He fell in the east with Yngvar. God help his soul.*
- *Tola had this stone raised for his son Harald, Yngvar's brother. Like brave men they journeyed for distant gold. And in the east they fed the eagle. In the south they died, in Serkland (Saracen Land).*

THE ORKNEYINGA SAGA

The largest collection of runic inscriptions is the set of thirty in the Maeshowe tomb on Orkney. Built in 2800 BC, the monument was reused to bury a Viking chief, with his treasure, in AD 950 and the inscriptions were made between then and about 1160.

The *Orkneyinga Saga* tells how at Christmas in 1153 Earl Harald and his men were making their way on foot from Stromness to the earl's palace at Firth, when they were caught in a terrible snowstorm. 'Two of his men went insane', and the party took shelter in the ancient and now empty tomb. Some of the graffiti may have been carved then.

- *Ofram the son of Sigurd carved these runes.*
- *Tholfir Kolbeinsson carved these runes high up.*
- *These runes were carved by the man most skilled in runes in the Western Ocean with the axe that killed Gaukr Trandkill's son in the south of Iceland.*
- *Crusaders broke into Maeshowe. Lif the earl's cook carved these runes. To the north-west is a great treasure hidden. It was long ago that a great treasure was hidden here. Happy is he that might find that great treasure. Hakon single-handed carried treasure from this howe. Simon Sirith.*

NAMES IN HISTORY

Runes were carved onto portable objects too. A bone comb-case found at Lincoln has a simple inscription: 'Thorfast made a good comb.' Viking runic writing has even been found in Istanbul and Venice. In the gallery at the church of Hagia Sophia, a Viking visitor inscribed his name in runes on the balustrade, just like a modern tourist.

More remarkable is the marble statue of a lion in Venice, which bears the name of another Viking visitor, though not to Venice. The Venetians collected the lion statue from Athens in 1687, and the sculpture had been signed there by a Viking 700 years before. Both are evidence that the Vikings reached the Aegean region, and left marks there that still survive.

PART 5.

CELEBRITY VIKINGS: KINGS & BARDS

CHAPTER 32

THE POWER OF THE VIKING KINGS

The Vikings certainly had kings, even if the meaning of the title varied. At the beginning of the Viking Age, Ireland and Wales were divided into several small kingdoms; England was divided into five (Northumbria, Mercia, East Anglia, Wessex and the Cornish), and Scotland was divided into three (the kingdom of the Picts, Dalriada and Strathclyde). A similar pattern was seen across the North Sea in the Viking homelands. There were many small kingdoms, each with its own king, who would act as battle-leader, law-giver and judge.

KINGS WITHOUT KINGDOMS

Kingship could sometimes be a matter of personal status, and there were some prominent figures who claimed the title as a personal badge, even when they had no kingdoms to rule. The Great Army that marched to Cambridge in 874 was led by three of these so-called 'kings', Guthrum, Oscytel and Anund, though none of them at that time ruled a particular kingdom.

After his famous treaty with King Alfred, the Treaty of Wedmore, Guthrum was able to establish himself formally as a king in East Anglia, carving out a kingdom for himself there known as the kingdom of Guthrum, but this did not happen until 879. There is a glimpse of this again in 954, when 'five kings' were allegedly killed along with Erik Bloodaxe, who was what we would think of as a *real* king.

KINGS WITH POWER

Some, especially in the late Viking Age, were kings in the great medieval tradition – kings with power, substantial kingdoms, and wealth. The Danish kings had strong power in Jutland by the eighth century and by the tenth century King Harald Bluetooth was able to proclaim on a rune-stone that he had 'won all of Denmark for himself'.

When the Danish King Harald Klak arrived at Ingelheim in Germany to be baptized, he received wonderful gifts: golden spurs, a magnificent sword, expensive robes, gold armlets and a crown. Receptions and ceremonies like this were an important part of European court life. The exchange of gifts meant a recognition of status, a guarantee of safe passage and a half-promise of future support.

ROYAL RELATIONS

Rune-stones tell us some of the relationships among the royals. A stone at Sonder Vissing in east Jutland says that Queen Tove, the wife of Harald Klak, was the daughter of Mistivoi, prince of the Slavic Obodrites. A generation later, the first wife of Sweyn Forkbeard was

Animal-head ornament found at Oseberg, Norway.

the daughter of Duke Mieszko I of Poland and sister to Mieszko's successor Boleslaw I Chrobry. One of Sweyn's daughters married a Slavic prince.

The Danish royal family strengthened its position by creating dynastic ties with the royal families of other countries; it was common practice throughout Scandinavia, and the continent as a whole. By the end of the Viking Age, the marriage ties of the Viking royals stretched across much of Europe.

ROYAL FOSTERING

Another medieval feature was the concept of royal fostering. This meant young nobles and princes being farmed out to learn courtly behaviour and foreign customs in the households of other kings or nobles, perhaps in other countries. The Norwegian King Hakon (934 – 961) was brought up as a Christian at the court of King Athelstan of England; he acquired the nickname 'Athelstan's foster-son'.

It has been suggested that Raedwald, the powerful Anglo-Saxon king of East Anglia who is believed to have been buried in 624 in the Sutton Hoo ship burial, was as a boy fostered in Sweden, where ship burial was already practised – well before the beginning of the Viking Age. Raedwald could in this way have imported to England a Scandinavian practice which he vividly remembered from his boyhood, and adopted it for his own dynasty.

Royal fostering was a common aristocratic practice that went on across northern Europe for hundreds of years. In Britain, the idea of sending upper-class boys away for courtly education has survived; the public school system is its pale descendant.

MONUMENTS TO A KING

The royal complex at Jelling in Denmark is a site that reverberates with the power of the kings of the Vikings. The monuments still standing consist of two colossal grass-covered mounds with, in between them, a stone church built in about 1100 and in front of it two impressive rune-stones. The larger of the two stones, sometimes described as Denmark's birth certificate, was erected by King Harald Bluetooth to commemorate his parents. The second stone was raised in about 950; 'King Gorm [Harald's father] made this monument in memory of Thorvi, his wife – Denmark's adornment.'

Underneath the North Mound there are the remains of Gorm the Old's timber burial chamber, the tree-rings in its timbers dating from 959. The king's burial was inserted into an already-existing bronze age barrow. Underneath the South Mound, there are some large boulders which formed part of an earlier stone setting that is believed to have been built in the form of a ship. The South Mound was not started until after 970, and it is possible it was intended for Harald's burial – or an assembly mound, like the Tynwald Hill on the Isle of Man.

BLUETOOTH'S CAPITAL

The Jelling royal complex, which included some large timber buildings, was contained within a large palisade enclosure 394 yards (360 meters) across and made of close-set vertical planks. So far only one entrance has been detected, a 6.5-feet-wide (2 meters) gateway to the north. The redesign of the complex as a whole has been dated to the 960s, the time of Harald Bluetooth's conversion to Christianity, and it is the largest known royal site of the Viking Age. This must have been Harald Bluetooth's capital. Its scale and geometrical layout are similar to those of the royal complexes that were built at the same time in Germany. Yet the Jelling royal complex was abandoned relatively soon after it was built. The centre of power shifted eastwards in Denmark, away from central Jutland. It also seems that Harald's successors had no need for monuments like this to enforce their power and authority.

CHAPTER 33.

IVAR THE BONELESS

(800 – 873)

Ivar Ragnarsson, Ivar the Boneless, was a Viking warlord of exceptional ferocity and cruelty, and reputed to be a berserker. The son of Ragnar Lodbrok (Ragnar Hairy-Breeches) and Aslaug Sigurdsdottir, he ruled over parts of what are now Denmark and Sweden. The strange nickname, Boneless, is very specifically explained in the Viking sagas: 'only cartilage was where bone should have been'. This may not have been meant literally, but a way of saying that he was unusually supple. One poem appears to take his bonelessness literally, and has him carried by his warriors on a shield, but if he was literally boneless he would have been seriously incapacitated and unable to fight, and he had a great reputation as a fighter.

He was very big, dwarfing all of his contemporaries. He had powerful arms, so that his bow was much stronger and his arrows heavier than those of other warriors.

INVADING EAST ANGLIA

In 865, Ivar crossed the North Sea with his brothers Halfdan and Ubbe to invade East Anglia with what the Anglo-Saxon Chronicle described as the Great Heathen Army, or a heathen host. According to legend, the raven banner Ivar unfurled in East Anglia was woven by three daughters of Ragnar Lodbrok. The East Anglians made peace with the Vikings.

The following year, Ivar led his army north and took the city of York. The kingdom of Northumbria was in a state of civil war, with Aelle usurping the throne from Osberht. In 867 they stormed the walls of the city of York, but the Vikings responded decisively, slaughtering everyone who had entered York and both of the Northumbrian kings, Aelle and Osberht.

RULING WITH ALL CRUELTY

Then the Great Army marched south into Mercia, establishing winter quarters at Nottingham. King Burgred of Mercia pleaded with Ethelred, the king of Wessex, and his brother Alfred, to help him. The West Saxons led an army into Mercia and laid siege to Nottingham, but the Vikings refused to fight. Ivar showed considerable cunning on this occasion, resorting to diplomacy to win peace from the West Saxons. The Mercians were relieved and agreed to pay the Vikings to go away. Then, in 868, Ivar returned to York, where he ruled 'with all cruelty'.

EXECUTING KING EDMUND

Ivar took his army back into East Anglia, where King Edmund was leading resistance against them. Edmund was captured and brutally executed at the village of Hoxne. Edmund bravely refused to become the vassal of a heathen or renounce his religion, declaring that his religion was dearer to him than his life. He was beaten with clubs, then tied to a tree, where the Vikings shot arrows into him until he died. Then they beheaded him. The Vikings contemptuously left Edmund's body unburied and his head was thrown into deep brambles. Monasteries were destroyed, and monks slaughtered. There was large-scale plundering.

IRELAND AND SCOTLAND

The following year, Ivar left the command of the Great Heathen Army in England to his brothers Halfdan and Ubbe, while he himself left for Dublin, from where he dominated the Irish Sea with his co-ruler, Olaf the White. He then launched an attack on Scotland, homing in on Dumbarton Rock, the ancient fortress-capital of Strathclyde, overlooking the River Clyde. The garrison held out for four months, though wasted by hunger and thirst. After that they surrendered and the stronghold was pillaged and destroyed. Ivar and Olaf stayed in Strathclyde for the winter, returning to Dublin weighed down with booty. Ivar was then in a position to exact tribute from Constantine I, the king of Scots.

The Annals of Ulster note that Ivar, or 'Imar' as he appears there, died in 873. The cause of his death was 'a sudden and horrible disease'. There has been speculation that this horrible disease may have been connected with his bonelessness, and one theory is that he suffered from brittle bone disease, *osteogenesis imperfecta*.

BURIED IN ENGLAND

The skeleton of a 9-foot-tall (2.7 meters) Viking warrior was discovered during excavations at the churchyard of St Wystan's in Repton in Derbyshire. The archaeologist Professor Martin Biddle and his wife Birthe Kjølbye-Biddle claim that the skeleton may have been that of Ivar the Boneless.

In 873 the Great Army is said to have travelled to Repton, where it took up quarters for the winter. A mass grave at Repton was initially uncovered in 1686 by a labourer named Thomas Walker but the grave was eventually covered over again and its existence forgotten. The *Saga of Ragnar Lodbrok* states that Ivar the Boneless was buried in England.

A SAVAGE AND BRUTAL DEATH

The 'nine foot long' man had disappeared by the time of the Biddles' excavation. They unearthed another body, of a man aged between 35 and 45, buried with a sword, a small Thor's hammer and a boar's tusk. The bones show that the warrior died a savage and brutal death. Two wounds on his skull were probably made by a spear and marks on the spine suggest the warrior was disembowelled after death.

A violent blow to the top of the thigh could have removed his genitals, perhaps the reason why the boar's tusk was discovered between the legs of the skeleton, an attempt by those who buried him to make his body whole before his journey to Valhalla. Viking beliefs stipulated that a body could not enter Valhalla if it was not whole.

The man was stabbed in the head, jaw, arm and thigh and disembowelled. Each of his toes and both his heels were split lengthways. Perhaps this 35 – 45-year-old warrior was Ivar. But the Biddles are reported to believe that the more important missing central burial in the mass grave was the grave of Ivar. Since that burial has vanished, speculation seems fruitless.

Viking brooch of the World Serpent, Oland, Sweden.

CHAPTER 34.

HARALD FAIR-HAIR

(858 – 942)

Tradition has it that Harald Fair-Hair controlled all of Norway in the late ninth and early tenth centuries. A thirteenth century history gives an early account of Harald, who was the first king of Norway, and it uses extracts from praise poems by Harald's skalds, his court poets, which date from Harald's time. One of them, *The Raven's Tale*, glorifies battle. Ravens, the birds of Odin, notoriously feed on the corpses of the battle-dead.

A STRANGE LEGACY

Harald was the son of Halfdan the Black, and he became king after Halfdan's death – king of a handful of separate scattered small kingdoms which his father had acquired. He was a boy when he inherited this strange legacy, and during his minority the kingdoms were ruled by a regent, his mother's brother Guthorm. As his nickname suggests, Harald's hair was a conspicuous feature. 'His hair grew thick, with a magnificent sheen very like silk. He was the handsomest of men, very strong and big of build.' He was a shrewd man, far-sighted and ambitious. The praise poems continue –

Listen, ring-bearers, while I speak
Of the glories in war of Harald, most wealthy

How is it with you, ravens? Where have you come from
With bloody beaks at the dawning of day?

HARALD 'SHOCKHEAD'

Harald proposed marriage to Gyda, the daughter of King Erik of Horderland, but she would only accept him if he was king over all of Norway. He was persuaded to take a vow not to trim or comb his hair until he became king and, until then, he was known as 'Shockhead' or 'Tangle-Hair'.

Much of Harald's life remains shadowy and uncertain: apart from the praise poems, virtually nothing was written down until three hundred years after his death. The poems unfortunately conflict with the version of events in the sagas, which also disagree with one another. What is known is that he had two sons, Erik Bloodaxe and Hakon the Good, who became kings after his death. It is also clear that he unified Norway into a single kingdom. This means that he was more than just the first king of Norway: he was its founder. He inherited a scatter of small kingdoms, and then went about the task of conquering more in order to consolidate and unify them.

SETTLING IN ICELAND

His nation-building project was under continual threat from outside, as many of his opponents had taken refuge outside Norway, in Iceland, Orkney, Shetland, the Hebrides and the Faeroes. His position was secured by a great victory in battle at Hafrsfjord near Stavanger in 872, yet he still needed to voyage to the west to clear the Scottish Highlands and Islands of Viking renegades who were hiding there.

The twelfth century *Islendingabók* comments that Iceland was settled during Harald's lifetime, with the clear implication that it was men dissatisfied with Harald's rule, particularly with regard to eroded property rights, who were emigrating to Iceland. Harald himself emerges as the driving force behind Viking settlement in Iceland.

LATE LIFE CRISIS

The sagas tell us that Harald's later life was troubled by strife among his many sons. He gave all of them the same title, king, and the instruction that they were to rule as his representatives. In old age, Harald handed over power to his favourite son, Erik Bloodaxe, whom he set up as his successor. Erik ruled jointly with his father when his father reached the age of 80. Harald died of old age about three years after this in 942.

Fierce human face carved on the Oseberg cart, Norway.

CHAPTER 35.

THORFINN SKULL-SPLITTER

(890 – 963)

Thorfinn Torf-Einarsson, known as 'Skull-Splitter', was Earl of Orkney in the tenth century. He appears as a character in the *Orkneyinga Saga* and briefly in *St Olaf's Saga*. These powerful stories were not written down until the thirteenth century in Iceland, and consequently much of the content is difficult to corroborate.

THE ORKNEY EARLDOM

Thorfinn was the youngest son of Torf-Einarr, who was the son of Rognvald Eysteinsson, the first Earl of Orkney. Two of Thorfinn's brothers joined with Erik Bloodaxe in a raid on an identified place in England. After Erik's death, his widow Gunnhild fled north to Orkney with her sons, who used the islands as a base for summer raids on the British mainland. Gunnhild and her family later travelled to Norway.

Thorfinn's five sons were Arnfinn, Havard, Hlodvir, Ljot and Skuli; there were at least two daughters as well. His wife Grelad was a daughter of Earl Dungad of Caithness and Groa, who was a daughter of Thorstein the Red. Grelad's Caithness connection may have helped Thorfinn's claim to the Orkney earldom. In the later days of Thorfinn's reign the sons of Erik Bloodaxe returned from Norway to Orkney, where they 'committed great excesses'.

FAMILY IN-FIGHTING

Thorfinn Skull-Splitter lived to be an old man and is believed to have died in 963. He is said to have been buried at the Howe of Hoxa on South Ronaldsay. *St Olaf's Saga* tells us that Thorfinn's sons became earls after him, but the earldom was weakened by dynastic fighting. Ragnhild had her husband Arnfinn murdered at Murkle in Caithness and married his brother Havard, who ruled for a time as Earl. Ragnhild then plotted with her nephew Einar kliningr, who killed Havard in battle close to Stenness. Then Ragnhild fell out with Einar and persuaded the other Einar, Einar hardkjotr, to kill Einar kliningr. Ragnhild was still not content. She then plotted with and married Ljot Thorfinsson and had Einar hardkjotr killed. So Ragnhild married three of Thorfinn's sons in succession. After Ljot became earl, no more is heard of Ragnhild.

MORE SCOPE FOR EXCESS

Modern scholars tend to believe the bloodthirsty story of Thorfinn's children. The earldom of Orkney seems to have been inherently unstable, with reigns usually ending in violence. In the tenth century, the earls of Orkney were gaining more freedom of action; there was less control from Norway as Scandinavian expeditions across the North Sea tended to be directed towards England. This by-passing of Orkney gave the earls more scope for independent action, more scope for dynastic in-fighting, more scope for 'excesses'.

Decorated silver sword hilt.

CHAPTER 36.

EGIL SKALLAGRIMSSON

(904 – 995)

THE GREATEST VIKING BARD

According to the thirteenth century medieval saga about his life, *Egil's Saga*, Egil was a fierce tenth century warrior, but he was also a gifted skald or court poet. Egil unwisely killed the son of King Erik Bloodaxe and was sentenced to death for this crime.

The saga tells us that Egil wrote a praise poem for King Erik. Egil recited this 'head-ransom' in front of the king. The poem was exceptionally fine, so Egil escaped execution and won his liberty. Some lines in the poem were untrue; Egil claimed that he had voyaged across the ocean to bring Erik a poem of praise.

I dragged my oak-ship to sea.
I loaded my vessel's hold
With its cargo of praise.

Then Egil praised Erik's valour in battle:

At arrows' weaving
Men sank to the ground.
In this battle Erik
Won a glorious name.

But the general nature of the verse is excused by the writer of the saga, who reminds us that Egil had only the night before to compose his poem. Most Norse poems are more carefully researched.

RAGING WE KILLED

Egil is, even so, regarded as the greatest of the Icelandic poets whose work has survived. He was born at Borg in western Iceland to a family traditionally opposed to the kings of Norway. On his journeys abroad he came in contact with Christianity, but these journeys made no impact at all on his beliefs. His poems show a purely pagan view of death and the afterlife. They are a celebration of core Viking Age values:

I have been with sword and spear
Slippery with bright blood
Where kites wheeled. And how well
We violent Vikings clashed!
Red flames gorged men's roofs,
Raging we killed and killed.

Egil Skallagrimsson led a turbulent life and when he died, old and embittered, he railed against Odin for taking from him the members of his family who should have supported him in his old age.

Now things go hard
with me. On the headland
Stands the sister of Odin's enemy.
Yet serene, in good heart,
undismayed,
I shall meet death face to face.

Viking sword with silver inlay on hilt.

CHAPTER 37.

VIKING SKALDS AND POETRY

The Viking skalds (court poets) composed their poems in what is called 'court metre'. It is intricately structured, using alliteration, and both internal rhyme and half-rhyme within lines that have a restricted number of syllables. The tight formality made the poems easier to learn and harder to alter. This was important if poems and narratives were to be kept unaltered. The verse was mainly committed to memory, not written down – or at least not written down until the Viking Age was over.

SCENE-SHIFTING

A problem for modern readers is the use of specific poetic vocabulary and allusions, or kennings. So, instead of referring to a raven directly, a skald might refer to a 'crane of battle' or a 'wound-gull'. By transposing images in this way a description can end up appearing to be about something else. If the raven on the battlefield becomes the 'wound's gull' and the raven's beak becomes a 'prow', the skald can scene-shift a battle into a seascape – then blood becomes brine.

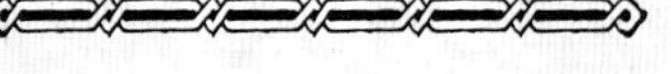

THE FUNERAL ODE

Much of the skaldic verse that we have survives from the Viking Age. Sometimes the saga-writers quoted long sections from a poem, occasionally an entire funeral ode. The funeral ode of the tenth century King Hakon of Norway has been preserved in this way.

Even though Hakon was brought up a Christian by King Athelstan, the skald Eyvind wrote him a pagan poem. In it, Odin sends out his Valkyries to choose a warrior brave enough to live with him in Valhalla, and they choose Hakon. The poem ends:

Freed from his chains,
To the home of men
The wolf Fenrir will run
Before there comes so good
A man of royal birth
To the desolate fields.

SAGA OF GUNNLAUG

The best skalds were much sought after and well-paid. They were welcomed by Scandinavian rulers to compose poems advertising their wisdom, battle exploits and ancestry. The thirteenth century *Saga of Gunnlaug Serpent-Tongue* portrays the life of a travelling skald. He voyages from Iceland to London (twice), and visits Dublin, Orkney, Uppsala and Trondheim.

At each place he recites his poetry in front of the rulers and is given a reward. In London, he praises Ethelred II as 'a battle-hasty ruler' and is given a scarlet cloak. In Dublin, he praises Sihtric Silkbeard; 'he feeds corpses to the troll-woman's steed [wolf]'. Gunnlaug's career is very much in the Viking tradition.

A SWORD OF SWORDS

The *Saga of Olaf Tryggvason* shows one of the skalds, Hallfred Ottarson, being difficult. Olaf gave him the nickname 'awkward skald'. Olaf asked if he still had the sword he had given him. Hallfred replied he did, but he had not fitted it with a scabbard yet. To which Olaf responded it was appropriate that the awkward skald had an awkward sword. He commissioned him to write a poem with the word sword in every line. Hallfred came up with this:

A Viking skald telling heroic sagas.

Olaf thanked him for the verse and as a reward gave him a richly decorated scabbard, but I can't help noticing that Hallfred left one line without the word 'sword'. That is awkward.

This is a sword of swords
That made me sword-rich.
For this swift Niort-of-swords
My verse becomes sword-full.
Not short of swords shall it be.
I shall be worth three swords
Should I get an inlaid
Sheath for this sword.

FOREMOST GREAT LORD

Cnut was a great patron of skalds. His administrators kept an 'Enumeration of Skalds' – a list of eight named individuals, some of whose poetry still survives. In one of the poems, Cnut is portrayed as a great warrior. The skald, by the name of Hallvard Harek's-Blaze, tells Cnut he is 'shaker of the ice of the sword-belt', but also 'the foremost great lord under heaven'.

It is easy to hear, behind a poem like this, an anxious private rehearsal in front of a courtier pressing for some adjustments in the interest of conveying the king's image correctly. Yes, King Cnut is a great warrior, but he is also a great Christian. Perhaps the skald might add a line saying so?

CHAPTER 38.

ERIK BLOODAXE

(910 – 954)

Erik was the eldest of the many sons of the Norwegian tyrant, Harald Fair-Hair. He became known as 'Bloodaxe' because of his savage feuding against his brothers. Having many brothers inevitably meant dynastic feuding.

AVENGERS OF BOLD BLOODAXE

Erik Bloodaxe ruled Norway for a few years after his father's death in the middle of the tenth century. But he was unpopular, and in the 930s was expelled by his younger brother Hakon the Good, who had been brought up in a Christian environment at the court of King Athelstan of England. Snorri Sturluson told the story.

Twenty-six years after Erik had been exiled, the sails of an avenging fleet were sighted, but no-one dared tell the upstart king, except Eyvind Finnsson, who told the king in verse:

Avengers of bold Bloodaxe
Demand a meeting of mail-coats
And scabbard-points. No chance
Of a sit-down for us. A problem for me, king,
To tell my lord of this attack. It's your honour I look to.
Quick, let's take up tried weapons.

King Hakon said, 'You're such a fine fellow, Eyvind, you wouldn't have told me of an attack if it were not true.' After a discussion, they decide to arm.

THE LAST VIKING KING

Exiled to England, Erik became King of York for a time, and issued his own coins. Erik has been virtually forgotten in England, but his rule and his death mark significant moments in English history. He died heroically in battle in 954, defeated by the Anglo-Saxons.

He was the last Viking king of Northumbria. His death marked one of the final steps towards a united England. His funeral ode described the preparations for King Erik's arrival, after his death in battle, among Odin's warriors in Valhalla.

'What dream was that,' said Odin, 'when I thought before dawn
I was making Valhalla ready for a slaughtered army?
I roused my great champions, bade the Valkyries wake,
Strew the benches, wash out the beer-mugs,
Bring out wine for a prince who is coming.
From the world I await such noble fighting men
As will make my heart rejoice.'

The sons of Erik and his widow Gunnhild became rulers of Norway. Curiously, Gunnhild was a very popular name in England well into the thirteenth century, so perhaps the great days of the last Viking king were not entirely forgotten.

Brooch in gold and precious stones from Ovre Eiker, Buskerud, Norway.

CHAPTER 39.

HARALD BLUETOOTH

(935 – 985)

Harald Gormsson was the son of King Gorm the Old and Thyra Dannebod, as he tells us in the runic inscription on the inscribed stone he raised in their honour. He ruled as king of Denmark from around 958 and king of Norway as well for a few years around 970. Some sources say he was forcibly deposed by his son, Sweyn Forkbeard.

The nickname is a puzzle. One explanation is that he had one bad tooth, which was dark in colour. But the name may originally have been 'Blue Thegn', in other words, the chieftain who wore blue, which was an unusual expensive dye. Harald may have habitually worn blue to emphasize his royal status.

A CHRISTIAN CONVERSION

The short inscription on the larger of the two Jelling Stones says that Harald turned the Danes to Christianity. Exactly how Harald was converted is unclear, as there are two medieval accounts and they are contradictory. Widukind of Corvey, a contemporary, said that Harald was converted by a cleric called Poppa. When Harald asked Poppa to prove the strength of his faith, Poppa carried a great iron weight heated in a fire, and did so without suffering burns. Adam of Bremen, writing a hundred years later, says that Harald was forced to convert by Otto I after he was defeated in battle. Harald's 'little son' Sweyn was baptized at the same time.

BURYING GORM THE OLD

When Gorm the Old died in 958, he was buried in the traditional pagan style in a mound with many grave-goods. The mound was already there, built in 500 BC. When Gorm was buried in it, Harald had the mound raised even higher and added a second mound beside it, probably for himself. Mound-building was a very ancient practice, dating back to 4000 BC, and in the tenth century there was a revival of the custom, probably as a reaction to the spread of Christian burial customs among the Danes' neighbours to the south, in Germany. But not long afterwards, in the 960s, Harald himself became a Christian and had his father's body exhumed and reburied in the church next to the empty mound.

Harald oversaw the building of ring forts in strategic locations, such as Trelleborg on Zealand and Aggersborg near Limfjord. The forts were all built to the same design, perfectly circular, with four gates and an enclosure divided into four. He also ordered the building of the oldest known bridge in southern Scandinavia, the Ravninge Bridge, which was 831 yards (760 meters) long and 16 feet (5 meters) wide.

MULTIPLE KINGSHIP

Harald turned his attention to foreign affairs, going to the aid of Richard the Fearless of Normandy in 945 and 963; according to the sagas, Normandy was a vassal state. When King Harald Greycloak of Norway was murdered, Harald Bluetooth managed to make himself king of Norway too, for a time. Viking kings often aspired to multiple kingship; one rarely satisfied their insatiable greed.

ST BRICE'S DAY DEATH

Norse sagas show Harald in a negative light. He was twice forced to submit to the Swedish prince Styrbjorn the Strong. On one occasion he had to give Styrbjorn a fleet as well as his daughter, Thyra Haraldsdatter.

On another occasion Harald had to give himself up as a hostage along with another fleet of ships. Then, when Styrbjorn arrived at Uppsala with all of these ships to claim the Swedish throne, Harald broke the oath he had given him and fled with his Danes to avoid fighting the Swedish army.

Harald eventually died in battle, fighting off a rebellion led by his own son. One of Harald's daughters married Pallig, Ealdorman of Devonshire, and it is thought that both of them died in the St Brice's Day Massacre in November 1002.

A FINAL VINDICATION

A female bog body, Haraldskaer Woman, was discovered in 1835. For a long time it was believed that this unfortunate sacrificial victim was Gunnhild, Mother of Kings, and that Harald Bluetooth was responsible for ordering her death. But in 1977 radiocarbon dating vindicated him. Harald was innocent of the crime, which was committed long before in 490 BC.

The big Jelling runic stone from the tenth century, raised by King Harald Bluetooth.

CHAPTER 40.

ERIK THE RED

(950 – 1002)

Erik Thorvaldsson, nicknamed 'the Red' because of his red hair and red beard, was the principal player in the Viking colonization of Greenland. He was born in south-west Norway in 950. His father, Thorvald Asvaldsson, was convicted of 'some killings' and banished in about 980. Thorvald sailed west from Norway, naturally taking his family with him, and settled in Hornstrandir in north-west Iceland.

BANISHED FROM ICELAND

But the pattern of violence continued in Iceland. In about 982 there was a feud with Thorgest, in which Erik killed both of Thorgest's sons and some other men too. This time the dispute was settled by a democratic assembly, which sentenced Erik to banishment from Iceland for three years.

He set sail with a band of followers for a land that lay to the west, which had been discovered sixty years earlier by Gunnbjorn Ulfsson. He had made landfall there by accident after being blown off-course while trying to sail from Norway to Iceland. But after Gunnbjorn's visit, it seems few others had been there. One other who made the trip was Snaebjorn Galti, who attempted to set up a colony, but the first European colony on the huge and still nameless island ended in disaster.

THE WESTERN GREEN LAND

Erik stayed in his island of exile for three years, spending much of the time exploring its incredibly long coastline, before returning to Iceland with tales of the Green Land. Erik chose this attractive name to encourage other Icelanders to go and settle there. It was, of course, an exaggeration.

There were small patches of grass round the coast, especially at the heads of the fjords, but by far the greater part of Greenland was a wilderness of rock and ice. The colonization began with twenty-five ships setting sail in the summer of 985. Only fourteen of them arrived.

SETTLING IN ERIKSFJORD

The two areas most suitable for habitation were round Julianehab Bay and Godthab Fjord, called the Eastern and Western Settlements, modern-day Qaqortoq and Vestribyggo. Unfortunately, they were 300 miles apart – too far away to support one another. Erik went back to the house he had built, 'took Eriksfjord by right of settlement and lived at Brattahlid', the estate he created in the Eastern Settlement.

Erik the Red was the paramount chieftain of Greenland, he became both respected and wealthy, and kept faith with the old religion, though his son became a Christian. New contingents of migrants arrived from Iceland. Unfortunately one of those arriving in 1002 brought an infection which killed many of the leading citizens in an epidemic, including Erik himself.

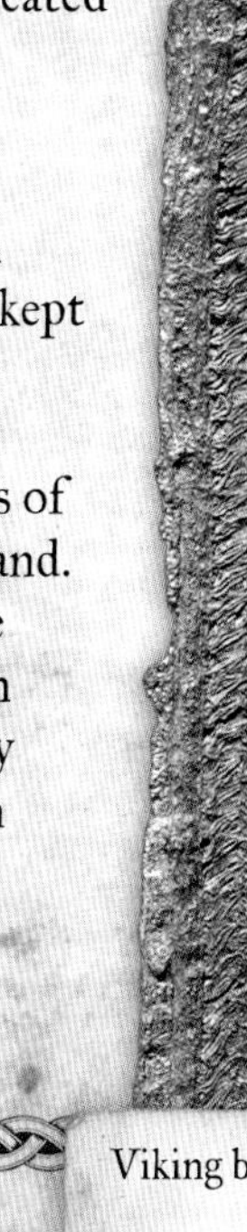

Viking battle sword.

CHAPTER 41.

SWEYN FORKBEARD

(954 – 1014)

Sveinn Tjuguskegg, Sweyn I Forkbeard was king of Denmark, England and parts of Norway. He was the son of Harald Bluetooth and the father of Cnut the Great.

KING OF THE DANES

In the 980s, Sweyn led a rebellion against his father, and succeeded in deposing him and driving him out. Sweyn had his own coins minted, bearing his own likeness and the inscription 'ZVEN REX DAENOR[UM]', 'Sven, King of the Danes'.

As a boy, Sweyn was baptized when his father converted to Christianity and, according to Adam of Bremen, Sweyn was given the Christian name Otto, in tribute to the German king Otto I, the first Holy Roman Emperor – but Sweyn never used this Christian name.

AN INTOLERANT EYE

Unfortunately, we cannot be sure that Adam of Bremen's account is reliable, and there are many aspects of Sweyn's biography that are uncertain because the sources are untrustworthy. As well as Adam of Bremen, there are the Anglo-Saxon Chronicle, the thirteenth century account by Snorri Sturluson, and several other conflicting later accounts.

On the whole, Adam of Bremen's account is a negative assessment, written by someone watching events in Scandinavia with a skeptical, unsympathetic and intolerant eye. He accused Sweyn of being a rebellious pagan, a persecutor of Christians, a usurper and betrayer of his own father. He alleged that Sweyn was sent into exile to Scotland for fourteen years by his father's German friends and deposed in favour of Erik the Victorious of Sweden.

But other, contemporary, documents do not support this scenario; Sweyn was ordering churches to be built in Denmark throughout the alleged period of exile – and he was also leading Danish raids against England.

DANISH ETHNIC CLEANSING

By 1000 he had acquired the allegiance of the Trondejarl, Eric of Lade, and Sweyn became ruler over most of Norway. Sweyn made great efforts to conquer England, leading raids in 1002 – 1005, 1006 – 1007 and 1009 – 1012, triggered in part by a desire to take revenge on the English for the St Brice's Day Massacre in 1002. This massacre was an episode of ethnic cleansing, in which the English tried to exterminate the Danish inhabitants of England.

The Danes naturally wanted to retaliate for this atrocity. Sweyn himself may have wanted personal revenge for the murder of his sister Gunhilde. But he was also short of money after paying a large ransom and he needed the revenue from the raids. The raiding yielded huge sums in Danegeld. He was active in East Anglia and Wessex in 1003 and 1004, but a famine forced him to sail home in 1005.

SWEYN'S SWEEPING ADVANCE

In 1013, Sweyn headed a full-scale invasion. According to the contemporary English account, the Peterborough Chronicle –

'Before the month of August came King Sweyn with his fleet to Sandwich. He went very quickly round East Anglia into the Humber's mouth and so upward along the Trent till he came to Gainsborough. Earl Uchtred and all Northumbria quickly bowed to him, as did all the people of the Kingdom of Lindsey, then the people of the Five Boroughs.

He was given hostages from each shire ... some of the invasion force as well as the hostages were with his son Cnut ... They went to Oxford and the town-dwellers soon bowed to him and gave hostages. From here they went to Winchester, and the people did the same, then eastward to London.'

London put up strong resistance, led by King Aethelred and Thorkell the Tall, a Viking leader who had defected to the English. So Sweyn took his army west to Bath, which submitted to him. By this time, the Londoners had reconsidered, and decided to surrender to Sweyn.

Aethelred wisely sent his sons Edward and Alfred on ahead to Normandy, for safety, then retreated to the Isle of Wight before following his sons into exile. Following the flight of Aethelred, Sweyn was declared king. So, on Christmas Day 1013, he became the first Danish king of England.

A HUGE NEW KINGDOM

He made his headquarters at Gainsborough in Lincolnshire, possibly on the site of the Old Hall, and from there he began the work of organizing his huge new kingdom. But he died on February 3, 1014, having been king of England for only five weeks.

There is no agreement about the cause of death. Some say he fell from a horse. Others say he was murdered in his sleep – by the ghost of St Edmund. His body was embalmed and returned to Denmark for burial in Roskilde Cathedral.

Sweyn's descendants continue to rule Denmark to the present day. One of his descendants, Margaret of Denmark, married James III of Scotland. This means that after James VI of Scotland inherited the English throne in 1603, Sweyn's bloodline was re-introduced into the English royal pedigree. The Viking bloodline lives on.

Sweyn himself is largely forgotten, partly because of his unusual cruelty and brutality; he thought nothing of burning women alive or impaling children on lances. His short-lived conquest unsettled England, tipping it into a phase of extreme political instability that would culminate in the Norman Conquest.

Dragon's head carving.

CHAPTER 42.

SIHTRIC SILKBEARD (960 – 1042)

KING OF DUBLIN

Sihtric II Olafsson, 'Silkbeard', was a son of Olaf Cuaran, the Irish-Norse king of both York and Dublin. He was a tenth to eleventh century king of Dublin, who had three periods of rule: 989 – 994, 995 – 1000 and 1000 – 1036. It was an incredibly long reign for those times, totalling 46 years, and even then it did not end with his death but with abdication in 1036. He died six years after that.

It was nevertheless a troubled and violent reign, with Sihtric's armies engaged in action in four of the five Irish provinces. In particular, he led raids in Meath, Ulster and Wicklow, and possibly across the Irish Sea into Wales. He also came into conflict with rival Viking kings, in Waterford and Cork.

OLAF'S PROTECTION

The Irish Annals tell us little about the early years of Sihtric's reign. The reason may be the major intervention in Irish affairs by Olaf Tryggvason, the future king of Norway. He was raiding the shores of the Irish Sea when he met and married Sihtric's sister Gytha.

Olaf's presence as a powerful Viking leader based on the Irish Sea coast meant that he was able to deter and plunder any Irish raiders who might venture out. In turn, Sihtric's Irish enemies and rivals were seriously weakened and this was a huge benefit arising from Sihtric's sister's marriage.

But then, in 994, Olaf Tryggvason returned to Norway, and left Sihtric exposed once more to predation by his enemies. His rival, Ivar of Waterford, was able to expel Sihtric from Dublin, even if only temporarily. Ivar is believed to have been in control in Dublin himself until Sihtric ejected him. In any case, Sihtric was back in Dublin within a year.

In 995, Sihtric and his nephew Muirchertach Ua Congalaich raided a church in County Meath. In a revenge attack, Mael Sechnaill went to Dublin and stole the ring of Thor and the sword of Carlus. Attacks like these made Sihtric realize that the wealth of Dublin made it – and him – attractive targets. He needed allies. So he formed an alliance with his wife's uncle, a king in Leinster.

THE BATTLE OF GLENMAMA

Sihtric was caught up in the failed Leinster revolt of 999 – 1000. The men of Leinster would not accept domination either by the O'Neill overkings or by the king of Munster. They allied themselves instead with the Vikings in Dublin and revolted against Brian Boru, the king of Munster. Brian's army inflicted an overwhelming defeat on the Leinster-Dublin armies at the Battle of Glenmama, following this with an attack on the city of Dublin. Brian captured Dublin and then occupied it for some weeks, plundering, burning, and expelling Sihtric.

RETURN TO DUBLIN

Sihtric fled to the north, seeking help first from the Ulaid tribe, then from Aed of Cenel nEogain, but neither of these tribes would offer him any support. It may have been at this moment that Sihtric turned pirate and led a raid against St David's in Wales. But there was no support for him in Ireland, and there was nothing for it but to return to Brian and submit. So, three months after Brian's occupation of Dublin had ended, Sihtric went to Brian and surrendered.

Sihtric's family arranged a double marriage alliance with Brian. Sihtric married one of Brian's daughters, and Brian married

Sihtric's mother, Gormflaith, who had already had two husbands.

SIHTRIC SEEKS REVENGE

There was a prolonged peace in Dublin while Sihtric's warriors served in Brian's armies. But Sihtric had not forgotten that the Ulaid had refused him aid when he fled from Dublin.

In 1002 he took revenge when his warriors took part in Brian's campaign against the Ulaid, and ravaged their lands. When the last of the Northern O'Neill kingdoms submitted in 1011, Brian Boru was recognized as High King throughout Ireland.

Then Brian divorced Gormflaith and she started to whip up opposition to him, even urging her son Sihtric to kill her ex-husband. She also urged him to go to Orkney to win the support of Earl Sigurd and then the Isle of Man to enlist Brodir and Ospak.

Sihtric arrived in Orkney in time for the Yule feast and he succeeded in gaining Sigurd's support, in spite of his initial strong reluctance. Sigurd's price was the hand of Gormflaith, which he had to have if they succeeded in killing Brian. Sigurd would also become King of Ireland.

Sihtric then travelled to the Isle of Man, where he made the same promise to Brodir. If they succeeded in killing Brian, Brodir should marry Gormflaith and become King of Ireland.

Naturally, Sihtric insisted that this agreement should remain secret. Open revolt against Brian broke out in 1012. Sihtric joined in, sending his son Oleif to burn the town of Cork, the location of Brian's naval power.

THE BATTLE OF CLONTARF

The two great armies, Brian and his followers on the one side and Sihtric, the Leinstermen and all their allies on the other, met at the Battle of Clontarf. This historic battle took place on Good Friday, 1014. Many fell in the fighting, including many of the leaders. Brian Boru and his son Murchad were both killed. On the Leinster-Norse side, Mael Morda, Sigurd and Brodir were all killed too.

According to Irish sources, Sihtric himself did not fight at Clontarf. He was holding the garrison in reserve in Dublin. From the ramparts there he was able to observe the movements of the battle standards. By wisely staying in the city, Sihtric survived. He lived to tell the tale.

THE SPOILS OF WAR

Yet, in spite of surviving the blood-bath of Clontarf, Sihtric's fortunes fell from that moment on. Mael Sechnaill was recognized as the new High King of Ireland. Then, within months, plague swept through Dublin. Exploiting this moment of vulnerability, the new High King marched on Dublin and set fire to its suburbs. Sihtric in turn attacked and plundered Kells, carrying off spoils and prisoners.

When Mael Sechnaill died in 1022, the situation deteriorated, with a large-scale power struggle for the High Kingship. Ireland descended into chaos as the many kings and chieftains battled for supremacy. Dublin itself became a prize for anyone wanting to be seen as a candidate for High Kingship. In 1029 Sihtric's son Olaf was taken hostage and Sihtric had to buy him back with a ransom of 1,200 cows.

ROMAN PILGRIMAGE

It was the custom in the dark ages for Christian kings and princes to go on pilgrimage to Rome at least once in their lives, especially towards the end. The risk was great, as a protracted absence was an invitation to usurpers. Sihtric went on his prilgrimage to Rome in 1028. His commitment as a Christian king is proved by his building of Christ Church Cathedral in Dublin.

MERCILESS SLAUGHTER

There was a revival of fortunes for Sihtric when in 1030 he formed an alliance with Cnut the Great, king of England; together they launched raids against Wales. He was able to found a Dublin colony in Gwynedd (north-west Wales). Sihtric had power again.

In Ireland, he was able to defeat a coalition of three kingdoms, without any allies of his own. And in victory he was not magnanimous. He slaughtered his prisoners without mercy and revived ancient feuds.

In Dublin he executed Ragnall, king of Waterford; Ragnall was the grandson of Ivar, who was Sihtric's earliest rival, who had competed with Sihtric for Dublin. It was ferocious revenge.

But in the end he had made too many enemies. He was forced to abdicate in 1036 by Ragnaill, King of the Isles, and go into exile. No-one knows where he went or where he died.

Death of Brian Boru at the Battle of Clontarf, Ireland.

CHAPTER 43.

LEIF ERIKSSON

(970 – 1020)

Leif Eriksson (Leifr Eriksson in Old Norse) was the first European to make landfall in North America, nearly 500 years before Columbus. Leif was born in Iceland in about 970, the son of Erik the Red and Thjodhildr.

GOING WEST TO GREENLAND

Erik the Red was an outlaw from Norway, and an explorer, and Leif was probably born at the farm Haukadal, where his mother's family lived. After Erik's second banishment, Leif went with his father to Greenland, where they settled at an estate called Brattahlid in the Eastern Settlement.

This was where Leif was brought up. He had at least two brothers, Thorsteinn and Thorvald. They were looked after mainly by one of Erik's thralls, Tyrker, who Leif later referred to as his foster father.

Leif voyaged from Greenland to Norway in 999. He was blown off course and landed in the Hebrides, where he spent the summer, then went on to Norway, where he converted to Christianity and accepted the mission to introduce the new religion to Greenland.

VOYAGE TO VINLAND

The famous voyage to Vinland is described in two different accounts written in about 1200, the *Saga of Erik the Red* and the *Saga of the Greenlanders*. The earliest purely factual account is found in the writings of Adam of Bremen, dating from 1075.

The *Saga of Erik the Red* tells us that Leif first saw Vinland after he was blown off-course on his way to introduce Christianity to Greenland. But he was not the first to sight Vinland. The merchant Bjarni Herjólfsson sighted land to the west of Greenland after being blown off-course, but never landed there. It was later that Leif, also blown off-course, made landfall there.

Leif claimed to have found 'self-sown wheat fields and grapevines', which sounds like a typical medieval traveller's tale. He then rescued two men who had been shipwrecked there before returning to Greenland. If we can believe this version of events, and the description of the crops makes it hard to believe, Bjarni saw North America west of Greenland, and the two shipwrecked sailors were the first Europeans to make landfall there (that we know of).

ROUTE TO NEW WORLD

After that initial experience, Leif purchased Bjarni's ship, recruited a crew of 35 men and organized an expedition to the new land. Erik the Red was intending to join his son, but fell from his horse and was unable to go.

Leif retraced Bjarni's route, landing first in a rocky place he named Helluland, Flat-Rock Land, which may have been Baffin Island. Voyaging on westwards from there, he landed on a forested coast which he called Markland, Forest Land, which may have been Labrador.

Then, after two more days' sailing, he landed in a luxuriantly vegetated place where there were many salmon.

Leif decided to overwinter there, and divided his party into two groups, one to stay at the camp, the other to explore. It was during the exploration that Tyrker found that the land was full of vines. This was why Leif called this land Vinland. In the spring, Leif returned to Greenland with a cargo of grapes and timber. On the way home, Leif rescued another Icelandic castaway and his crew.

DISCOVERING AMERICA

In the 1960s, the Norwegian explorer Helge Ingstad and his wife, the archaeologist Anne Ingstad, discovered a Norse settlement at the northern tip of Newfoundland. They identified this site, which is today called L'Anse aux Meadows, as Leif Eriksson's settlement, Leifsbudir.

Some scholars now think it more likely that Vinland was the area of the North American mainland along the shores of the Gulf of St Lawrence. If so, L'Anse aux Meadows may have been a ship repair station and an interim waypoint for voyages to Vinland.

Others think Vinland was a larger area, as the sagas describe, and that it encompassed several settlements. The *Saga of Erik the Red* mentions two more settlements, Straumfjordr and Hop.

Statue of Leif Eriksson and Hallgrimskirkja Church, Reykjavik, Iceland.

CHRISTIAN MISSIONARY

Leif was a wise, considerate and strong man with a striking appearance. During his summer stay in the Hebrides, he fell in love with the noblewoman Thorgunna. She bore him a son called Thorgils, who was later sent to join Leif in Greenland.

Following his first voyage to the New World, Leif went back to Brattahlid, where he began his mission to spread Christianity. His father would hear none of it, but his mother converted almost at once and built a church that was named after her, Thjódhild's Church.

The last time Leif is mentioned as living is in 1019, and by 1025 the chieftancy was held by his son Thorkell. Nothing is said in the sagas about his death, but it must have happened between those two dates.

FIRST CONTACT

Leif's expedition to Vinland encouraged other Norse Greenlanders to make the voyage across to North America. It seems the first contact by the Vikings with the native North Americans, the people the Vikings called *skroelingjar*, was made by Leif's brother Thorvald. Typically, given the Viking way of doing things, this led to hostility, violence and bloodshed.

Perhaps, if more diplomatic relations had been established, the Norse colony settlements might have endured. As it was, there were no long-lasting Norse colonies on the mainland. But there were occasional foraging voyages, at least to Markland (Labrador), and these went on for hundreds of years.

A VAST CONTINENT

These early contacts with North America were referred to fairly casually, as if their significance in the context of later history had not been guessed at. Indeed, there was no reason for people in the tenth, eleventh or twelfth centuries to have that developed sense of the historic nature of these voyages.

Apart from anything else, the lands they were seeing and landing on were probably understood as just some more islands, like Iceland or the Hebrides. The Vikings had no way of knowing that they had set foot on the threshold of a vast new continent, and no way of knowing that the history of its colonization would have global implications.

PATHFINDING FOR COLUMBUS

Yet the early landfalls in Markland and Vinland may have been remembered in European seaports through to the fourteenth and fifteenth centuries, where Columbus might have heard about them. In fact Columbus claimed to have visited Iceland in 1477, and it is even likelier that stories and traditions of the voyages west to Greenland and Vinland were preserved there. Columbus did not sail off into a void.

Leif's early landing in North America had a great effect on the self-perception of much later Scandinavian migrants to the United States. The first statue of Leif Eriksson was raised in 1887, in Boston; this was because many Americans then believed that Vinland was the Cape Cod area. A second casting of the Boston statue was erected in Milwaukee.

Another statue was raised in 1901 in Chicago. It was originally commissioned to coincide with the arrival of a reconstruction of a Viking ship from Norway in 1893 as part of the World's Columbian Exposition. As America celebrated the 400th anniversary of Columbus's famous voyage of discovery, many were reminded that Columbus was, after all, *not* the first European to set foot on North American soil.

President Coolidge said just that at the 1925 Minnesota State Fair, in a speech to mark the centenary of the first official organized migration of Norwegians to America; Leif was the first known European to arrive in America.

CHAPTER 44.

CNUT THE GREAT

(975 – 1035)

Cnut the Great (Knut Sveinsson) often referred to as Canute, became king of a huge sea-empire consisting of England, Denmark, Norway and parts of Sweden, and sometimes called the North Sea Empire. Great though he was, and great though his empire was, he left little in the way of a lasting legacy. His heirs died soon after him, and in England the Norman Conquest erased all trace of his reign.

INVASION OF ENGLAND

Cnut was the son of Sweyn Forkbeard, King of Denmark; it is not known who his mother was. In fact very little is known about Cnut's early life until 1013, which is when he joined a Scandinavian force led by his father to invade England. This was the climax of a long series of Viking raids against England.

When King Sweyn's fleet arrived in the Humber, the kingdom quickly fell to the Vikings. Towards the end of that year King Aethelred fled to Normandy, leaving Sweyn in possession in England. While Forkbeard consolidated his position, Cnut looked after the fleet and the army base at Gainsborough. Sweyn Forkbeard lived only a few months, dying early in February 1014.

In Denmark, he was succeeded by Harald, though Cnut was elected king by the Vikings – and the people of the Danelaw in England. The English aristocracy had other ideas, recalling Aethelred from Normandy to reinstate him as king.

CNUT'S CASUAL SAVAGERY

Aethelred swiftly led an army against Cnut, who fled with his army to Denmark, leaving the hostages his father had taken on the beach at Sandwich, after cutting off their hands, ears and noses.

This looks like casual savagery, but Cnut was making the point that, in Danish eyes, the English had broken an agreement in recalling Aethelred from exile; they had behaved dishonourably.

But the English view would have been that their agreement had been with Sweyn. Sweyn's death released them from their obligation, and Cnut was not himself instated as king, so they were free to recall Aethelred.

INTENSE INVASION CAMPAIGN

Back in Denmark, Cnut approached his brother Harald and it is believed that he proposed a joint kingship, but Harald disliked and rejected the idea. Harald offered Cnut the command of his army and navy for a new invasion of England, on condition that he abandoned his claim to the Danish throne.

In 1015, Cnut sailed for England with an army of perhaps 10,000 Danes, Swedes and Norwegians in 200 longships, making landfall at Sandwich. Then he sailed round the coast of Kent and Sussex to Wessex, where he launched a campaign of an intensity not seen since the days of Alfred the Great.

AT CLOSE QUARTERS

This formidable Viking army fought at close quarters with the English for over a year. Most of the battles were fought against the eldest son of Aethelred, Edmund Ironside. While the Danes rampaged through England, London remained unconquered, safe behind its Roman walls. After Aethelred's death, Edmund was elected king there on April 23, 1016.

Cnut pursued and fought Edmund relentlessly. Eventually, after Edmund was wounded in battle in October, he agreed terms; Cnut was to have the north of England and Edmund could keep the south for his lifetime, after which it too would pass to the Danes. Within weeks Edmund was dead – it is suspected that he was murdered – and Cnut became king of the whole of England for the next 19 years.

MILITARY MIGHT

Cnut was still only a prince of Denmark in 1016, when he won the English throne, largely thanks to the cumulative attrition of hundreds of years of Viking attacks. Then, two years later, when Harald II died, he acceded to the throne of Denmark, making it plain that he would be stopping any future raids against England. He was not immediately popular in Denmark, but his position was secure enough for him to return to England within the year.

Cnut maintained his power over the two kingdoms not just by military might but by forging cultural bonds of wealth and custom. Then, in 1028, after ten years of conflict with opponents in Norway, Cnut was able to claim the Norwegian throne too.

Before that, in 1026, Cnut travelled to Rome for the coronation of the Holy Roman Emperor. To mark the occasion, Cnut wrote a letter to his subjects, declaring himself to be 'King of all England and Denmark and the Norwegians and of some of the Swedes.'

GREATER PROSPERITY

Cnut was described as 'exceptionally tall and strong, and the handsomest of men, all except for his nose, which was thin and rather hooked.' The great advantage in having a Viking king was that he was in a strong position to protect England against Viking

King Edmund Ironside meets King Cnut in 1016.

raids, which had been weakening the country for thirty years. So Cnut's accession led to an immediate improvement and greater prosperity.

He consolidated his position by marrying Emma, Aethelred's queen, and removing any challenges from survivors of the Anglo-Saxon Wessex dynasty. There were executions. Aethelred's son Eadwig fled from England, but was pursued and killed. Edward the Confessor, another of Aethelred's sons, survived by living with relatives in Normandy. In his place, Cnut presented Harthacnut, his son by Emma, as his heir. Two other sons, by Aelgifu, were fallback heirs.

THE GREAT REFORMER

Cnut reformed and streamlined the administration of England by grouping the many shires together into four large provinces, each under an ealdorman, and these were based on the old kingdoms that had preceded the unification of England.

Another change was calling all the ealdormen 'earls', which was a Viking word already in use in some parts of England. After Cnut had purged the Anglo-Saxon nobles he thought untrustworthy, he allowed the remainder, who were trusted, to assume rulership of his earldoms.

THE WISDOM OF CNUT

When Cnut died at Shaftesbury in Dorset in November 1035, he was remembered as a wise and successful ruler, in England and in Scandinavia. If someone was working treacherously against him, like the influential Danish nobleman Ulf, he could act swiftly and decisively. He had Ulf assassinated in church at Roskilde on Christmas Day 1026.

Cnut was a Christian king, baptized 'Lambert', a name he never used, and he was keen to make it easier for his subjects to go on pilgrimages – and to trade. In 1027, in a brilliantly successful visit to Rome, he negotiated with the Pope to make European travel easier. In his own words:

'I spoke with the Emperor himself and the Lord Pope and the princes there [in Rome] about the needs of all people of my entire realm, both English and Danes, that a juster law and securer peace might be granted to them on the road to Rome and that they should not be straitened by so many barriers along the road, and harassed by unjust tolls; and the Emperor agreed and likewise King Robert [a mistake for Rudolph of Burgundy?] who governs most of these same toll gates. And all the merchants confirmed by edict that my people, both merchants, and the others who travel to make their devotions, might go to Rome and return without being afflicted by barriers and toll collectors, in firm peace and secure in a just law.'

THE BEST OF BOTH WORLDS

Cnut's relationship with the Church was not easy. As a Viking he was regarded as an enemy, and his brutal treatment of the overthrown Wessex dynasty further alienated the Church. His bigamous marriages with Aelgifu of Northampton, his northern queen, and Emma of Normandy, his southern queen, also brought him into conflict with the Church.

Cnut did what he could to win the Church round by repairing all the monasteries and churches that had been damaged in Viking raids, and restoring to them their plundered treasure.

He adopted a similar approach in Denmark, proving his Christian credentials by overseeing the rebuilding of Roskilde Church in stone; its patron was his sister Estrid. He was exceptionally generous with gifts to churches.

Whether Cnut was motivated by faith or politics is unclear. The praise poems written for him show a respect for pagan mythology, while he actively negotiated for Christian pilgrims to have freedom of movement. Perhaps he wanted the best of both worlds.

CHAPTER 45.

EMMA OF NORMANDY (988 – 1052)

Emma of Normandy's father was Duke Richard of Normandy, descended from its Viking founder, Rollo. Her mother Gunnora was said to have been Danish. Emma was married to two kings of England, the English Aethelred and the Danish Cnut.

SECURING THE SUCCESSION

Her marriage to Aethelred was a political one; by marrying Emma, Aethelred hoped to pacify Normandy. During this marriage, she had to leave England with her children in 1013 in response to Sweyn Forkbeard's invasion; they went back to Normandy where they were shortly afterwards joined by Aethelred. Sweyn died in 1014 and the family was able to return to England.

When Aethelred died in 1016, Emma was free to remarry. But first she had a struggle on her hands to ensure that the succession of her sons was recognized. Aethelred had nominated all of his sons by his previous marriage as heirs in precedence over Emma's children.

So Aethelred's oldest son Aethelstan had been heir apparent until his death in 1014. Now the heir apparent was Edmund Ironside. Emma tried to get her own son Edward (the Confessor) recognized. This had strong support from Aethelred's chief advisor, Eadric Streona, but it was opposed, naturally, by Edmund Ironside.

MURDERING EDMUND

Cnut was meanwhile virtually shaking the gates of London while this went on. Edmund agreed a fatal deal with Cnut and was himself dead by November 1016. Then Emma tried to retain Anglo-Saxon control over London while her marriage to Cnut could be arranged.

Queen Emma being presented with the *Encomium Emmae Reginae*.

Cnut was a ruthless eliminator of rivals, and it must be strongly suspected that he had Edmund murdered.

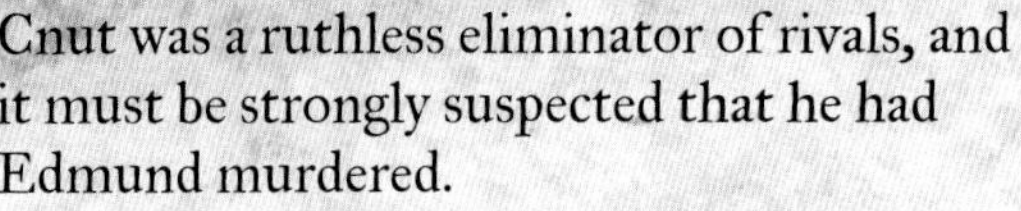

UNDER ROYAL PROTECTION

Emma's marriage to Cnut was at least in part a means of ensuring a measure of protection to her sons Edward and Alfred. If so, it worked, because Cnut spared their lives and allowed them to live in exile, but they made the mistake of returning to England in 1036 to visit their mother.

Alfred was seized and blinded with a red-hot iron. He later died of his injury. Emma believed this was Harold Harefoot's attempt to remove two unwanted claimants to the throne. Edward escaped and returned to Normandy, returning only after the throne had been secured for him.

QUEEN CONSORT

Through Cnut, Emma became queen consort of England, Norway and Denmark. She was also the mother of two more kings, Harthacnut and Edward the Confessor.

With Cnut, she was a great patron of the Church. After Cnut's death, she commissioned the *Encomium Emmae Reginae,* which was an account of the Danish kings in England in the tenth century. She made sure that her own portrait was included in the manuscript.

Emma has a strong claim to be the leading female Viking celebrity. After Cnut's death, there was an attempt at joint rule by Harthacnut and Edward the Confessor, and this worked mainly because Emma herself was a third co-ruler, acting as the common tie between the two kings; she was the mother of both of them. Emma was a remarkably powerful and effective figure, in some ways centuries ahead of her time.

Part of a ninth-century, copper-alloy, Viking horse bridle.

CHAPTER 46.

HARALD HARDRADA

(1015 – 1066)

Harald Sigurdsson, nicknamed Harald Hardrada, 'hard ruler', was one of the most famous Viking leaders. He was born at Ringerike in 1015, the son of the petty king, Sigurd. He was later to rule Norway as King Harald III (1046 – 1066), and he unsuccessfully claimed the thrones of both Denmark and England. He was rebellious and tremendously ambitious. His two older brothers, by contrast, were unambitious, and like their father they were content to live quietly as farmers.

BATTLE WOUNDS

Before his reign as king of Norway and the spectacular climax of his life, his death at the Battle of Stamford Bridge, Harald spent many years in exile. He was fifteen years old when he took part in the Battle of Stiklestad in 1030 with his half-brother Olaf Haraldsson (later to become St Olaf).

Olaf was attempting to reclaim the Norwegian throne, which he had lost to Cnut, the Danish king, two years earlier. Olaf and Harald were defeated at Stiklestad; Olaf was killed, but Harald managed to escape and lie low while his battle-wounds healed. He travelled over the mountains into Sweden and from there into an obligatory exile.

Harald and his followers arrived at the court of Prince Yaruslav of Russia, who welcomed them as mercenaries.

By the next year, battle-happy king,
You were in the Russian towns.
I never knew a peace-destroyer
Bolder than you.

CELEBRITY IN SERKLAND

Then in 1034 Harald moved on to Constantinople, where Zoe the Mighty was the empress, ruling jointly with a succession of emperors. The emperor at the time Harald was there was Michael IV, 'the Paphlagonian'. Harald asked the emperor to put him and his men on contracts as mercenaries, which was agreed, and Harald quickly rose to become commander of the Varangian Guard.

His royal identity and reputation were by now well-known; he enjoyed real celebrity status. The Viking contingent was then ordered to man the Byzantine warships. According to the saga, Harald took his men into the Caliphate, 'Serkland', where they took eighty Arab strongholds, and to Jerusalem, where the whole country was given to him.

Harald visited the holy places in Jerusalem, and went to the River Jordan, where he bathed. The Byzantines were then able to repair the Church of the Holy Sepulchre.

JEALOUSY OF AN EMPRESS

Harald then returned to Constantinople, where he became involved in dynastic disputes. He was accused of holding onto gold that rightfully belonged to the emperor. Harald had indeed amassed great wealth, which he had shipped out to Russia for safe-keeping.

Zoe also accused him of making love to her niece Maria; Harald had indeed proposed marriage and been refused. But Zoe may have been motivated by jealousy and frustration; it was rumoured that she herself wanted Harald.

The current emperor, Constantine IX Monomachos, had Harald thrown into a dungeon along with Ulf and Halldor Snorrason. They were rescued by a woman with two servants, who let a rope down into the dungeon. According to the saga version of events, Harald and his friends escaped, went to the palace, killed the guards, seized the emperor and put out his eyes.

The Byzantine documents give a slightly different version of events from the Icelandic sagas. There was indeed a rebellion in Byzantium in 1042 and during the course of it the emperor was indeed mutilated, but it was Michael V, not Monomachos, and he was castrated, not blinded. These Byzantine documents nevertheless confirm that Harald was a real historical figure and performing great military exploits, calling him 'Araltes'. These documents record that Harald asked the Emperor Constantine IX Monomachos for permission to return to his own land, but the emperor would not give it.

MAGNUS THE GOOD

Harald finally left Byzantium in 1042, returning to Russia to prepare an attempt to claim the throne of Norway. He had probably heard that in his absence the throne had been restored from the Danes and given to Olaf's illegitimate son Magnus the Good, who was also king of Denmark.

Four years later, Harald returned to Scandinavia and began raiding the coast of Denmark. Magnus was unwilling to fight his uncle and agreed to share the throne of Norway with him; in return Harald was to share his wealth with Magnus.

This co-rule ended suddenly and conveniently a few months later when Magnus died (falling overboard from his ship), leaving Harald sole ruler of Norway.

Harald probably hoped to recreate Cnut's North Sea Empire, and as a step towards this claimed the throne of Denmark, but he was unable to achieve it. He spent every year until 1064 raiding the Danish coast, battling against his one-time ally, Sveinn, but never succeeded in conquering Denmark.

HAROLD GODWINSON

Then, momentously, Tostig Godwinson, brother of the new English king Harold Godwinson, pledged his support for Harald Hardrada and invited him to claim the English throne. Harald accepted this challenge and arrived in the North of England in September 1066, successfully defeating English forces in the Battle of Fulford.

His success drew Harold north to confront him. Harold Godwinson defeated and killed Harald Hardrada at the Battle of Stamford Bridge, but the huge effort involved in marching north, fighting the battle and marching south meant defeat for Harold at Hastings.

Harald Hardrada's career was remarkable in many ways, shaping the history of northern Europe, but it was also a classic action-packed Viking adventure, full of voyaging, spectacular daring and violence. He was the last great Viking.

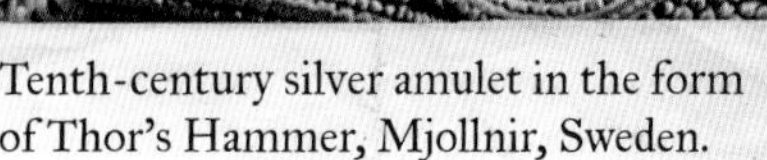
Tenth-century silver amulet in the form of Thor's Hammer, Mjollnir, Sweden.

CHAPTER 47.

SVEINN ESTRIDSSON

(1019 – 1074)

Sveinn II has the distinction of being the last Viking king of Denmark, reigning from 1047 until his death in 1074. Cnut the Great was his uncle, and Cnut's sister Estrid was his mother – hence his surname, Estridsson. He was a tall and powerfully built man, but he walked with a limp. The most notable feature of his personal life is that he was married three times and fathered over twenty children, including no fewer than five future kings.

STRUGGLING FOR POWER

Sveinn's public life was dominated by a long and wearying power struggle with Harald Hardrada; they were in competition for the Danish crown. Sveinn almost succeeded in capturing Harald in 1050, when Harald attacked the coast of Jutland. In a sea-chase, Sveinn very nearly caught up with Harald, so Harald ordered his men to throw overboard all his captured loot, thinking that Sveinn would stop to collect it and allow him to escape.

But Sveinn ordered his men to ignore the goods and continue pursuing Harald. Then Harald ordered his men to throw overboard all the Danish captives he had taken during the raid. Sveinn stopped to pick up the released captives and this allowed Harald to escape.

THE LAST BATTLE

Harald goaded Sveinn into meeting him in what was intended to be a final determining battle, a showdown. Sveinn came close to losing his life in this battle, the sea-battle of Niså, in 1062. Sveinn lost the battle, but managed to keep Denmark. A deal was struck in 1064. Harald relinquished his claim to the Danish throne, recognizing Sveinn as king of Denmark, in exchange for Sveinn's recognition of Harald as king of Norway, as Harald III.

STAMFORD BRIDGE

Then, having failed to collect the Danish crown, Harald sailed off to try to claim the English crown instead. He had to fight King Harold of England for it and he lost, dying in the Battle of Stamford Bridge in 1066. By diverting and exhausting Harold and his army, Harald Hardrada made William of Normandy's success at Hastings likelier.

King Sveinn, in turn, had seen himself as a possible successor to King Edward the Confessor; he too might have become king of England, but he was outflanked by Harold Godwinson. So the royal ambitions of both Sveinn Estridsson and Harald Hardrada were intimately entangled, both with each other and with the destiny of England.

THE FIRST MEDIEVAL KING

Sveinn has been described as the last Viking king of Denmark but also the first medieval king. His reign saw the conversion of Denmark, and he was responsible for ordering the building of hundreds of small wooden churches. Yet the notorious Viking raids continued, including the looting of churches and monasteries.

Viking battle axe-head.

CHAPTER 48.

WILLIAM THE CONQUEROR

(1028 – 1087)

THE NORMAN CONQUEST

In 1066, after defeating the Norwegian invasion force at Stamford Bridge, Harold of England raced south to meet a French invasion force under Duke William of Normandy at Hastings. This is sometimes represented as another Viking invasion.

The dukes of Normandy made much of their Viking ancestry. Duke William claimed descent from Rollo, a Viking leader who was ceded lands in northern France by Charles the Simple in 911. On the face of it the Normans were the same Scandinavians as those raiding the coasts of England and settling the Northern Isles. Normandy takes its name from the Vikings, Northmannia, land of the Northmen. There are some place-names of Scandinavian origin in Normandy, but mainly near the coast.

William's ancestry was mixed; he had many French aristocrats in his family tree, and his contemporaries described the duke and his followers as Frenchmen. The Bayeux Tapestry confirms this by showing the Battle of Hastings as being between '*Angli et Franci*', the English and the French. Nor was anyone in eleventh century Normandy speaking Old Norse. There was nothing Viking about the Normans – except the predatory nature of their attack on the English.

THE END OF THE VIKING AGE

The Viking threat to England did not end with the Norman Conquest of 1066. Three years later a Danish royal fleet sailed into the Humber to support an English revolt against the Normans. If there had been a Danish alliance with Harold, three years earlier, instead of the disastrous distraction of Stamford Bridge, Harold would probably have defeated William at Hastings.

But the Vikings had not entirely disappeared – at least not until 1070. In that year the Danish king, Sveinn Estridsson, led an invasion fleet to England with the idea of becoming king of England as well as Denmark, and was bought off by William. Finally, Cnut, Sveinn's son and successor, cancelled his plan to invade England in 1085 – and that brought the Viking Age in England finally to an end.

INCREASINGLY CHRISTIAN

With Christianization came a shift in identity. Cnut the Great was already taking on the persona of a Christian king in the 1020s. Commerce in an increasingly Christian Europe meant that Vikings had more dealings with Christians. Viking mercenaries served in the armies of Christian kings. There was missionary activity. It was a gradual process of change, but by the eleventh century, the time of Cnut the Great, Harold of England and William of Normandy, most of Scandinavia had been converted to Christianity.

The last raids on England were those organized by Cnut the Holy, king of Denmark from 1080 to 1086. After the failure of his invasion he was murdered in Odense by a group of angry yeomen incensed not by the failure of the invasion but by Cnut's imposition of a military service tax.

THE WARRIOR IDEALS

When Cnut the Holy was subsequently canonized, the reason given was that his purpose in invading England was to reawaken the old warrior ideals of the Danes. These were of course pagan ideals, but Cnut's courtiers and admirers saw them, and Cnut's mission to conquer England, as pleasing to the Christian God.

Traces of paganism lingered, especially in Sweden, but the mainstream of Scandinavian culture was now Christian. It is fortunate that so much was written down in the two centuries that followed, so that the old pagan folk tales and myths were recorded before they had been entirely forgotten.

William the Conqueror on the Bayeux Tapestry, Calvados, France.

PART 6.

THE LASTING LEGACY

CHAPTER 49.

MEDIEVAL VIEW OF THE VIKINGS

We have two medieval views of the late Viking Age from contemporary or near-contemporary writers. The two chroniclers were Adam of Bremen, writing in the eleventh century, and Snorri Sturluson, an Icelandic writer of the thirteenth century.

ADAM OF BREMEN

A German who moved to Bremen in 1066, Adam died there about twenty years later. He was a canon of the cathedral church of Bremen and wrote a book about his church's history.

The See of Bremen had taken responsibility for the mission to convert the North, so a good deal of Adam's writing views Scandinavia from later than the Viking Age. Not surprisingly, some of the detailed geography is shaky, and there are the usual travellers' tales about the fabulous far north.

Even so, it is a useful account and there is a lot of accurate information about southern Scandinavia that was provided by Sveinn Estridsson, the last Viking king of Denmark, with whom Adam had a number of conversations, perhaps at Roskilde.

ADAM'S DENMARK

Sjaelland [Zealand] is an island, large in area, lying in a bight of the Baltic Sea ... well famed for the toughness of its men and the plenty of its crops. Its biggest town is Roskilde, seat of the kings of Denmark ... There is a great deal of gold piled up there as a result of pirate raids.

The pirates themselves, whom they call Wichingi and we call Ascomanni, pay tribute to the Danish king for leave to plunder the barbarians, who live in large numbers round this sea-coast. It can just as well happen that the licence they apply to their enemies recoils on themselves. So little faith has each in the other that anyone, if he can capture someone else, will quickly sell him without compunction into a state of slavery either to a comrade or to a barbarian.

Both in their laws and their practices the Danes hold to many other things that are contrary to virtue and justice. There seems no point in my speaking of any of them save to note that they immediately sell any woman who has yielded to seduction. Men who have been apprehended for high treason or some other crime would rather be beheaded than flogged.

There is no other sort of punishment there but the axe or slavery, and when a man is condemned it is his glory to put on a cheerful face. For tears and complaint, and other signs of remorse which we generally regard as wholesome, the Danes so loathe that no-one is allowed to weep either for his sins or for the dear departed.

From Sjaelland to Skåne there are many routes. Skåne is the prettiest province of Denmark, strong in its men, rich in crops and wealthy in commodities – and now full of churches. Skåne has twice as many as Sjaelland – three hundred churches.

ADAM'S SWEDEN

The whole region is full of imported merchandise. You can say the Swedes are poor in nothing but pride. For all the materials of empty pomp (that is to say, gold, silver, regal steeds, the pelts of beaver or marten), things that drive us [Germans] mad with desire, they think nothing of.

Only in their relations with women do they know no bounds. Any man may have at the one time two, three or even more, depending on the extent of his powers; the rich and the nobles innumerable. Even the sons of such unions they accept as legitimate. Yet it is a capital offence for a man to know another's wife or to take a virgin by force.

Though all Northmen are noted for their hospitality, our Swedes are supreme. To them, worse than any infamy is to deny hospitality to travellers, so there is rivalry as to which of them shall have the honour of entertaining a guest. To him they extend all the courtesies for as many days as he wants to remain there and they take him to their friends in their various homes. Good things like this are part of their tradition.

There are many men outstanding in strength and warfare. As excellent fighting-men they are equally good on horseback or shipboard. Indeed that is why they seem to keep the rest of the Northmen under their thumbs. They have kings of ancient family. Their [the kings'] power, however, is dependent on the will of the people. What everyone has approved by common agreement the king must confirm; unless his decision turns out to be more sensible, when the people sometimes accept it, though reluctantly.

When they [the fighting-men] go to war, they display complete obedience to the king. If in battle they find themselves in peril they call for help to one of the host of gods they worship. After victory they then remain faithful to that one, setting him above the rest. Yet now, by common consent, they claim that the God of the Christians is stronger than any others.

ADAM'S NORWAY

The land produces the most powerful fighting-men, who are not enfeebled by any luxury of produce. They hold no ill-will towards their neighbours the Swedes, though they are sometimes tested by the Danes. They are forced by daily lack of commodities to travel the whole world, bringing back from their forays a plentiful supply of the riches of all countries. Since their conversion to Christianity, however, they have been inspired to love peace and truth and be content with their poverty ...

The metropolitan city of the Norwegians is Trondheim, which is now graced with churches and crowded with a great press of people. In it lies the body of the most blessed Olaf, king and martyr.

SNORRI STURLUSON

A different view of the Vikings comes from Snorri Sturluson, the thirteenth century Icelandic prose-writer, skald and politician. He was writing from just after the Viking Age, but from within a culture with a strong Viking legacy. Snorri expounded the mythology of the Vikings and the history and legends of the Viking Age as he understood them.

Snorri's writings are extremely valuable, because they incorporate poetry that was written a couple of centuries earlier, and through Snorri we are able to hear the authentic voice of the Icelandic Vikings.

THE ROYAL PUBLIC PERSONA

Snorri explains that the skalds were expected to write praise poems about their kings and how we should evaluate what they wrote.

It is the practice of court poets to praise most fulsomely the man they are reciting to, but no-one would dare to tell in a man's presence anything about his exploits that everyone who listened knew to be falsehood. That would be mockery, not praise.

This is specious of course; we know from today's public figures that they are only too happy to cultivate a favourable public persona, even when they know it to be false and their behaviour has been reprehensible. On the other hand, we can believe Snorri when he tells us that skalds were often left to tell their rulers bad news when other courtiers were afraid to do so.

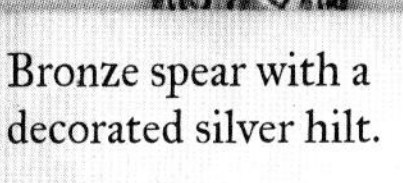

Bronze spear with a decorated silver hilt.

CHAPTER 50.

THE NINETEENTH CENTURY VIKING CRAZE

THE EIGHTEENTH CENTURY

The word Viking only came into use in modern English in the eighteenth century and did not appear in the Oxford English Dictionary until the beginning of the nineteenth. This was the time when North Europeans discovered a North European antiquity, and began to feel their way towards an ancestral identity. 'Celticness' became popular.

The possibility of an alternative Viking ancestry in the Old North emerged at the same time. In the crucial revolutionary year of 1789 John Pinkerton wrote that the British had been 'misled by a puerile love of the Romans' which had led them to undervalue their legacy from barbarian Northern Europe.

Before the outbreak of Viking fever in the nineteenth century a raft of issues regarding the Old North had emerged. Developments in the study of language and literature raised the possibility that there might be a common poetry.

There was also speculation that a common court culture might be shared by Britain and Scandinavia and that ideas about chivalry might have evolved from the Old North rather than Normandy, as had previously been assumed.

SCANDINAVIAN ROOTS

It was emerging that British culture might be founded on Anglo-Saxon or Scandinavian or Norman cultures. Was the Old North perhaps more civilized than had been assumed? The old idea of Southern Europe as more civilized than Northern Europe might be challenged.

Alongside these cultural shifts there was a developing literary interest in the sagas of the Old North, both Germanic and Nordic. The ground was prepared for the Viking craze.

It is hard now to imagine it, but interest in the Vikings and enthusiasm for their culture swept through the nineteenth century like a bushfire. At the beginning of the century no-one was writing about Vikings, yet within fifty years there were books, poems, plays, learned papers and encyclopaedia entries – all about the Vikings.

A PUBLISHING SENSATION

By the end of the nineteenth century, there were scores of books. *The Vikings* was published in 1852, *The Baptism of the Vikings* in 1890, *Ivar the Viking* in 1893, *The Last of the Vikings* in 1895. Viking was the buzzword, and it covered a wide range of moods and mindsets: buccaneering, disillusionment, flamboyant paganism, austere piety, relentless jollity.

An Orkney cleric with the improbable name of Alexander Pope associated Vikings with everything that was negative – wickedness, murder, invasion, robbery, massacre, piracy and every kind of villainy.

The literature was sometimes based on rigorous scholarship, but sometimes the Vikingness was no more than a spray-on Nordic additive. Tension between the probity of scholars and the garish populism of the commercial interests existed in the nineteenth century just as it does in the twenty-first.

WALTER SCOTT'S VIKINGS

The Celtic Society of Edinburgh was founded in 1820, its members dining in kilts. In 1820 – 22, the novelist Walter Scott worked away at the tartaning of Scotland in the run-up to a landmark visit by George IV, when even the fat king would be wearing full Scottish tartan.

The idea was to retrieve the ancient British, Celtic, Gaelic past. At the same time, Scott was working on retrieving and reviving the residual Viking spirit of Orkney and Shetland. If there was colour and tradition to bring back to life, Scott was the man to do it.

Scott's novel *The Pirate* (published in 1821) became one of the definitive texts in the nineteenth century British view of the Viking past. Astonishingly, Sir Walter Scott played a leading role, simultaneously, in the Celtic revival and the Viking revival.

In *The Pirate,* Scott showed the Viking past powerfully resonating among Orcadians and Shetlanders and, although it was a complete fiction, it was what people wanted to hear. *The Pirate* became the first and most popular Viking novel of the century. It was an instant hit.

It was painted, set to music, dramatized; it immediately entered the popular culture and stayed there for the rest of the century. George Bernard Shaw was sitting in the little port of Thurso, waiting for the ferry across to Orkney; he passed the time, like so many pilgrims of his day, '*re*-reading *The Pirate*'.

NORNA OF THE FITFUL HEAD

Scott handled the settings with gusto – the lonely rock-cut tomb of the Dwarfie Stane on Hoy, the weirdness of the Stones of Stenness stone circle, the dark corners of Kirkwall Cathedral. He had a richly textured narrative that was equally rich in exotic names. The story's central matriarch is called Norna of the Fitful Head, and she clashes with a mainland technocrat called Triptolemus Yellowley.

Meanwhile the feast given by Magnus Troil is attended by a clutch of old men with 'shaggy hair and beards, cultivated after the ancient Norwegian fashion'. Together they listen to the songs of Halcro the skald.

Scott seems to have been the very first to draw attention to the Viking longships and it is remarkable that he whipped up instant nostalgia for them; 'I would it were possible to see our barks, once the water-dragons of the world, swimming with the black raven standard waving at the topmast, and their decks glimmering with arms, instead of being heaped up with stockfish ...'

He conjures the image of the great, long-lost ships, and shows them, or their successors, degraded, reduced to humble fishing vessels.

GOKSTAD DISCOVERY

The British public latched onto this wonderful image. Then, in 1880, came the discovery of the first actual longship, the Gokstad ship, which caused a sensation, not least because it fully met the expectation created by Scott's description.

Silver-plated iron brooch with enamel and precious stones.

Norse explorer Thorvald Eriksson fighting Native Americans, *c.*1003.

Here was a real ship, just as Scott described, just as the sagas described. It was a moment like Schliemann's well-publicized 'discovery' of Troy, just a few years before, a revelation that suddenly made it seem that Homer was true.

SAMUEL LAING'S VIKINGS

Samuel Laing, born in 1780, wrote a *Chronicle of the Kings of Norway*, which gave a political edge to the Viking revival. Laing made it seem as if there was a natural unity and continuity between the Scots and their Viking ancestors.

He argued that Anglo-Saxon lethargy had developed out of monasticism – he was anti-Catholic – and the monasteries functioned under an excessively powerful and oppressive elite. The Vikings had rescued the English nation by intervening and only the monkish bias of the chroniclers had hidden this truth until now. The Vikings were not barbarians. How could the sagas have been written by barbarians?

Laing was relentless in his criticism of everything German. Too much time had been spent searching for the roots of pre-Conquest England in Germany. The roots of nineteenth century Britain's imperial power, its dynamism and social cohesion were traceable to Norway. It was the Vikings who had provided England with its key institutions, and traditions like assemblies to articulate public opinion, and trial by jury – not the Anglo-Saxons.

Laing even brought North America into his sweeping argument. Iceland and New England, he said, were the only colonies ever founded on principle – and they were colonies set up by the Vikings.

Whether it was true or not, Samuel Laing's argument was persuasive and influential. It remained influential from the 1840s until the end of the nineteenth century.

REVISITING SNORRI STURLUSON

In 1864 Jules Verne's *Journey to the Centre of the Earth* was published. This epic journey was prompted by a piece of paper with runic writing on it that fell from a copy of Snorri Sturluson's *Heimskringla*. It was Viking Iceland that provided the physical and cultural setting for Verne's walk on the wild side.

Snorri's book had been available in English since 1844, thanks to Samuel Laing's translation, and more and more people were reading it. Laing's translation of Snorri's work became one of the key access points to Viking culture in Victorian Britain. Laing was one of the founding fathers of the berserker school of modern European Viking enthusiasts, those with an extravagant and uncritical admiration for Vikings.

RAMPAGING ANARCHY

The medieval stereotype was still being perpetuated in art. The stereotyped Vikings (violent hit-and-run marauders) stood well outside the national narratives that dominated the accepted history of the British Isles; the Viking heritage went largely unnoticed, and certainly under-emphasized.

There was a tendency for Vikings to be shown as rampaging anarchic criminals who destroyed monasteries and created diversions and mischief for hard-working and patriotic English kings like Alfred and Harold.

A classic image is the one painted in the 1880s by the Danish artist Lorenz Frølich. *Strand hungst* shows the archetypal Viking warrior, a huge helmeted and bearded barbarian striding along, dragging a captive monk and a half-naked woman to captivity or worse. In the background is a scene of murder and mayhem, including a burning monastery.

The Viking anti-hero brandishes a spear, wears a bishop's mitre to show his scorn for the Christian church and even stretches one leg forward in an exaggerated way as if foreshadowing the Nazi goose-step. It is a cartoon of destructive philistinism and savage cruelty, a wild, uninhibited, and worryingly exhilarating, brutality.

CHAPTER 51.

SCANDINAVIAN ANCESTRAL AWARENESS

ENHANCED VIKING STATUS

In the early nineteenth century, the Swedish writer Erik Gustaf Geijer wrote his poem *The Viking*, which showed a very positive side to the Viking culture. This helped to popularize a romantic image of the Norse adventurers.

The Danish antiquarian Carl Christian Rafn argued that the Vikings had crossed the Atlantic and explored some of the North American coastline, hundreds of years before Columbus. Rafn aired his ideas in a book entitled *Antiquitates Americanae*, published in 1837.

This was the earliest scholarly statement about the Vikings' Atlantic expeditions. It enhanced the status of the Viking culture and established a credible case for an alternative, non-Columbian origin for modern North America.

Antiquitates Americanae also became a starting-point for regarding Leif Eriksson as a noble discoverer as shown in Christian Krohg's 1893 painting of *Leif discovering America*.

Statues of Leif were erected in Boston in 1887 and Chicago in 1901. October 9 was nominated as Leif Eriksson Day, specifically in commemoration of the first organized immigration voyage of Norwegians to the USA on October 9, 1825.

SEARCHING FOR AN IDENTITY

For Norwegians, the rediscovery of their Viking past began in the nineteenth century, in parallel with what was happening in Britain, and at a time when Norway saw a rise in nationalism. For 400 years Norway had been joined with Denmark, under a personal union with the Danish king. Then Norway had been politically united with Sweden under the Swedish king. With independence, the Norwegians began to search for a national identity of their own.

As if presenting itself as the answer to this question, in 1867 the first Viking ship was uncovered, at Østfold: the Tune ship. Then in 1880 the Gokstad ship was discovered, again in Norway, and a replica of this longship was sailed across the Atlantic in 1893 to be shown at the World's Columbian Exposition in Chicago.

VIKING ICON

The longship was now internationally established as the icon of Viking culture. This was clinched by the discovery of the Oseberg ship burial in 1904 – 5: an incredibly graceful ship, with its hull almost intact, complete with a wonderful curving prow, carved in something uncannily close to the contemporary Art Nouveau style.

It was as if the Vikings were still among us.

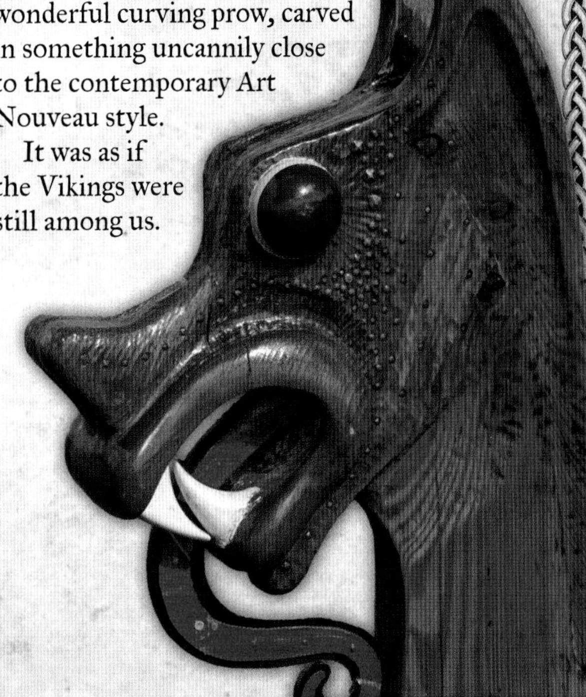

Replica of ship's dragon head.

CHAPTER 52.

THE NINETEENTH CENTURY MYTH MAKERS

THE RING OF THE NIBELUNG

The nineteenth century composer, Richard Wagner, was strongly influenced by both Nordic and Germanic sagas in the writing of his huge tetralogy of operas, *The Ring of the Nibelung*. One source was the *Atlakvida*, among the oldest surviving heroic poems, dating from the tenth century.

It is about a revenge struggle between Burgundians and Huns in the fifth century. In the poem the king of the Burgundians is Gunther, who appears in Wagner's final opera, *Twilight of the Gods*. Atli, the Hunnish king, is greedy for an ancestral treasure owned by Gunther, and this wealth is ascribed to a clan called the Niflungar: Wagner turned this clan into a race of dwarves, the Nibelungs.

PLUNDERING HISTORY

Sigurd, who becomes Wagner's Siegfried, wins the treasure from the dragon Fafnir. The saga is only Viking in the sense that the subject appealed to the Vikings. Norse poets used material that was centuries old and not strictly Norse in origin. The Vikings in effect plundered European proto-history and pseudo-history to forge their heroic poetry; then Richard Wagner, a different kind of Viking, plundered it back again.

Wagner was full of admiration for the old German epic, the *Nibelungenlied*, and it was as its name suggests one of the sources for *The Ring of the Nibelung*. Wagner started his exploration of the saga world in the 1840s. In October 1848 he wrote a sketch called *The Nibelung Legend* and straight away, the same month, turned it into a prose sketch for a Sigurd-Siegfried opera that he gave the provisional title *Siegfried's Death*.

REVOLUTION IN DRESDEN

He was, incredibly, at the same time, deeply involved in stirring up a political revolution in Dresden, which broke out in April 1849. The revolution failed and, as one of the ringleaders (though he later downplayed his part in the fiasco), he had to flee to Switzerland to avoid arrest and a long prison sentence. In real life, Wagner was actually behaving rather like one of his borrowed saga heroes while he was planning his great saga-based *Ring*.

THE SOURCE OF THE RING

Wagner wrote *everything* down. In 1856 Franz Müller was preparing a book on the libretto of *The Ring*, and to help him, Wagner wrote out a list of the sources he had used. Among them was the *Nibelungenlied*, but also in the list were the Viking *Edda*, *Volsunga Saga* and *Heimskringla*, along with several scholarly books about the saga heroes and German mythology. Wagner was drawing on old Germanic myth, but on Norse myth as well.

WILLIAM MORRIS'S VIKINGS

In England there was another saga creator or re-inventor, William Morris. His trade was his decorating firm, which designed and manufactured textiles and furniture in a medieval English vernacular style. Morris's familiar and deservedly popular textile designs were based on the English countryside – foliage, thrushes, cuckoos, daisies.

But, deep inside, William Morris was not an Englishman at all. He was a Northman, drawn to the harsh high-latitude scenery of rocks and ice, where no songbirds sang and no daisies flowered. He certainly looked rough and woolly enough to be a seasoned seafarer, roving the empty Arctic wastes.

His great friend, the Pre-Raphaelite painter Edward Burne-Jones, often poked fun at him for his wild appearance. Once, as Morris was rolling along a street in Kensington, a passing fireman stopped him to ask, 'Beg pardon, sir, were you ever captain of the *Sea Swallow*?' From his appearance, he might well have been.

Morris's 1870s sea-roving took him to Iceland by mailboat, a four-day journey to Reykjavik. In part, this was an escape from the stress caused by the breakdown of his marriage; Janey was now living openly with the artist Gabriel Rossetti.

SNORRI LOOK-ALIKE

William Morris learned Icelandic and with help from an Icelander, Eiríkur Magnusson, he translated several of the sagas into English prose. He was completely at home in Iceland and when he returned to England his friends teasingly complained that he now even looked like Snorri Sturluson.

Morris wrote his own four-part Icelandic epic *Sigurd the Volsung and the Fall of the Nibelungs*, which was published in 1876, coincidentally the year when Wagner's *Ring of the Nibelung* was staged complete for the first time.

TANGLED UP STORYLINES

Morris's 10,000-line epic poem in rhyming couplets was based on stories from the *Edda* and the *Volsunga Saga*. It dealt with the Norse hero Sigmund, his son Sigurd and Sigurd's wife Gudrun. All three characters featured in Wagner's treatment too, as Siegmund, Siegfried and Gutrune.

Early in the plot, Odin arrives in disguise and plants a sword in a tree, which no-one can draw except Sigmund, elements used by Wagner too. In Book 2, Sigurd is raised by a cunning old man called Regin; Wagner has his young hero Siegfried raised by a cunning old dwarf called Mime instead.

Sigurd has to pass through an unearthly blaze on a mountain to reach a beautiful armour-clad woman. Wagner similarly has Siegfried plunging through the Magic Fire to reach Brunnhilde.

The fourth and final book of Morris's epic has a scene similar to the closing scene in Wagner's *Twilight of the Gods*, in which the mead-hall is burnt down and the heroine commits suicide.

In 1870, Morris and Magnusson published their translation of the saga itself, under the title *The Story of the Volsungs and Niblungs*. They claimed in their preface, 'This is the Great Story of the North, which should be to all our race what the Tale of Troy was to the Greeks.'

WAGNER CONDEMNED

It seems that by 1873 Morris had become aware of what Wagner was doing. He condemned Wagner's project; he condemned the operatic staging of the story. It was 'nothing short of desecration to bring such a tremendous and world-wide subject under the gas-lights of an opera: the most rococo and degraded of all forms of art ...'

He ridiculed the spectacle of 'a sandy-haired German tenor tweedledeeing over the unspeakable woes of Sigurd'. Two committed enthusiasts of the saga world at odds with each other. But each leading something of the pirate's perilous roving life style, each with Viking blood in his veins. Each a berserker.

SIR HENRY HOLLAND

Enthusiasts for things Viking might find that they had little sympathy with one another. In 1871, there was an odd meeting in Reykjavik between two of Victorian Britain's keenest Icelandophiles, William Morris and Sir Henry Holland. Holland was a physician with a distinguished patient list. He attended six British Prime Ministers, an American President, Prince Louis Napoleon, King

Wagner's Vikings. The 1896 female cast of *The Valkyrie*.

Leopold of the Belgians, Queen Victoria, Prince Albert and William Wordsworth.

As a committed socialist, William Morris was unimpressed by this and unimpressed by Holland as a person, who seemed to have no enthusiasm, no fire. Morris described him as 'the courtly old carle, Sir Henry Holland, whose age (eighty-four) I thought was the most interesting thing about him.'

Morris was there to visit the bleak farmsteads that were the historic locations of scenes in the sagas that he and Magnusson had been reading and translating. Morris was profoundly moved by the sight of Grettisbaeli, a conical hill in western Iceland which had been the retreat of a Viking warrior who for more than two years had taken refuge there from his enemies. Morris wrote two fine sonnets about it. Holland described it too but added, 'let it pass for what it is worth'. To Morris it was worth a great deal.

WINGED HELMETS

Wagner and Morris in effect reshaped the old Norse myths, as well as retelling them. They were adding bits of their own invention too. What is not clear is where the idea of winged or horned Viking helmets came from. The Vikings never wore either.

Winged helmets first appeared in eighteenth century depictions of Vikings and became common in the nineteenth century in pictures of not just Viking helmets, but Germanic and Celtic helmets too. They seem to have been favoured by artists to emphasize that the warriors underneath them were from the barbarian North.

It is possible that the wings were borrowed from Roman depictions of the god Mercury. Just occasionally wings are found on real ancient helmets but, ironically, on Attic (Greek) helmets from the fourth century BC, and belonging very much to the classical, Mediterranean world, to the so-called civilized South and not to the barbarian North.

HORNED HELMETS

Horned helmets were based on some Scandinavian figurines discovered in the eighteenth century and at that time assumed to be Viking. The figurines have now been dated to the early iron age, 800 – 500 BC, which is much earlier than the Vikings. Horns are sometimes found on helmets belonging to the iron age, like the fine helmet found in the Thames. The Swedish artist Gustav Malmström seems to have been the first to give horned helmets to the Vikings, in the 1820s.

MAGNIFICENT WINGS

Wagner was partly responsible for reinforcing the winged and horned helmet tradition. He gave his first Wotan a helmet with a magnificent pair of wings, which totally dominated his costume. There are picture postcards showing this incredible outfit.

Wagner's wife, Cosima, was unsettled by the appearance of the gods in the first production of *The Ring*; she thought Wotan and the other gods looked too much like American Indian chiefs. It was Wagner who gave a horned helmet to Tristan, in his opera *Tristan und Isolde*, even though this hero was supposed to be a Celt, not a Viking. Confusion reigned.

The general intention seems to have been to create a barbarian world that was exotic and refreshingly distinct from the classical world – but it was very much a modern creation.

SUTTON HOO HELMETS

The helmets that the real, historical, Vikings wore were very different. Some of the raiders probably did not wear helmets at all. Those who did wore a peaked, bullet-shaped helmet with cheek-pieces, neck-guard and 'spectacles' to protect the eyes. They were to all intents and purposes indistinguishable from the Anglo-Saxons, all wearing helmets of Sutton Hoo type.

CHAPTER 53.

THE THIRD REICH AND THE ARYAN VIKING CULT

In the late nineteenth century, Wagnerian mystique regarding the barbarian dark ages, based in part on the ambiguous message of *The Ring*, was merging with Friedrich Nietzsche's ideas about the superman. Germans began to see themselves as the destined inheritors of the world, the *Herrenvolk* – the Master Race. A credible ancestry was needed for this, a fake history, and the rapacious, dynamic Vikings were called up as racial forebears and role models for twentieth century Germans.

The Black Sun runic insignia of the Nazi SS, Wewelsburg Castle, Germany.

CREATING AN ARYAN HISTORY

Hitler and his followers drafted these ideas into political and then military service after 1933. Once in power, they launched a campaign against the decadence of modern European culture, replacing it with a version of what they called Aryan culture, which was based on a mix of Vikings, Old Norse mythology and German peasant culture. Wagner's *Die Meistersinger*, projecting an idealized and rosy picture of well-regulated German town life in the middle ages, became a ready-made anthem to the newly-branded Germany. It became the official opera of the Nuremberg party congresses.

AUTHORIZED BY THE FUHRER

The Potsdam congress ended with a performance of *Die Meistersinger* in March 1933. Benno von Arent's sets and costumes for the opera were personally authorized by Hitler. The Festival Meadow, with its row of flags receding into the distance and massed extras closely resembled a Nuremberg rally. The Nazis' Aryan culture was cobbled together out of some extraordinarily variegated elements.

When the Germans invaded Scandinavia, they were conscious that they were entering and taking the Viking homelands – a kind of return to adoptive roots. Key Viking sites such as Hedeby in Denmark and Borre in Norway became foci for Nazi propaganda activity.

POST-WAR REHABILITATION

After the Second World War and the annihilation of Nazism, a new kind of Viking world was needed, a non-violent one. There was a reaction to the blood and thunder Viking-ism and, thanks to archaeological discoveries, a more civilized side to the Vikings came to light. A process of rehabilitation was under way.

A VIKING SHOWCASE

The Jorvik Centre at York was set up to celebrate the Viking heritage of York as revealed by the 1970s Coppergate excavations – a show-case for the house-trained Vikings. It has been very successful in showing the domesticated face of Viking culture at the time when York was under Viking rule (866 – 927 and 939 – 954), and has become one of the most popular heritage attractions in the UK. It is a persuasive re-creation of part of tenth century York, with houses, shops, pots and pans, people, clothes, middens and even voices speaking authentic Old Norse (taped in a pub by distinguished language scholars).

SPECTACULAR REMAINS

The Dublinia Centre similarly embraces Dublin's Viking past, and there have been efforts to reconstruct Viking houses at a number of heritage parks. In places where Viking sculpture has survived, they too have become tourist attractions.

The spectacular discoveries of preserved ship remains have led to the construction of replica ships, notably at Roskilde. These are startlingly beautiful, impressing everyone who sees them with their grace and technical refinement. They, in themselves, constitute an overwhelming argument against viewing the Vikings as barbarians. Modern Scandinavians naturally prefer to stress the more constructive aspects of their ancestors' culture.

CULTURAL SIMILARITIES

The Anglo-Saxons demonized the Vikings, representing them as very different from themselves. But documentary and archaeological evidence shows many parallels between the two cultures. Many of the Anglo-Saxons' ancestors had come from the same homelands only 200 years earlier.

Their ships were broadly similar; they had kings, some of whom were buried in their ships; they had large, barn-like royal halls with high-pitched roofs and walls held firm by stout raking posts; they had

high-ranking nobles, called ealdormen in England, earls in Scandinavia; they both had areas of local administration, the Viking *wapentakes*, the Anglo-Saxon *hundreds*, each with a democratic assembly, the Viking *thing* and the Anglo-Saxon *moot*.

PARALLEL NARRATIVES

Who were the real Vikings – the bloodthirsty ruffians who leapt from their longships and looted monasteries, or the quiet Scandinavian colonists who made skates and model boats for their children? Perhaps we do not need to choose. Perhaps we can accept these parallel narratives as two sides of a complex culture.

Certainly the warrior class had ideals that were distinct. The rune-stones tell us that voyaging long distances was a deed for which a great man might be remembered. Finding death in a far-off land was a proof of strength and courage. The Swedish Gudbjørn 'stood bravely at the prow of the ship, and now lies buried in the west'.

Other heroes were remembered for the wealth they gathered while they were a-viking. Another Swede called Ulf 'took three [Dane]gelds', which he shared with Toste, Thorkil and Cnut. Yet another was praised for travelling far to gain his wealth and leaving a trail of corpses behind him. To sum it up, the good life of the Viking aristocrat depended on killing, seafaring, travelling long distances and acquiring wealth.

CONFLICTED IMAGE

The current image of Vikings is divided, conflicted, partly because, like our forebears, we find it hard to shake off traditional views and images. Even if we have read about the archaeology, and know that the image is wrong, part of our mind still sees a cross-gartered, ginger-bearded ruffian with a horned helmet and an axe, rampaging across a beach or through a burning monastery, felling monks and seizing women.

The image is partly true, but there is another image which is gradually being fleshed out. This is the sophisticated trader, craftsman or poet, keen to get rich but also to adjust and assimilate. There are two Viking worlds, because different social classes behaved in different ways.

The modern view inclines to see the Vikings as heroic adventurers, as they saw themselves. So now they are less 'salt-water bandits with brutal vices', and more 'stout-hearted gentlemen of the north'.

They are also seen as more diverse. We can see a more violent and barbarous side to their supposed victims, people like the Anglo-Saxons, who were equally capable of savage atrocities.

A VERY STRANGE SYNERGY

An interesting tension exists, and it feeds the management of heritage sites and museums, and stimulates the writers of books about Vikings. All have to try to portray the Vikings accurately and fairly, while at the same time meeting popular expectations for commercial reasons. The Jorvik Centre exemplifies this interesting tension.

Its managers try conscientiously to present to the public the peaceful, civilized, workaday aspect of the Viking life-style, but they also, for some years, sold merchandise that pandered to the old image, merchandise that portrayed the wild barbaric side as somehow lovable and entertaining. Rather in the way that the British Museum Shop (at the time of writing) is selling a Viking warrior bath-duck. A traditional yellow plastic duck kitted out with a round shield, sword and helmet; it may look cute but it takes us to a very strange place indeed.

Viking sword with double-edged blade.

CHAPTER 54.

A LEGACY OF WORDS AND PEOPLE

There is a Viking legacy in the language we still use today. The 'English' pronouns *they*, *them* and *their* are Old Norse words. This came about by Old Norse continuing to be spoken in some areas of Britain in the middle ages.

OLD NORSE DERIVATIONS

In areas where Vikings settled there are still places with names derived from Old Norse. The Orkney island of Rousay was originally Hrolf's Ey (Hrolf's Island). Stromness on Mainland Orkney was Straumr Nes (Current Headland).

A cluster of names in Lincolnshire ending in the suffix *-by* (farm) is also Norse: Osgodby (Asgautr's Farm), Claxby (Klakkr's Farm), Walesby (Valr's Farm). In a slightly different class is Normanby (Northmen's Farm), which suggests naming by Anglo-Saxon neighbours but using the Old Norse form.

Some Lincolnshire place-names combine the names of Anglo-Saxon people and the Norse ending: Kingerby (Cyngeard's Farm) and Usselby (Oswald's Farm). There are also some later names dating from after the Norman Conquest that use Norman personal names with the Old Norse place-name formula: places like Robberby and Piersby. So what we think of today as English place-names were developing while Viking speech was still in use.

PLACE-NAME LEGACY

The street names in the city of York bear testimony to the Viking legacy. Gillygate, Jubbergate, Goodramgate, Back Swinegate, Deangate all come from Viking names. The place-name legacy is not confined to the north. Swansea in South Wales is derived from 'Sveins-ey', Svein's Island.

The names scattered across the map show, more vividly than anything else, that England is a melting-pot of peoples, languages and cultures. Take, as an example, a road sign on the A540 main road on the Wirral, a windswept peninsula between the estuaries of the Dee and the Mersey – it clearly shows the Viking legacy.

The sign points straight ahead to Meols (pronounced 'mells'), a coastal site that has produced a huge range of Viking artifacts. 'Meols' is Old Norse for sand dunes. The sign also points ahead to West Kirby; the name Kirby comes from Old Norse – *kirkju-byr*, meaning a village with a church. The word kirk is still used in Scotland today meaning church.

TURNING BACK IN TIME

Turn right on the same road for Frankby, Greasby and Upton. Frankby combines Old English *franca* (Frenchman's) and Norse *byr* (farm). Greasby is odd – a later substitution of the Norse farm name *byr* for what appears in the Domesday Book as Gravesberie, which is Old English *graefe burh* (the stronghold in the wood). Upton is Old English for the farm on the hill.

Turn left for Caldy, which is another Norse name, possibly meaning Cold Islands or Cold Arse. Not far away are Thingwall, the site of the local Viking assembly mound, and Landican, which started life as a Brythonic (ancient British) name, Llan-Tegan, the church of St Tegan.

MIXED HERITAGE

The place-names on the road signs show north-west England's mixed heritage: some Old English, some ancient British, and a lot of Viking. This is partly because the Viking Age did not come to an end all at once in 1066, or in 1100 either. Stamford Bridge in 1066 and the death of Magnus Bare-Legs in 1103 were certainly milestones in the ending of the Viking adventure, but in many areas Viking settlements continued.

The native and Norse population of Scotland remained mixed until 1500. The Viking settlers were gradually assimilated into the states or provinces now occupying the islands of Britain and Ireland. Even after all these centuries of assimilation, the Viking legacy is strong.

St Magnus Cathedral, Kirkwall, Orkney.

TRACING DISTANT ANCESTORS

DNA studies have added enormously to our understanding of ancestry. Most of our DNA consists of a mixture of genetic characteristics inherited from each of our parents. Their DNA similarly mostly consists of a mixture of their parents' DNA, and so on back through the generations. This is what we would expect from the visible results of family relationships, such as tall parents generally having tall children. But there are two segments of our DNA with a much simpler inheritance pattern.

One is the Y-chromosome, the one that determines whether a person is male, and which is passed down from father to son to grandson, down the line. I am male and my Y-chromosome looks very much like my father's, and so on, back through countless generations.

Similarly, the mitochondrial DNA which is passed down through the female line can be traced back to a distant female ancestor. This is useful, in that the Y-chromosome and the mitochondrial DNA can link a person living now with their paternal and maternal ancestors who lived long ago.

VIKING DNA ANALYSIS

Recent large-scale population movements in West Lancashire make it hard to detect Viking colonization there a thousand years ago. In 1921 there were seventy times the number of people who were living there in 1545. It is possible to identify long-term Lancastrian families from their names. By selecting the Y-chromosome DNA of paternally inherited names that were in use in West Lancashire in the fourteenth and fifteenth centuries, we can be sure we are looking only at the DNA of 'medieval' Lancastrians.

This kind of DNA analysis shows that among men now living in the Northern and Western Isles, North-West Scotland, the Isle of Man and North-West England, there is a high proportion with Norwegian Viking ancestry. There must have been a lot of Viking settlers there. It is much harder to identify the Danish Viking contribution in eastern England, because the Danish and Anglo-Saxon chromosome types are too similar.

MATRIARCHAL ANCESTORS

Parallel research among Icelanders shows a high proportion of women with maternal ancestors who originated in Britain or Ireland, significantly higher than for Icelandic men, whose DNA suggests a Norwegian ancestry. The forensic evidence suggests what the texts are telling us, as we saw earlier, that women were collected, whether voluntarily or not, by Scandinavian-born Vikings during their raids on Britain and Ireland, before they went on to colonize Iceland.

The Icelandic DNA studies in their turn revealed a fascinating anomaly. As so often in science, it is the odd results, the results that don't fit, that prove to be the most interesting. One of the researchers found that all the modern Icelanders carrying the 'C1' (ultimately Asian) lineage can be traced back to four women who were living in Iceland in 1700. These four in turn were descended from a single matriarchal ancestor.

CULTURAL EXCHANGE

As the Vikings visited Canada around the year 1000, the best available explanation is that the errant lineage links back to a Native American woman who was collected and taken back to Iceland when the Vikings returned there from the New World.

This means that the Vikings did not just go to Labrador and Newfoundland, and look; they actually met and engaged with the Native Americans. They met, they journeyed together, they cohabited, they had children together. This was real and meaningful contact between the peoples of Europe and North America.

Up Helly Aa, Lerwick, Shetland.

CHAPTER 55.

THE VIKINGS IN MODERN POPULAR CULTURE

UP HELLY AA!

At Lerwick, in Shetland, there is an annual fire festival with a powerful Viking theme, Up Helly Aa. It takes place on the last Tuesday in January. The day of the festival starts with a procession through the streets of Lerwick of the Guizer Jarl and his Jarl Squad, all dressed in Viking costume. The Guizer Jarl is given the freedom of Lerwick for 24 hours.

In the evening there is a torch-lit procession featuring a galley, a mock-up of a Viking longship, which is sometimes a canvas-covered timber framed structure and sometimes an old boat; this is finally burned with the torches. The event has something of the flavour of the Lewes Bonfire Processions, in East Sussex, and perhaps not by chance.

The origins of Up Helly Aa are unclear. The modern festival can be traced back to the 1880s. It seems there was in rural Shetland a celebration known as Antonsmas 24 days after Christmas, so the January date for the modern festival may relate to that, though there is no evidence that the people in Lerwick celebrated Antonsmas in any way.

The very rowdy New Year celebrations seem to have begun following the demobilization of soldiers and sailors at the end of the Napoleonic Wars. So, from 1815 onwards there were outbreaks of banging on drums and kettles and gunfire each January.

TORCH-LIT PROCESSIONS

After 1840, flaming tar barrels were added. The inhabitants of Lerwick objected that this was dangerous in the narrow streets and by the 1870s tar-barrelling had been stopped. In the 1880s disguise was brought in, giving rise to words like 'guizing' and 'guizer'. Torch-lit processions replaced tar-barrelling. Then in the late 1880s the Viking longship was added.

The Viking connection is persuasive. The Guizer Jarl, who heads the procession, was given Viking armour in 1906, and this has subsequently been upgraded. He carries an axe and a round shield and wears a spectacular raven-winged helmet.

Each year at Up Helly Aa, the Guizers sing, 'From grand old Viking centuries, Up Helly Aa has come ...' But the festival has no ancient ancestry at all. The nineteenth century was the beginning of it, and there is no real Viking legacy here. There is no connection.

BORROWING THE BONFIRE

Up Helly Aa is only Viking by adoption, and may in fact have been borrowed from Lewes by Shetlanders serving in the army or navy in south-east England during the Napoleonic Wars.

A 16-year-old Lerwick boy joined the Royal Navy and served on HMS *Ardent*, escorting merchantmen from the Thames to Scandinavia. On shore leave, the boy would have mixed with soldiers and sailors conscripted or impressed all over Britain.

This was a time of extreme mobility for the common man. The 3,000 Shetlanders demobilized in 1815 returned home full of ideas picked up in other places – and Bonfire may have been one of them.

THE LEWES TRADITION

Though separated by 650 miles, the Lewes Bonfire tradition in Sussex shows several parallels with Up Helly Aa, but it begins earlier. After the Catholic plot to overthrow the Protestant King James I was discovered, an Act of Parliament was passed appointing November 5 each year as a day of thanksgiving for 'the joyful day of deliverance', to be celebrated by bell-ringing and bonfires.

The Act remained in force until 1859. Lewes had a particular reason to celebrate the suppression of the plot – the memory of the martyrdom of seventeen Protestants in the 1550s during the reign of Mary Tudor. In the street in front of the old Star Inn, now the Town Hall, the Protestant martyrs were cruelly burned to death. Lewes has never forgotten.

The Lewes Bonfire celebrations always had a high level of energy, often getting out of hand; some years they turned into riots. The tradition waned during the eighteenth century but, just as in Shetland, there was a surge of activity in the wake of the Napoleonic Wars.

By the 1820s, Bonfire Boyes let off fireworks and lit bonfires in the streets. The *tableaux vivants* of the Enemies of Bonfire had their roots in the *auto da fe*, a ritual parade of penance of condemned heretics during the Mary Tudor persecutions.

The *auto da fe* involved a public procession of those found guilty and a reading in the town square of their sentences. The Lewes *tableaux vivants* probably started as a parody of this Catholic practice. From 1711, effigies of the Pope, the Devil and the (Catholic) Stuart Pretender were carried in procession and then burnt.

BONFIRE SOCIETIES

The disorder at Lewes Bonfire worried the authorities. 1829 brought a Bonfire Night riot, when a local magistrate tried and failed to stop the celebrations on Cliffe Bridge. In 1832, the authorities again tried and failed to prevent Bonfire from happening. More riots took place in 1847, when the Metropolitan Police were drafted in.

In response to this threat, two bonfire societies were formed, the Cliff and the Town (now the Borough). In 1906 street bonfires were banned, along with the custom of dragging burning tar barrels through the streets – another parallel with Up Helly Aa.

In spite of all attempts to abolish the custom in the interests of safety, public order and staunching anti-Catholic sentiment, Lewes Bonfire continues. There have been changes. The bonfires are not in the street any longer and political correctness demands the recognition of Bonfire Belles as well as Boyes.

Seventeen flaming crosses are carried in procession, commemorating the martyrs. There are also effigies of Guy Fawkes and Pope Paul V, who was pontiff at the time of the Gunpowder Plot. The five main bonfire societies each display effigies of current Enemies of Bonfire; contemporary villains have included Osama bin Laden. According to their own dress codes, the members of the bonfire societies parade as Tudors, Zulus, Greeks, Moors, Monks, Smugglers – and of course Vikings.

THE LORD OF THE RINGS

In popular fiction there is a more thoroughgoing Viking legacy – the books of J. R. R. Tolkien, where there are many dark passages that are similar in mood and texture to Viking and Anglo-Saxon poetry. Tolkien was an Oxford academic and his specialist fields of knowledge were philology and early Germanic literature, especially poetry and mythology.

The influence of ancient Norse mythology is palpable in *The Lord of*

Viking sword with decorated hilt.

The Lord of the Rings : The Return of the King (2003).

the Rings. When he was still a boy he read and translated Old Norse. He also read the *Volsunga Saga* in what was then the only English translation available, by William Morris and Eiríkur Magnusson.

The Volsunga Saga supplied Tolkien with some of the names he used. The elves and dwarves were borrowed from Norse and Germanic myth. The central figure of Gandalf is closely based on Odin in his incarnation as The Wanderer, an old man with a long white beard, a wide-brimmed hat and a staff. Odin appears, only called Wotan, in the same Wanderer guise in Wagner's *Siegfried*. Tolkien vehemently rejected any suggestion that he was influenced by Wagner.

Tolkien may have drawn mainly from the original sagas, but there were certainly some developments of the myth that he took from Wagner. One was the idea of the Ring giving mastery of the world, which was Wagner's contribution to the myth, and not in the original. Another was the corrupting power of the Ring; this Tolkien also borrowed from Wagner.

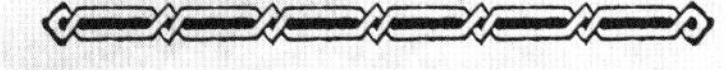

THE ENDLESS JOURNEY

Other influences were at work on Tolkien as well, such as Catholic ideas of mercy, pity, justice, free will and wrestling with temptation. Tolkien's story-telling was influenced by the sagas, but also by lighter adventure writers such as Jules Verne, Rider Haggard and John Buchan.

The Viking thread in Tolkien was one of many threads, but the weary plodding of the endless journeying in Tolkien is clearly borrowed from the Viking world. This is Viking poetry;

Swift man of battle, I beg
This noble fellowship to hear
These verses that I made on my journey.
I suffered teeming rain.
I was sent to ski across the field
Of the swan, eastwards,
Far away, to Sweden.
There was little sleep for me that autumn.

WIDE SCREEN VIKINGS

In the nineteenth century, the Vikings were popularized in novels and paintings. In the twentieth century popularization continued through the medium of film. The genre of film epics lends itself to stories about the Vikings. The Vikings are big-screen, Technicolor, Cinemascope through and through.

In fact, the 1928 film *The Viking* was the first feature-length Technicolor film with a soundtrack. There is no talking, but there is singing and a certain amount of hubbub from extras, but above all there is continuous music: an orchestra playing snatches from various Wagner operas with relentless vigour.

The film is based on a novel, *The Thrall of Leif the Lucky*. Lord Alwin, Earl of Northumbria, is captured during a Viking raid and taken to Norway as a slave. There he is bought by Helga, whose guardian is Leif Eriksson (Donald Crisp). There is a complicated love triangle, and they all set off together in a longship to discover America.

THE TEETH OF THE TEMPEST

An opening caption tells us, 'These were men of might, who laughed in the teeth of the tempest and leaped into battle with a song.' The costumes have an authentically nineteenth century Viking flavour, with an interesting mix of helmets, some without horns, some with small horns, some with big horns and some with wings.

Several of the best scenes are filmed at sea on board a full-sized longship, which is an adventure in itself. The pagans on board are afraid of falling off the edge of the world, so they throw Leif's crucifix into the sea in the hope of making him turn back, but he refuses. Land is sighted and the happy ending shows Leif solemnly planting a huge improvised cross on the beach; the anchored longship is in the background on the right and his Viking followers stand on the left with banners. The tableau is a conscious reworking of the conventional depiction of Columbus's landing in the New World.

The Viking is a spirited and salty film, still watchable, and it ends with Leif Eriksson building a watch tower. It still stands, the film tells us, in Newport on Rhode Island. This is the round stone tower in Touro Park. Some like to think that it dates from the early medieval period, which its round arches suggest, but all the archaeological and documentary evidence points to it having been built in around 1660 by Benedict Arnold, whose house stood nearby; in 1677 he mentioned 'my stone-built windmill'.

VIKING MOVIES

A steady stream of Viking films followed: *The Saga of the Viking Women* (1957), *The Vikings* (1958), *The Last of the Vikings* (1961), *Erik the Conqueror* (1961), *The Viking Queen* (1967), *Hagbard and Signe* (1967), *Tarkan versus the Viking* (1971), *The Saga of Gisli* (1981), *Berserker* (1987), *In the Shadow of the Raven* (1988), *Erik the Viking* (1989), *The White Viking* (1991), *The Viking Sagas* (1995), *The 13th Warrior* (1999), *Vikings: Journey to New Worlds* (2004), *A Viking Saga* (2008), *Valhalla Rising* (2009), *Severed Ways: the Norse Discovery of America* (2009) *Thor, the Hammer of the Gods* (2009), *The Saga of Biorn* (2011), *The Hammer of the Gods* (2013), *Vikingdom* (2013).

STRAIGHT FROM THE SAGAS

The Viking Sagas, written and directed by Michael Chapman, is a dark, serious, sincerely told warrior tale persuasively set in some uncompromising harsh and raw Arctic landscapes. *The 13th Warrior*, based on a Michael Crichton novel, *Eaters of the Dead*, is a loose re-working of *Beowulf*.

One of the most successful Viking films was the 1958 film *The Vikings*, which had not only an outstanding adventure story as its plot, but some archetypal images lifted straight from the sagas. Kirk Douglas loses an eye, which makes him like Odin. Tony Curtis loses a hand, which makes him like Tyr.

Then in 1963 came *The Long Ships*, a swashbuckling treasure-hunting Viking action film with Richard Widmark and Sidney Poitier. Much more recently there was the 2013 TV series *Vikings*, which traced the rise of Ragnar Lodbrok. What is clear from the list of film titles is that not only is the subject of enduring appeal but the very word 'Viking' is a major box office attraction.

TWO KINDS OF VIKINGS

The Jorvik Centre has already been mentioned as a determined effort to show the domestic side of Viking life. It would be possible to present a convincing picture of the Vikings with a focus on houses, arts and crafts, with foreign travel added in as mainly peaceful trade or exploration.

But it would be misleading to do this, and dishonest to omit the fact that many families emigrated from the Viking homelands to settle abroad, and that raiding parties and armies, sometimes of huge proportions, roamed for generations across Europe and beyond.

In 2014 a major exhibition about the Vikings was mounted at the British Museum. The publicity for it was perhaps consciously trying to swing the pendulum back again, away from the Jorvik-domestic, and back to the swashbuckling: 'for 300 years their sails were feared on four continents'.

COMMERCIAL PROMOTION

The name 'Viking' has a wide commercial use, exploiting the association of the name with power, strength, speed, single-minded determination. Rover cars were promoted with a discreet logo showing a silver Viking ship with a red sail. Countless small businesses use the name 'Viking' to sell a huge range of products and services.

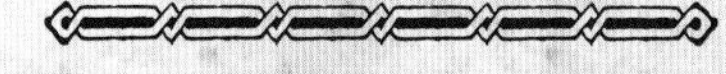

UNRELIABLE SOURCES

We are so familiar with images imprinted from popular culture that it is very hard to separate the stereotypes from the historical realities. Even early medieval sources may be unreliable. As we have already seen, much of what we think we know has come from sources heavily biased against the Vikings, because most of the chroniclers were monks.

Churchmen wrote some fearful accounts. But even Arabic sources, describing Vikings encountered in the Middle East, are unreliable, because the authors were ready to borrow stories about other people and attach them to the Vikings.

CONVERTING GUTHRUM

The real Vikings were capable of robbery with violence – they made a living out of it – but they could also be flexible and adaptable when the situation demanded. They were willing to change religion. The best-known documentary record of a conversion is that of Guthrum, the Viking leader who was defeated in battle by King Alfred in 878.

The terms of the truce that followed were dictated by the victor; they involved an agreed frontier to Danish-controlled England (Watling Street) and Guthrum's conversion to Christianity. Viking settlers in England rapidly followed suit in the years that followed.

BAPTIZING THE KING

Soon all of England was Christianized, except Cumbria. In 826, the king of Denmark, Harald Klak, was baptized. This was promoted as a conversion of Europe-wide significance, and the occasion was appropriately grand. The baptism took place in the abbey at Mainz in the presence of the Carolingian emperor, Louis the Pious, and his entire family and household. The newly baptized king and his sponsors, then processed to the Carolingian palace at Ingelheim. A major part of the pomp was dedicated to showing off the imperial palace, which would have been conspicuous at the top of the slope during the proceedings.

WOODEN STAVE CHURCHES

The change from paganism to Christianity left its traces in metalwork, literature and carvings. There was wonderful new architecture too. As Christianity caught on, the Scandinavian homelands were covered with wooden stave churches. The church at Borgund in Norway is a fine example. The roof is often broken up into several roofs at different levels, with gabled doorways. The roofs are steeply-pitched, lofty and culminate in tiny spires.

Most distinctive of all are the finials on the gable-tops, which are dragon heads similar to the ones the Vikings put on the prows of their ships. They represent a distinctive style of architecture that has an almost oriental exoticism.

The colonial Vikings were equally capable of assimilating not only Christianity but Christian architecture too. The Viking Earls of Orkney had St Magnus' Cathedral built at Kirkwall. It was dedicated to the murdered Earl Magnus of Orkney, after he was canonized in 1135. The cathedral is a conventional, mainstream European Romanesque building.

CULTURAL MELTING POT

It may be that pagan Vikings started wearing Thor's hammer in response to Christians wearing crosses. Some of the pendants seem to be transitional, with characteristics of both hammer and cross, and there must have been many people who were undecided as to what they believed. A tenth century Thor's hammer pendant made of silver and found at Hedeby has a simple punched decoration with a discreet cross in the centre.

The artwork was often ambivalent. There were even saga characters who were ambivalent. An early Icelandic settler called Helgi the Skinny named his farm Christ's Headland, but he did not entirely give up Thor, whom he consulted on all serious matters.

The Gosforth stone cross is an impressive monument that incorporates elements of

both Christian and pagan religions. The overall cross shape indicates Christian belief, while the pictorial carvings on it show scenes from pagan mythology.

PAGAN CHRISTIAN FUSION

When pagan Vikings settled in countries that were Christian, conversion was often part of the assimilation process. We saw how the Vikings cruelly put to death the Christian Anglo-Saxon king of East Anglia, yet within two decades they were minting coins with crosses on them, commemorating the martyrdom of St Edmund. Many Vikings settling in Britain and Ireland became Christians, and it was groups of mixed belief who set off to colonize Iceland.

One of the early sources (*Landnámabók*) tells us this –

Men who know say that some of the first settlers who colonized Iceland had received baptism. Named among them are Helgi the Skinny, Ørlyg the Old, Iorund the Christian, Aud the Deeply-Wealthy, Ketil the Daft and others too who sailed from the western colonies [*Britain and Ireland*]. *And some continued in Christianity right to their deaths. But that did not spread through their families, because the sons of some of them put up temples and carried out sacrifices and the land was completely heathen for a hundred years.*

Borgund Stavekirk in Norway is one of the best preserved stave churches. It was built just before 1150, and dedicated to the Apostle St Andrew.

CHRISTIAN ICELAND

So the flexibility went in both directions. Olaf Tryggvason tried to Christianize Iceland but the appointed missionary, Thangbrand, had an unfortunate temperament and had to be recalled after a year 'having killed two or three men who slandered him'. King Olaf was later persuaded by two leading Icelanders to try again, as Ari Thorgilsson tells in his *Islendingabók*.

The next summer they went west to Iceland, bringing with them a priest called Thormod, and they landed in the Vestmann Islands [off the south coast of Iceland] when it was ten weeks into summer and they had a good voyage. The previous summer it had been enacted that men should attend the Althing when it was ten weeks into summer. They went straight away to the mainland and on to the Althing. They prevailed upon Hialti to stay behind at Laugardal with eleven men because at the Althing the previous year he had been outlawed for blasphemy. The case against him was that he had recited the following couplet at the Law-rock:

'Blasphemy is not for me,
But what a bitch must Freyja be.'

... It was declared that everyone should be Christian and accept baptism, but the old law should still stand as regards exposure of [unwanted] infants and eating horseflesh. If they wished, men could sacrifice in secret, but suffer the sentence of outlawry if anyone witnessed it. But a few years later these aspects of paganism were abolished like the rest. These were the circumstances under which Christianity came to Iceland.

NO MORE ROAMING

The Viking Age came to an end around 1100. The difference between the Vikings and the other peoples they came into contact with had in some important ways diminished. They had initially been pagan and their victims mainly Christian.

That religious difference enabled the victims to demonize the Vikings, and at the same time the Vikings' religion had given them a focus on military glory, on aggression, in order to win them seats in Valhalla. There had been polarization. The conversion to Christianity removed much of this, and the differences blurred.

The Viking homelands, the Scandinavian kingdoms, were gradually absorbed into the Europe-wide project of the Crusades. There was another political shift too: the new focus on imperial ambitions in the Baltic region and eastern Europe. The westward roaming petered out.

MASTERS OF THE SEA

The Vikings are unalterably identified with the sea, and with mastery of the sea. That powerful image remains. Their sea-roving and their adventurousness bring their way of life very close to the culture of Homer's sea-going Greeks of two-and-a-half thousand years earlier. Like the Vikings, the bronze age Greeks taunted their enemies before doing battle; they dared to cross the sea to raid and pillage foreign lands, killing, destroying, seizing women and treasure.

Sometimes the poetry of the Vikings shudders with the swell of the sea, just like Homer's. The Vikings were a manifestation of an ancient European way of life. They were a continuation of that deep, visceral and ancient cultural groundswell – barbarian Europe.

Often I was glad when out
On the fjords the harsh storm
Drove the wind-filled sail of the king
Of the Strinda-men across the water.
The sea-stallion made a fine gallop.
The keels made Lista's neck-ring shudder
As we sailed our pinnace, fiercely rushing
Out across the ocean.

Sigurd killing the dragon Fafnir, in a wood engraving from the *Volsunga Saga*.

FURTHER READING

There is a huge reservoir of information available about the Vikings, much of it very new. Some, such as the DNA research, is scientific and technical, but much of the literature is non-technical and easy to read. The two journals *British Archaeology* and *Current Archaeology* supply a steady stream of new archaeological discoveries and ideas, presented in an attractive and accessible way.

Anon. (2014) News: A Potted History of Viking Scotland. *Current Archaeology* 297, 6. [The Dumfries and Galloway hoard]

Anon. (2014) Viking Victims at Ridgeway Hill? *Current Archaeology* 290, 7.

Bowden, G.R., Balaresque, P. et al. (2008) Excavating past population structures by surname-based sampling: the genetic legacy of the Vikings in northwest England. *Molecular Biology and Evolution* 25, 301–309.

Carroll, J., Harrison, S.H. & Williams, G. (2014) *The Vikings in Britain and Ireland.* London: British Museum Press.

Catling, C. (2014) From the Trowel's Edge. *Current Archaeology* 290, 52–53.

Graham-Campbell, J. (2013) *The Viking World.* London: Frances Lincoln.*

Graham-Campbell, J. (2013) *Viking Art.* London: Thames & Hudson.

Hadley, D. & Richards, J.D. (2013) Viking Torksey: Inside the Great Army's Winter Camp. *Current Archaeology* 281, 12–19.

Hall, R. (2013) *Exploring the World of the Vikings.* London: Thames & Hudson.

Haywood, J. (1995) *The Penguin Historical Atlas of the Vikings.* London: Penguin.*

Hills, C. (1986) *Blood of the British: From Ice Age to Norman Conquest.* London: Guild Publishing.*

Kershaw, J. (2010) On the Trail of Viking Women. *British Archaeology* 115, 18–23.

McEvoy, B., Brady, C. & Moore, L.T. (2006) The scale and nature of Viking settlement in Ireland from Y-chromosome admixture analysis. *European Journal of Human Genetics* 14, 1288–94.

Milman, N. & Pedersen. P. (2003) Evidence that the Cys282Tyr mutation of the HFE gene originated from a population in southern Scandinavia and spread with the Vikings. *Clinical Genetics* 64, 36–47.

Page, R.I. (1995) *Chronicles of the Vikings: Records, Memorials and Myths.* London: British Museum Press.*

Pálsson, H. & Edwards, P. (editors) (1981) *Orkneyinga Saga: The History of the Earls of Orkney.* Harmondsworth: Penguin Books.

Pálsson, H. & Edwards, P. (editors) (1985) *Seven Viking Romances.* Harmondsworth: Penguin Books.

Parsons, A. & Newman, R. (2014) Buried Vikings: Excavating Cumwhitton's Cemetery. *Current Archaeology* 294, 12–18.

Symonds, M. (2014) The Sacking of Auldhame: Investigating a Viking Burial in a Monastic Graveyard. *Current Archaeology* 293, 20–23.

Williams, G., Pentz, P. & Wemhoff, M. (2014) *Vikings: Life and Legend.* London: British Museum Press.*

Wilson, D. (1970) *The Vikings and their Origins: Scandinavia in the First Millennium.* London: Thames & Hudson.

Williams, G. (2014) *The Viking Ship.* London: British Museum Press.

* specially recommended for accessibility

The Vikings TV series (2013).

INDEX

O

P

R

S

T

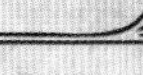

U

V

W

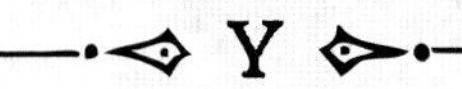

Y

Picture Credits

Cover: Front: © Interfoto / Alamy/ © Andy Buchanan / Alamy; Back: Dave Donaldson/Alamy

Internal: 7 © Mary Evans Picture Library / Alamy/ 11 © Don Douglas / Alamy/ 12 © ClassicStock / Alamy/ 17 © Daniel Valla FRPS / Alamy/ 20, 25, 27, 30, 33, 63, 67, 68, 71, 83, 87, 91, 102, 103, 105, 112, 125, 127, 140, 148, 150, 157, 159 © Heritage Image Partnership Ltd / Alamy/ 22 © All Canada Photos / Alamy/ 32, 94, 118, 132, 165 © The Art Archive / Alamy/ 36, 49 © Classic Image / Alamy/ 42 © Falkensteinfoto / Alamy/ 47 © Yolanda Perera Sánchez / Alamy/ 57 © Ivy Close Images / Alamy/ 60 © Stocksolutions / Alamy/ 62 © David Lyons / Alamy/ 64 © Cindy Hopkins / Alamy/ 66 © Jason Lindsey / Alamy/ 74 © Iconotec / Alamy/ 82 © National Geographic Image Collection / Alamy/ 89 © Andrea Magugliani / Alamy/ 98 © Yvette Cardozo / Alamy/ 100 © Jorge Royan / Alamy/ 106 © Tor Eigeland / Alamy/ 110 © Bernie Epstein / Alamy/ 114 © Howard Davies / Alamy/ 122 © World History Archive / Alamy/ 38, 51, 76, 77, 86, 98, 107, 126, 129, 131, 170, 177, 184 © Interfoto / Alamy/ 134 © Niels Quist / Alamy/ 137 © Stephen Giardina / Alamy/ 142 © JLImages / Alamy/ 145 © Art Directors & TRIP / Alamy/ 153 © Hemis / Alamy/ 160 © The Print Collector / Alamy/ 163 © Adrian Davies/ Alamy/ 169 © Germany Images David Crossland / Alamy/ 172 © Doug Houghton / Alamy/ 174 © CountrySideCollection - Homer Sykes / Alamy/ 178 © New Line Cinema/ The Kobal Collection/ 186 © Irish Film Board/ Take 5 Productions/ World 200 Entertainment/ The Kobal Collection.

This edition published in 2015 by
Chartwell Books
an imprint of Book Sales
a division of Quarto Publishing Group USA Inc.
142 West 36th Street, 4th Floor
New York, New York 10018
USA

ISBN-13: 978-0-7858-3235-5
ISBN-10: 0-7858-3235-1

Printed in China